MW01165593

Williamsport

"PARTNERS IN PROGRESS" BY
JOSEPH P. LAVER, JR.
PICTURE RESEARCH BY JOHN F. PIPER, JR.,
WITH
THE PHOTOGRAPHIC ASSISTANCE OF
MICHAEL G. ROSKIN

SPONSORED BY THE
WILLIAMSPORT-LYCOMING CHAMBER
OF COMMERCE
WINDSOR PUBLICATIONS, INC.
WOODLAND HILLS,
CALIFORNIA

Williamsport

FRONTIER VILLAGE
TO
REGIONAL CENTER

Robert H. Larson • Richard J. Morris •

John F. Piper, Jr.

Overleaf: *Downtown Williamsport is captured in this woodcut as it appeared in 1843. Looking east on Third Street, the view features the first Lycoming County Court House on the left, and the Eagle Hotel, the first columned building on the right. Courtesy, James V. Brown Library*

Windsor Publications, Inc. — History Books Division
Publisher: John M. Phillips
Staff for *Williamsport: Frontier Village to Regional Center*
Editor/Picture Editor: Susan L. Wells
Editorial Director, Corporate Biographies: Karen Story
Design Director: Alexander D'Anca
Assistant Director, Corporate Biographies: Phyllis Gray
Editor, Corporate Biographies: Judith Hunter
Editorial Assistants: Kathy M. Brown, Patricia Buzard, Lonnie Pham,
   Pat Pittman
Marketing Director: Ellen Kettenbeil
Sales Manager: William Koons
Sales Representative: Glen Edwards
Sales Coordinator: Joan Baker

Layout Artist: Ellen Ifrah

Larson, Robert H., 1942-
Williamsport : frontier village to regional center.

   Bibliography: p. 204
   Includes index.
   1. Williamsport (Pa.)—History. 2. Williamsport (Pa.) —Description. 3.
Williamsport (Pa.)—Industries. I. Morris, Richard J., 1947-. II. Piper, John F.,
1936-. III. Title.
F159.W7L37   1984   974.8'51   84-21930
ISBN 0-89781-110-0

© 1984 by Windsor Publications
All rights reserved.
Published 1984
Printed in the United States of America
First Edition

CONTENTS

"TO OUR STUDENTS"

ACKNOWLEDGMENTS

Left: *The Williamsport Recreation Commission developed a number of ice-skating rinks in the city beginning in the mid-1950s, in part because the recently completed flood control system prevented skaters from reaching the frozen river. This view features the rink at the Penn Street Armory in December 1955. Courtesy, Grit Publishing Company*

Our interest in this project is long standing and grows largely from our work with history students in our senior seminar at Lycoming College. Many have written fine papers on the Williamsport area that serve as sources for much of the story we tell. The papers we relied on most heavily were written by: Joseph Shannon, Michael Collins, Paul Roman, David Richards, Christine Updegraff, Werner Garben, William Inglis, David Wilson, Bonnie White, George Ebbert, Gregory McDonald, Frank Nunan, Robert Kane, John Protastio, Gerry Rhian, Mary Ann Smith, and Craig Weaver.

During the writing process itself and in securing pictures for the book, we have had the help of many knowledgeable and gracious individuals and institutions. Miriam Mix, John Troisi, Mary Winner Stockwell, James P. Bressler, Helen Youngman Carlson, Clifford A. Thomas, Thomas Rickey, Paul Bloom, Naomi Woolever, Amelia Mitchell, Paul Fullmer, Harry L. Rogers, Carl E. Stotz, Frank Cummings, Ann Williams, Founders Federal Savings and Loan, and The Williamsport *Sun Gazette* provided information, photographs, and family papers which have enhanced the book immeasurably. Special thanks must go to Marlin D. Fausey for his assistance in providing a plane for aeriel photography, and to Ralph E. Menne for his help with our color photography. The book was also enriched by the fine photographic collections at the James V. Brown Library, The Grit Publishing Company, and the Lycoming County Historical Museum. At the museum the D. Vincent Smith Collection was particularly useful. The successive directors of the museum, Andrew W. Grugan and Joseph L. Zebrowski, were especially helpful and kind. Paul G. Gilmore, William A. Turnbaugh, Marc L. Sheaffer, Joseph P. Laver, Andrew W. Grugan, and Richard L. Mix read copies of the manuscript, offered stylistic suggestions, and saved us from many errors in fact. Michael G. Roskin, our photographer, lent to the project a degree of artistry that is matched only by his patience with our perpetual desire for one more picture from one more angle. Madlyn Wonderlich, Nancy Morrett, and Judy Knittle at Lycoming College, who typed various versions of the manuscript, are not only skilled professionals but warm and agreeable co-workers. At Windsor Publications our editor Susan Wells was enormously supportive throughout the project.

CHAPTER ONE

The Land and the River

Left: *This view of the West Branch Valley looking west shows two of the major arteries of the Valley, the Susquehanna River and the Beltway. Visible are the three bridges, beginning with the Market Street Bridge, connecting Williamsport on the right with South Williamsport on the left. Courtesy, Marlin D. Fausey and Michael G. Roskin*

The first white settlers struggled up the Susquehanna River in the 18th century in search of new farmland. They saw the West Branch Valley as an area of great promise. Their needs were relatively simple, and their ability to utilize the land was limited to what a few individuals and animals could accomplish. Few, if any, thought about the broader geographic character of the region and how it might affect the future of the communities which they were establishing. As more people came into the valley and the nation began to industrialize, that character became increasingly important. In hindsight, it is clear that geography, specifically the mountains and waterways, played a complex and extremely important role in Williamsport's history. It explains the extent and pattern of the city's development, the reasons for its great period of prosperity during the lumber era of the late 19th century, and many of the problems it has had, and opportunities it has enjoyed since that time.

THE MOUNTAINS

Williamsport is located in the Appalachian Mountains, an old and complex mountain chain that stretches southwestward from the St. Lawrence River in Canada to the Gulf Coastal Plain in central Alabama. Geographers divide the chain into three long bands, each running the entire length of the system. The band nearest the coast, called the Older Appalachians, contains the foothills and piedmont section of the system and lies well outside Williamsport's region. The central and western bands are very important to the story of Williamsport, because the city lies almost exactly on the dividing line between them. The central band, known as the Folded or Newer Appalachians, consists of a series of high-crested ridges and long, narrow valleys which run in the same direction as the chain itself. The ridges range in elevation from 1,600 to 2,100 feet and rise steeply 1,000 or more feet above the valleys which separate them. The most prominent of these ridges in Williamsport's region of Pennsylvania is Bald Eagle Mountain, which, beginning just west of the Susquehanna River opposite Muncy, curves southwest in a great arch for 140 miles. The western band of the chain, called the Appalachian Plateau, is a mass of high ground varying in

elevation from 2,000 to 2,400 feet which extends to cover much of Western and Northwestern Pennsylvania. Its beginning is marked by the Allegheny Front, a sharp rise in the ground which can be seen about six miles north of Williamsport.

Although these mountains have provided Williamsport and the surrounding communities with one of the most picturesque settings in the eastern United States, they have also significantly limited many types of economic activity. Their poor soil, steep slopes, and height make them largely unsuitable for agriculture. Their north-south axis, a barrier against east to west movement of people and goods, caused the entire region to be bypassed during America's great westward migration. Consequently, the region achieved only a limited place in the commercial development that followed. Finally, with the great exception of lumber, the mountains lack sufficient natural resources to attract and support large numbers of people. While the impact of lumber on the economic expansion and development of Williamsport can scarcely be exaggerated, it is no less important to realize the limited duration of that impact.

The continuous effect of the mountains can still be seen on the region's population distribution. Although Pennsylvania has a population of almost 12 million, making it the fourth most populous state in the nation, most of its residents are concentrated in its eastern, southern, and western fringes. The north-central part of the state remains one of the least populated areas in the entire East. As recently as 1970, the Lycoming County Planning Commission reported that 95.4 percent of the county was still undeveloped.

THE WATERWAYS

The other geographic feature which has played a dominant role in Williamsport's history is the region's system of waterways. These streams have offered the best and sometimes only routes to and through the area, and their adjacent lands provide most of the fertile soil and flatland that is suitable for agriculture and settlement.

The main components of the water system are the West Branch of the Susquehanna River and its major tributaries: Bald Eagle, Pine, Lycoming, Loyalsock, and Muncy creeks. All but Bald Eagle originate in the Allegheny Plateau region. Together with their subsidiary streams, these creeks drain 5,680 square miles of North-Central Pennsylvania, and except for their headwaters, they drop gently for most of their course. The stretch of the Susquehanna for the 17 miles between Pine and Lycoming creeks is almost level, leading the Indians to give it the name "Long Reach." Many of the subsidiary streams fall very rapidly, some as much as 1,000 feet in a mile, and are thus capable of sending large amounts of water into the system in a short period of time. This has been an important fact of life for the people in the region.

Most geographers treat the West Branch Valley as part of the Ridge and Valley band of the Appalachians, but local archeologist William Turnbaugh, who has carefully studied the area, believes it constitutes a distinct geographic region separate from those to the north and south. Calling it the Susquehanna Section, he defines it as the area from where the river emerges from the Allegheny Plateau to where it curves south around the end of Bald Eagle Mountain, that is from Lock Haven to Muncy, and from Bald Eagle Mountain north to the Allegheny Front. The area is marked by the river, its floodplain, and the terraces and foothills immediately to the north. The valley reaches its maximum width of six miles in the vicinity of Williamsport. This distinction is extremely useful in explaining the attractiveness of the valley for settlers moving into the region in search of farmland. In addition, the mountains provided an inducement to settlement because they act as a shield against cold air moving down from the north. Although most Williamsporters may understandably be forgiven for not appreciating that fact on a blustery January day, the city's winters are significantly milder than towns only a few miles north. It has, for example, an average of 26 fewer days of killing frost annually than Canton, which is only 30 miles to the north.

Thus, if the mountains explain where the people have not

Facing page: *The long ridge of Bald Eagle Mountain reaching off to the southwest is seen from Loyalsock Township. The view shows the dramatic rise of the mountain from the Susquehanna River floodplain. Two of the major local gaps are clearly visible. The first one from the left is at South Williamsport and the one next to it is at DuBoistown.*

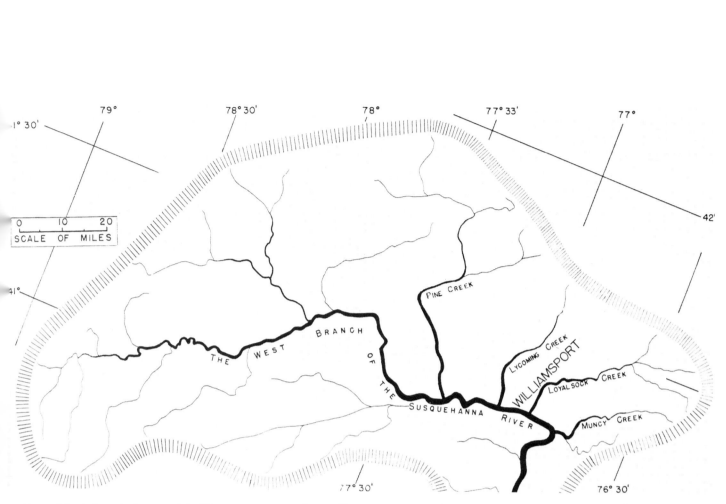

Above: *The drainage basin map of the West Branch of the Susquehanna shows the concentration of tributaries in the vicinity of Williamsport. The size of Lycoming Creek and the extensive drainage of Pine Creek were very favorable to the development and success of the lumber industry. Courtesy, William F. Plankenhorn*

Left: *The Loyalsock Creek Valley is seen here looking north from the mouth of the Creek to the Appalachian Plateau Province. The Valley retains a relatively broad alluvial plain almost until it reaches the Plateau. Montoursville is on the right. Courtesy, Marlin D. Fausey and Michael G. Roskin*

gone, the valleys explain where they have, an observation supported by the fact that 90 percent of Lycoming County's population is concentrated in only 3 percent of its total area along the river.

The waterways and adjacent lowlands present several problems, however. First, they do not penetrate the entire highland region. The West Branch Valley essentially ends at Lock Haven. Lycoming Creek Valley, which reaches north to New York, is a difficult route. Colonel Thomas Hartley, the commander of an expedition up that valley in 1778, likened it to crossing the Alps. Also, however suitable for agriculture the river valley may be, it is simply not large enough to support more than a limited number of people. Finally, as Williamsporters have been regularly reminded throughout their history, there is a flooding problem. Part of this problem is due to geography. The highlands to the north tend to conserve snow longer into the spring when the warm weather causes it to melt quickly. The rapid fall of the small streams of the highlands and the absence of any natural lakes to store the water produce a rapid runoff into the tributaries of the Susquehanna and then in the river itself. When this is combined with heavy spring rains, which are fairly common, the result is flooding of both the Susquehanna and its tributaries.

13

Floods have regularly disrupted the communications network of the citizens of the Williamsport area. The great flood of 1889 destroyed the Market Street Bridge over the Susquehanna and left its shattered remnants in the river. This scene looks south toward South Williamsport and the Bald Eagle Ridge. Courtesy, James V. Brown Library

Between 1886 and today, the river overflowed its 20-foot-banks 25 times. Fortunately, most of these were not major floods, but in 1889, 1894, 1936, and 1946 the results were disastrous. In 1972 the river reached a record high of 34.75 feet. Although contained by recently completed levees, flooding of the tributaries caused severe problems in many local areas.

In sum, the geographical characteristics of North-Central Pennsylvania indicate that the West Branch Valley was attractive to limited numbers of settlers. Within the valley, settlers were drawn to the area between Lycoming and Loyalsock creeks, because this area possesses the most extensive flatland and the best routes to the outside world.

Williamsport has clearly grown far beyond such a limited scale. A major reason for this was the growth of the lumber industry. Again, this was the result of geography. Many of the same climatic and topographic qualities which made the Allegheny Plateau unsuitable for agriculture made it ideal for the growth of high quality white pine and hemlock which covered the mountains. Moreover, the drainage system of the area was well suited for transporting the logs. The annual spring flooding of the rapidly descending streams was, with the addition of small dams, perfect for carrying the logs down to the creeks and then to the Susquehanna. Once there, it was desirable to turn the raw logs into lumber before shipment to users, or manufacture into wood products. To do this, three things were needed: storage areas for logs waiting to be processed; level land on which to build sawmills and factories; and access to markets outside the immediate region. Williamsport's location, only a short distance downstream from

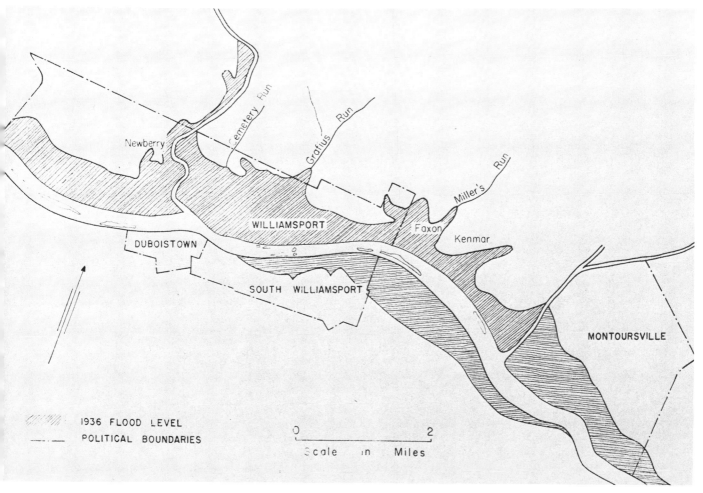

1936 FLOOD LEVEL
POLITICAL BOUNDARIES

Scale in Miles

Pine Creek at the mouth of Lycoming Creek, provided these three requirements. "Long Reach" provided a stretch of quiet water which could be used for constructing storage facilities. This was enhanced by the construction of a dam to back up the river and by a seven-mile-boom to pen the logs. River islands provided secure anchors for the boom, and a gentle northward curve of the river caused the logs to push against its south bank rather than the boom, so more logs could be stored. Swampy areas adjacent to the river were easily converted into logging ponds to serve as log storage. The widening of the valley plain at this point provided the room for mills, factories, and worker housing. Finally, the canal and railroads provided means of shipping finished products to the major markets of the East.

Thus, the land and the river, which had earlier limited Williamsport's growth, spurred economic activity during the late 19th century. Once the prosperous lumbering years ended, the city's traditional geographic disadvantages reasserted themselves, and go far to explain the problems Williamsport has faced since.

The Susquehanna River crested at 33.9 feet in the Saint Patrick's Day flood of 1936. The map shows how much of the city was inundated. Water rose as high as 10 feet in some industrial and commercial areas of the city. Courtesy, William F. Plankenhorn

CHAPTER TWO
Frontier Days

Left: *Russell Inn, built by James Russell in 1796 on the corner of Third and Mulberry streets, served many purposes. It was the first house in Williamsport, the site of early Lycoming County Court sessions, the first inn, and the first tavern. This major city landmark was destroyed in the great fire of 1871. Courtesy, James V. Brown Library*

The earliest settlers in the Susquehanna Valley were the Indians of the Laurentian, Lamoka, Shenks Ferry, Susquehanna, and Iroquois cultural traditions. For the most part, they were hunters and gatherers who flourished in a valley that abounded in oak, hickory, beech, bear, deer, turkey, and fish. The natives originally covered broad expanses of territory in their search for food, but as they became better adapted and developed a primitive agriculture, they reduced the range of their movement to a single large watershed. Generally women and children tended vegetable gardens near the major settlements while the men continued the tradition of obtaining foodstuffs from the forest.

When Charles II of England established the Colony of Pennsylvania and granted proprietary rights to William Penn in 1681, the Iroquois had recently driven out the Susquehanna Indians but had not moved into the area themselves. Instead they had granted settlement rights to various tribes including the Delaware, Shawnee, Chickasaw, and Leni Lenape, who had been displaced from their home areas by whites or other Indian peoples.

Penn required commissioners to extinguish Indian claims before he would provide whites with land titles. The Penn family purchased the West Branch Valley from Governor Thomas Dongan of New York, who had previously been granted it by the Seneca and Susquehanna Indians. The Iroquois protested that the land was theirs by right of conquest, and the Penns, as was their habit, also secured the Iroquois claim in a series of treaties in 1736 and 1768. The area did not attract much white habitation until after the French and Indian War, when a group of officers returning from service asked for land along the West Branch of the Susquehanna. Their request was heeded and soon surveyors were sent to prepare the territory for sale.

By this time the area was the subject of a heated dispute between the colonies of Pennsylvania and Connecticut. Both claimed the land on the basis of vague colonial charters and purchases from the Iroquois. Such conflicting claims among colonies were a common occurrence. Indeed, Pennsylvania had

Members of the North-Central Chapter No. 8 of the Society for Pennsylvania Archeology are shown on a dig on Canfield Island, east of Williamsport on the north side of the Susquehanna River. James P. Bressler, excavation director, records the discovery of a Laurentian burial site, dating approximately 3,000 B.C. Bob Demmien carefully chips away the packed earth in search of artifacts.

similar disputes with New York, Delaware, Virginia, and most notably with Maryland, which was only settled after the surveying of the Mason-Dixon Line. This problem with land claims lay partially with the Indians, who lacked a concept of private property and viewed land as a resource similar to water and air. Thus they believed they were merely granting the right to utilize this resource and saw no reason why various groups could not do so concurrently.

The European concept of private property and the practice of intensive land use made property claims most important to the colonists. The conflicting claims to the area by residents of Pennsylvania and Connecticut led to a series of sporadic raids between the citizens of the two states that marked the first, 1769-1772, second, 1775, and third, 1784, Yankee-Pennamite Wars. The disputed territory encompassed most of northern Pennsylvania including the present site of Williamsport. Battles raged at various times between the Scranton-Wilkes-Barre area and Muncy, about 10 miles east of Williamsport. Conflicts like these in the 1760s and 1770s convinced the British that the colonists could never unite to sustain the strong military effort needed to establish independence. Although the federal government under the Articles of Confederation settled the colonial claim dispute granting the land to Pennsylvania in 1782, it took more than 20 years and a series of complicated

Bull Run Indian Village is shown as it may have looked in about 1400 A.D., when it was inhabited by the Shenks Ferry people. The village, located on Bull Run in Loyalsock Township east of Williamsport, may have been the site of Madame Montour's Village. This diorama in the Lycoming County Historical Museum depicts typical domestic scenes: hunters returning with a deer; women preparing food; a man making projectile points; women hoeing a cornfield; a burial; and children playing. Courtesy, Lycoming County Historical Museum

This model in the Muncy Historical Museum depicts Fort Muncy, which was built in 1778 to protect the Muncy Valley during the American Revolution. The fort was abandoned when the area was invaded by a party of about 100 British and Tories and 200 Indians in the summer of 1779. Although the invaders destroyed the fort, the settlers quickly rebuilt it, but it fell into decay after the Revolution. Courtesy, Muncy Historical Museum

agreements to settle individual titles.

While the claim disputes were raging, the American Revolution erupted. Many settlers moved from New Jersey into the region to avoid the ravages of foraging parties of the American and British armies. This population influx bred conflict between Indians and whites. Throughout American history when the two cultures met, the Native Americans were usually driven west into conflict with other tribes. If they stayed in the east, they were forced into areas far too small to allow them to meet their nutritional requirements. This resulted in malnutrition, disease, and for some cultures, extinction. Many of the Indians in the region, like the Delaware and Leni Lenape, had already been forced west at least once, and so resisted. The British apparently supported this action. They had frozen settlement along the Appalachians in 1763, and were supplying the Indians with arms against the Americans.

This conflict produced two of the most famous events in West Branch Valley history, the Plum Thicket Massacre and the

"Big Runaway," both of which occurred in the summer of 1778. The massacre, one of the first recorded events in what was to become Williamsport, occurred near the present corner of West Fourth and Cemetery streets. It followed a protracted series of raids between the Indians and whites, and resulted in the loss of seven lives, including two men, three women, and two children. During the massacre two other children were taken captive but both were recovered in Canada by their father seven years later. Such attacks spread panic and fear through the West Branch Valley. When a group of British, Tories, and Indians defeated an American force near the Wyoming Valley on the North Branch of the Susquehanna, Colonel Samuel Hunter ordered the settlers out of the West Branch Valley for their own safety. Many settlers who joined the "Big Runaway" were critical of Hunter, arguing the danger did not warrant evacuation. Within a month they began returning to their homes.

At the time of these conflicts in the valley, the site of the original town plat of Williamsport was being surveyed and sold. The first owner was the surveyor, George Gibson, probably the western explorer and Indian fighter from Lancaster County, who acquired title to the land in 1769. Gibson sold it to Matthias Slough, a prominent merchant and land speculator, also of Lancaster, less than two years later. Slough held the land for about 16 years before selling it to William Winter, a tavern keeper whose place of business was located about a mile west of his recent purchase. Shortly before his death, Winter sold the site to Michael Ross, who had been a resident of the area for about 14 years. Ross had served a seven-year indenture with Samuel Wallis, the wealthy surveyor and speculator from Muncy. Apparently Ross learned much from his former master, because almost immediately he sought to exploit the land's location between the two major drainage systems in the inhabited part of the area. He supported the movement to establish a new county in the western section of what was then Northumberland County and requested that 111 acres of his purchase be named the county seat. He was encouraged in this effort by a river survey of 1790 which convinced many that the Susquehanna would become a great inland waterway.

The legislature established Lycoming County in 1795, and the governor appointed five commissioners to select the seat of justice. Four sites vied for the designation, including Dunnstown, Newberry, Jaysburg, and Ross' town. The contest for county seat was quickly reduced to the two locations on the river near the population concentration of the region: Jaysburg, situated south of Newberry at the confluence of Lycoming

Michael Ross, founder of Williamsport, was drawn by an itinerant artist. Born in 1759, he and his mother were living in Philadelphia in 1772 when he agreed to move to Muncy Farms to work for Samuel Wallis. When he completed his indenture in 1779 Wallis gave him 100 acres of land, which likely became the basis of his fortune. He believed in the future of his new town largely because of its river front and he reserved in his deeds all "fisheries and ferries" for himself. Courtesy, Lycoming County Historical Museum

The deed to "Virginia," the name of the tract of land Michael Ross purchased from William Winter, is dated March 7, 1794. The deed is in the Lycoming County Historical Museum. Courtesy, Lycoming County Historical Museum

Creek and the Susquehanna, and Ross' farm. Ross' town had several advantages, including more high, dry ground nearby for expansion. Ross surveyed the largest townplot and had made the most generous contribution of lots for county buildings. According to tradition, Ross had the support of former Pennsylvania State Senator William Hepburn, who owned land, a grist mill, and a distillery abutting Ross' plot. Hepburn knew that if Williamsport was named county seat the value of his land and the volume of his business would increase. He also had been named president judge of the court as soon as the county was created, but before a seat of justice had been named, and he may have preferred not to cross Lycoming Creek to Jaysburg for court sessions.

Jaysburg long claimed foul play after the commissioners

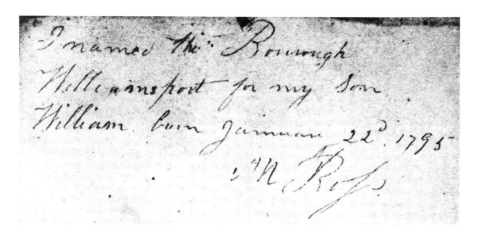

Above: *William Hepburn was born in County Donegal, Ireland, in 1753. He arrived in the West Branch Valley around 1773, achieved a local reputation as a soldier and businessman, and was elected state senator from Northumberland County. It was in this position that he served as the primary force in establishing Lycoming County. Courtesy, Lycoming County Historical Museum*

Above left: *Local historians have long disputed the origin of the name Williamsport. Some believe local citizens named the town for William Hepburn. Others believe Michael Ross named it after his close friends Joseph Williams and William Ellis who surveyed the town. Still others argue it was named for William Russell, a boatman who frequently docked at the lower end of Pine Street. This document appears to settle the issue, for Michael Ross in his own hand says he named the town for his son William. Courtesy, Lycoming County Historical Museum*

selected Williamsport as the center of county government. Its residents contended Williamsport was situated on low ground and was susceptible to flooding, and secured an affidavit to this effect. The messenger carrying the affidavit to the commissioners was waylaid by the Williamsport group, provided with ample drink, and awoke to find his saddlebag torn open and the document missing. This is a great tale and it may well be true, but even if the commissioners saw the affidavit they may still have selected Williamsport because the bulk of both town plots were situated 25 feet above normal river level. Williamsport did have a low section that flooded during high water, but this inlet also provided safe harbor for rivercraft, making it an asset as well as a liability. Jaysburg, like many aspiring frontier communities whose future was bound to the acquisition of a county seat, a canal dock, or a railroad terminal, soon passed out of existence. It is now the site of the Williamsport sewage treatment facility.

When Williamsport was designated county seat, it had only one building, the newly-completed Russell Inn. Michael Ross moved immediately to assure his new town's success. On July 4, 1796, he held an ox roast and land auction, selling 16 lots. That same year, he also named the town Williamsport in honor of his young son, William. Still, it took several years to build the courthouse, so in the meantime court sessions were held at Jaysburg, and later a mile west of town at the widow Eleanor Winter's tavern. In 1797 the court finally met in the new county seat for the first time at the Russell Inn. Civil offices and the jail were situated in Jaysburg until 1800. In that year Williamsport became seat of government in locale as well as name.

The 1800 federal and state census data reveal that Williamsport was becoming an economic center. The city contained 131 people, including three or four tavern owners, a

The first Lycoming County Court House was built on the plan of the courthouse in Harrisburg. The first court session in the new building appears to have been held in 1804. In 1858 the commissioners, faced with a growing county government, debated whether to expand or replace this building. They had the roof removed so that they could examine the condition of the walls and found them so weakened by age that they had the building torn down. Courtesy, James V. Brown Library

hatter, a tailor, two carpenters, a blacksmith, a tanner, a merchant, a surveyor, a distiller, and two attorneys. As in most nascent frontier communities, specialization was a luxury few could afford. Workers usually produced and sold their own specialty and many practiced several occupations. Robert McElrath, the hatter, for example, served as town jailer and kept an inn for a while. He also cooked the viands for the courthouse raising in October 1802.

One hundred and thirty-one people situated on 111 acres in such an unspecialized economic environment hardly conveys the image of a burgeoning metropolis, but it was 131 more people than had lived in Williamsport when Ross applied to have his tract designated county seat five years earlier. To gain a full appreciation of Williamsport's relative size it is important to realize that Lycoming County had a population density of about one person for every two square miles. The 1800 federal census listed 5,314 people, excluding Indians, in a geographic area roughly twice the size of Connecticut.

As county seat and river way station, Williamsport continued to attract settlers. Its population increased by 86 percent to 244 in 1810, by 156 percent to 624 in 1820, and by 83 percent to 1,140 in 1830. This growth was real but unimpressive when compared to western river cities like Cincinnati, Lexington, Louisville, and Pittsburgh. Indeed, many of the city's early historians lamented Williamsport's slow growth during these years. Michael Ross must have been particularly disappointed in 1810 because he was the largest taxpayer solely because of his assessment for 116 vacant lots. In 1820, two years after his death, his estate was still assessed for 47 empty lots. Surely Williamsport had grown, but it had not achieved the size and significance he had envisioned in surveying the original plot.

Williamsport's mediocre growth resulted from a variety of factors, many arising from its geographic conditions. There were also the rivalries with other river towns like Muncy to the east and Jersey Shore and Newberry to the west, all of which were linked to the north by wagon roads which gave them a trading advantage over Williamsport.

As a result, there simply were not enough people in town to fund projects such as the building of bridges and turnpikes needed to link an Appalachian county seat surrounded by creeks and mountains with a broader economic network. The total tax receipts for the county amounted to $2,393 in 1796 and in 1806, when Williamsport first became a borough, its receipts amounted to a mere $86.70. This was at a time when the county was faced with the immediate expense of building a courthouse, which when completed in 1806, cost $20,417. While the public sector was in tight circumstances, private investors questioned the financial feasibility of establishing toll bridges and roads through the area.

Nevertheless, Williamsporters displayed a burst of civic activity that fostered growth and economic development. They established a newspaper, the Lycoming *Gazette,* in 1801, and secured borough status for the community in 1806 to achieve greater home rule. They ran a stage line east to Northumberland in 1809, a trip which took 14 hours in good weather. They founded Williamsport Academy, the forerunner of Lycoming College, in 1812. They also bridged Loyalsock and Lycoming creeks between 1812 and 1813. Although Williamsporters sought subscriptions to bridge the Susquehanna at various times, a real link to a broader economic world did not occur until the West Branch Canal opened in 1834.

In these decades, Williamsport was in some ways the egalitarian society that historians have often envisioned frontier communities to have been. It was egalitarian in that the leading citizens like Michael Ross, Williamsport's founder, and William Hepburn, the first president judge of the county court, had both risen from obscurity. Hepburn, a Scotch Irish immigrant, first appeared in Williamsport digging a channel for a mill at the mouth of Mosquito Creek before the American Revolution. The background of other affluent citizens is also very obscure, indicating humble beginnings. Indeed, it is impossible to discover background data on William Wilson, the first United States congressman from the city, who served from 1815 to 1819.

Another indication of the egalitarian nature of the society lies in patterns of wealth distribution. The early 19th-century tax books reveal a society where wealth was as equitably distributed as in agrarian areas in Pennsylvania and far more equitable than in more urbanized areas in the state and elsewhere along the eastern seaboard. In 1810 and 1820 the wealthiest 10 percent of the population in Williamsport held between 25 and 30 percent of the taxable wealth, while in Chester County, Pennsylvania, the wealthiest group held as much as 48 percent. In major cities like Boston, New York, and Philadelphia, this group held up to 70 percent of the taxable property.

Williamsport's economic democracy resulted largely from the nature of its migrants and the frontier economy. In Eastern cities shipping merchants amassed huge fortunes and dominated the economic elite in these years, but in 1810 in Williamsport the 10 richest men included two distillers, one of whom also owned a store, three tavern keepers, two store owners, one of whom was the local postmaster, a blacksmith, an attorney, and land speculator and surveyor Michael Ross.

Despite the relative economic equality in the new borough, a social aristocracy seems to have emerged soon after settlement. This is evident from an analysis of marriage patterns among the city's wealthy families. Michael Ross' daughters all married affluent Williamsporters. Elizabeth married Peter Vanderbelt, Jr., son of the sixth wealthiest man in town in 1810, Margaret married James Huling, the richest man in town in 1820, and Anna married Major Charles Low, a fairly successful shoe manufacturer. The second wealthiest man in town, Andrew D. Hepburn, was William Hepburn's nephew. Hepburn married Martha Huston, the daughter of the fourth most affluent Williamsporter, in 1810. The third wealthiest man was William Wilson. After the death of his wife Rebecca, Wilson married Henrietta Van Horne, the widow of Espy Van Horne, a former local congressman. Robert McClure, the fourth in total taxable wealth, wed Mary Hepburn, who was the daughter of Judge William Hepburn. A full analysis of the experience of the ten wealthiest families reveals no instance where a son or daughter of an affluent Williamsporter married poor. Williamsport's society began taking firm shape almost as soon as the town was founded.

Another indication of Williamsport's stability during the frontier era was that a large portion of the town's citizens tended to remain in the county seat. Of the 10 wealthiest men in town in 1810, eight were still present in 1820 and at least one of the other two had died. Persistence rates for others in the town were also quite high during this era. More than half the

The Lycoming County Historical Museum recreated this frontier period blacksmith shop. Peter Vanderbelt was the local blacksmith and may have used some of this equipment since most of it was collected from the local area. Courtesy, Lycoming County Historical Museum

adult males remained during each of the first three decades of the 19th century, providing a very stable social situation.

Thus Williamsport's birth and early history were similar to many frontier villages. An entrepreneur hoping to improve his economic situation surveyed his farm into city lots and sought to make it the political and economic center of a region. In 1830 Williamsport resembled an early colonial settlement in many ways. It was geographically isolated, wealth was relatively equally distributed, the population was stable, and the town was rather self-sufficient. However, the city was on the brink of breaking its isolation and of being thrust into a rapidly changing economic and intellectual climate in America during the presidency of Andrew Jackson.

CHAPTER THREE
Routes to the World

Left: *This photograph captures the busy curbstone markets of Market Street north of the Square in the horse and buggy days of the early 1860s. The church spire belongs to the Second Presbyterian Church. The Masonic Temple was built on the site of the Second Presbyterian Church after it was destroyed by fire. Courtesy, Lycoming County Historical Museum*

The Age of Jackson was a time of enormous optimism, when people believed in a benevolent God and a decent, capable humanity. Such an outlook encouraged the democratization of the American political system, producing the growth of popular nominating conventions, popular rather than state legislative selection of the electoral college, and the election of men like Andrew Jackson, who scorned the Eastern aristocracy of wealth and power. The hope of the era also led to the abandonment of established religions in states where such institutions continued, and produced tremendous local church growth throughout the nation. At the same time, church and secular leaders united in their attempts to reform society. Temperance advocates, abolitionists, prison reformers, women's rights advocates, and pacifists all pursued various methods of achieving individual and social perfection.

Economically, this optimism encouraged many to carve existences from the trans-Allegheny West. Others opened factories on a scale American entrepreneurs had hardly contemplated a generation earlier. States and private individuals undertook massive internal improvement projects to bind the nation together and provide the transportation system necessary for the economic growth and development which seemed to be both America's mission and destiny.

In Williamsport the spirit of the age materialized in the work of the abolitionists, the programs of local temperance advocates, the growth of Anti-Masonry, and the birth of new religious congregations. This spirit also produced a pattern of public and private investment that allowed Williamsport to become the commercial center its founders envisioned, and spawned an industrial sector that would nourish economic development in the future.

The most productive abolitionist work in Williamsport was that of the Underground Railroad, a way of helping slaves escape from the bondage of the south to the freedom of Canada. The line was supported by some of the city's most prominent citizens including Tunison Coryell, county prothonotary, and Abraham Updegraff, president of the West Branch Bank, and president of the board of trustees of

Right: *Daniel Hughes was a powerful man, a few inches short of seven feet tall and weighing about 300 pounds. His farmhouse north of Williamsport was the center of "Hughes Territory" on the Underground Railroad. Caves cut into Grampian Hill not far from the farmhouse were used to hide fleeing slaves. The caves have since been sealed. Courtesy, Lycoming County Historical Museum*

Far right: *Abraham Updegraff was one of many successful businessmen who supported public works and contributed to charitable projects. Manager during the early stages of the Williamsport Bridge Company, he was also associated with the Williamsport Water Company. In addition, he worked with the Underground Railroad and Dickinson Seminary. He also found time to be superintendent of the Lycoming County Sunday School Association, and to establish Wildwood Cemetery.*

Dickinson Seminary. Daniel Hughes, an American Indian who was married to former slave Annie Rotch, also did much work for the line. Hughes was a river rafter who picked up slaves on trips to Maryland, transported them to his farm on what is now Freedom Road in Williamsport, and hid them in caves cut into the eastern side of Grampian Hill in preparation for the next leg of their journey, to Elmira, New York. In this effort, the Underground Railroad was aided by Robert Faires, president of the Williamsport and Elmira Railroad.

Closely associated with abolitionism in this period was the temperance movement. Temperance advocates sought to reform society by prohibiting the use of alcoholic beverages, which they believed made people violent and lazy. Perhaps the area's most prominent temperance advocate was John J. Pearce, a Methodist minister from Lock Haven and Jersey Shore who won endorsement of the local Whig and Know-Nothing Parties and was elected to congress in 1855.

One of the major manifestations of political reform was the growing mistrust of the Masons. The Masonic Order was an organized brotherhood which described its mission as "enlightening the understanding, cultivating the mental faculties, and improving the moral virtues of men, and teaching them their duties and relations to each other, in connection with their religious obligations." Suspicion of the Masons was originally based on the members' pledge of secrecy and the belief that they were aristocrats who threatened to control society through a system of mutual rewards.

Anti-Masons, ardent temperance men, were bitter about rumored alcoholic excesses in the Masonic ceremonies. The Anti-Masons were usually abolitionists and egalitarian Democrats who viewed the more affluent and politically conservative Masons with hostility. In Williamsport Anti-Masonry was particularly strong. In 1835 the city supported the successful Anti-Mason gubernatorial candidacy of Joseph Ritner. But the clearest indication of the strength of the movement occurred on June 17, 1829, when a group of Anti-Masons broke into the Williamsport Masonic lodge, which was located on the second floor of the courthouse, and vandalized it, throwing most of the "furniture, papers, records, and working tools" out the windows. So strong was local feeling that the Masons suspended their meetings for 17 years.

Closely associated with the social and political reform of the day was the growth of existing religious congregations and the proliferation of new ones, many of which adhered to liberal views of God and human nature so prevalent in Jacksonian America. The earliest churches in the area were Presbyterian and Methodist Episcopal. The first Presbyterian congregation erected a log building in Newberry in 1792. The Presbyterians established their own congregation in Williamsport on Third

The first Pine Street Methodist Church was erected on the northwest corner of Pine and West Edwin streets in 1826. It was the first brick church in the borough. The pulpit was in the rear of the church and was so high that a child could not see the preacher until he stood to preach. The church was replaced by another brick structure in 1843. Courtesy, Pine Street United Methodist Church

and Mulberry streets in 1833. The Second Presbyterian church was organized in December 1840. The latter body was initially composed of migrants from western New York who belonged to the New School Branch of the church. The Methodist Episcopalians apparently met in the cabin of Amariah Sutton just east of Lycoming Creek around the time of the American Revolution. In 1776 Sutton set aside an acre and a quarter of land for a church, schoolhouse, and cemetery. The congregation was formally established in 1791. The first Methodist Episcopal church in Williamsport proper was built on Pine Street in 1826.

Other churches were formed at about the same time. The Reformed Church was built on West Third Street in 1827 jointly by German Lutherans and Reformed. A Protestant Episcopal church was organized in 1842. The Evangelicals built a church on Market Street near the Railroad in 1845. Saint Boniface Roman Catholic Church was organized in 1853, and Saint Marks Lutheran and the First Baptist churches were built a year later.

The optimism which gave birth to the social and political reforms also encouraged a series of public and private economic endeavors which broke Williamsport's geographic isolation and bound it to a broader economic world. The first and perhaps grandest accomplishment of this nature was the building of the West Branch Canal. The town's first settlers dreamed of a bustling trading center along the West Branch of the Susquehanna. Yet, the river was not easily tamed. It had so many shallows, rapids, bars, and islands that had to be removed or circumvented that it was beyond the means of the settlers in the region to make the waterway navigable for anything but rafts and canoes until the state took an active role in internal improvements.

The state stepped into the transportation business during the 1820s after many false starts and only after the Erie Canal to the north proved an immediate financial success, threatening to draw off much of Pennsylvania's trade. The Erie was paying the interest on its debt even before the entire canal was opened in 1825, and tolls covered the cost of construction within nine years. Equally important, freight rates between Buffalo and New York City declined drastically, leading many farmers in western Pennsylvania to ship their goods north to the lakes and from there to New York City by way of the Erie. Partly as a result, between 1820 and 1830 New York City doubled its population and raced ahead of Philadelphia as the nation's largest port. Hoping to end the loss of its own trade and to emulate the economic development of its neighbor to the north,

Pennsylvania embarked on its own canal system linking Philadelphia and Pittsburgh and sending feeder lines, among other places, along the North and West branches of the Susquehanna River.

The story of the building of the Pennsylvania Canal system is filled with political compromises. Legislators from areas a considerable distance from the main canal voted appropriations only if feeder lines were promised for their districts. The agreement worked well initially, but briefly in 1831 many legislators refused to fund the branch canals. At this point prominent citizens from branch canal towns took action. In Williamsport, William Packer, editor of the Lycoming *Gazette,*

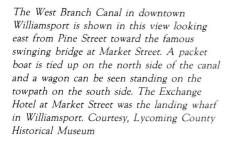

The West Branch Canal in downtown Williamsport is shown in this view looking east from Pine Street toward the famous swinging bridge at Market Street. A packet boat is tied up on the north side of the canal and a wagon can be seen standing on the towpath on the south side. The Exchange Hotel at Market Street was the landing wharf in Williamsport. Courtesy, Lycoming County Historical Museum

and Tunison Coryell, who made 12 trips to Harrisburg at his own expense to lobby for passage of the West Branch appropriation, organized the citizens to place all the pressure at their disposal on the governor and legislature to secure the West Branch funding. They succeeded. Governor George Wolf called a special session of the legislature and an appropriations bill was quickly passed and signed.

William Packer was in charge of construction of the West Branch Canal from Sunbury to Lock Haven. A trench was excavated measuring four feet deep, 28 feet wide at the base and 40 feet at the top. A total of 600 million cubic feet of dirt were moved by hand and wheelbarrow. Locks were built, culverts

William Fisher Packer was one of Williamsport's best known citizens. Newspaperman and civic booster, he was superintendent of the West Branch Canal. He later served Lycoming and nearby counties in the State House of Representatives (1846) and the State Senate (1849), and served all the citizens of Pennsylvania as their governor (1857). He died in Williamsport in 1870. This portrait, an original Currier and Ives, hangs in the Lycoming County Historical Museum. Courtesy, Lycoming County Historical Museum

were established over small streams, and aqueducts over the larger ones. The towpath was graded and finally on October 15, 1834, the canal was filled. Within a few days the first boat passed into Williamsport. The opening of the canal was celebrated by local bands and military groups and large numbers of the citizenry, who turned out for the event.

At the same time Williamsporters actively sought a variety of railroad connections, most importantly a link to a Great Lakes' port to the north. In November 1836 Williamsporters held a railroad convention urging the development of the line from Philadelphia to Sunbury to Williamsport and then to Erie. Governor Joseph Ritner signed a charter for the Sunbury and Erie in April 1837, but construction was delayed by the demise of the Bank of the United States, a main source of the line's funds. The subsequent Panic of 1837 and the lengthy depression that followed kept funds scarce, delaying the commencement of construction until 1852. The line was completed from Sunbury to Williamsport in 1855 and the remainder of the line to Erie was finished in 1864.

During the time the Philadelphia and Erie was being planned, Robert Ralston and some of his friends from Philadelphia developed iron mines and a blast furnace just north of Williamsport and built a railroad line from Ralston to Williamsport to expedite movement of pig iron to the canal at the river city. The line was poorly constructed and mules hauled the freight along the tracks for years because the engine was too heavy for the rails. The line failed financially for a variety of reasons and was sold at auction for $6,000. It was reorganized, renamed the Elmira and Williamsport, and extended to the former city in September 1854. At Elmira, Williamsport traffic was linked to all the important points on Lake Erie and Lake Ontario by way of the New York lines.

While the railroads were being completed, Williamsport's leading citizens were finding other ways to bind the city to the outside world. In 1833 the state legislature appointed Joseph Anthony, James Armstrong, Joseph Wallis, William Wilson, Jeremiah Tallman, William Piatt, Jr., Hugh Donley, Henry Hughes, and William Packer commissioners to sell shares of stock in a private toll bridge across the Susquehanna and to construct a turnpike south to the Union County line. Once the stock was subscribed the legislature passed an act of incorporation and the bridge was completed in July 1849. Two years later, the Susquehanna River, North and West Branch Telegraph Company ran a telegraph line to Jacob Mussina's jewelry shop on Market Square.

NEW ROUTE

FROM

ELMIRA, WILLIAMSPORT, DANVILLE & CATAWISSA:

TO

NEW YORK

AND TO

PHILADELPHIA:

VIA

Williamsport and Elmira, Catawissa, Quakake, Lehigh Valley, and Central Rail Road of New Jersey,

TO

☞ NEW YORK, ☜

OR VIA

NORTH PENNSYLVANIA RAIL ROAD

TO

PHILADELPHIA.

ON AND AFTER

Wednesday, December 22, 1858,

Passengers for Philadelphia, will take Cars of Catawissa Rail Road at Williamsport, at 10.30 P. M., to Quakake Junction; thence by Quakake Rail Road to Mauch Chunk, arriving at 4.50 A. M.; then take Lehigh Valley Rail Road to Bethlehem, in time for breakfast, and Express Train of North Pennsylvania Rail Road, and arrive in Philadelphia at 10 A. M..

Passengers for **NEW YORK** continue on the Lehigh Valley Cars to Easton, thence by New Jersey Central, arriving in New York at 11.30 A. M.

RETURNING

Leave Philadelphia from FRONT AND WILLOW STS., at 2.15 P. M., and New York, Pier No. 2 NORTH RIVER, at 12 Noon.

Arriving at Williamsport soon after Midnight.

Many new routes to the world opened up for Williamsport in the 1850s. This 1858 advertisement announced a new connection between North-Central Pennsylvania and New York City or Philadelphia. Travelers could reach either of these major port cities in about 12 hours. Courtesy, Lycoming County Historical Museum

With links downriver and beyond the mountains, Williamsporters began to provide urban services for the industries and people they knew would soon arrive. In 1856 two private institutions, the Williamsport Water Company and the Williamsport Gas Company, were incorporated, providing a supply of energy and clean water to the city.

Despite these developments, population growth was slow between 1830 and 1850 when it rose by only 475 to 1,615. But a few years after the canal's completion the city began its transformation to a commercial and manufacturing center. Between 1820 and 1840 the number of people engaged in manufacturing jumped from 83 to 216, an increase of nearly 260 percent, when the population had barely doubled. Between 1830 and 1840 the number of working men aged between 15 and 45 increased 71 percent, while the population increased by only 19

Physician John Crawford came to Williamsport in 1849 after practicing medicine in Cambria, Luzerne County, for 15 years. His home and office are shown in the 1860s (left) and today (right). He organized the Lycoming County Medical Society and served as its president. He also was president of the State Medical Society. He was killed in 1879 while crossing a railroad on the way to visit a very sick boy. The child died shortly after Dr. Crawford. Courtesy, James V. Brown Library

percent. The canal attracted industries which foreshadowed Williamsport's golden age. John B. Hall from Geneva, New York, established a foundry in the city in 1832 which was devoted at first to the production of wood cutting machinery. Similarly, four Philadelphians built the Big Water Mill in 1838, which contained four waterwheels powering four saws to process lumber. Major James Perkins, of South New Market, New Hampshire, who later purchased the mill, built a temporary boom on the Susquehanna River in March 1849 to stop the logs destined for his saws. Following his success a group of businessmen formed the Susquehanna Boom Company and established a boom of their own in December 1849.

Between 1850 and 1860, the coming of the railroads and telegraph, the bridging of the Susquehanna, the development of an array of private utilities, and the establishment of the lumber boom prepared Williamsport for a sustained period of growth. The population more than tripled during the 1850s, rising from 1,615 to 5,664, as many new industries developed. Peter Tinsman opened a steam sawmill in early 1852 and Garret Tinsman and Runyon Woolverton opened another later that year. John and Charles Dodge also established a steam sawmill that year and replaced it with a larger one in 1854. In 1859 Peter Herdic, George W. Lentz, John White, and Henry White formed a partnership and established extensive mills near the river above Center Street. In 1855 George Banger of Philadelphia established the first planing mill and in 1859 John Otto commenced the manufacture of furniture.

While the population grew and industry developed, Williamsport extended its geographic boundaries. The original city was bordered by the river and what are now West Street, Little League Boulevard, and Academy Street. But between 1822 and 1860 the annexation of a series of farms to the north, east, and west more than tripled the size of the community.

This period of growth was fostered by a new generation of Williamsporters led by William Packer, Tunison Coryell, Joseph B. Anthony, James Armstrong, and Robert Faires. Each one of these men was a founder or initiator of two or more of the public works or utilities completed during the 1850s. These men all migrated to Lycoming County and most seem to have risen from relative obscurity but benefited from links to powerful families in the area. Joseph B. Anthony, a graduate of Princeton, studied law with Samuel Hepburn in Milton. After establishing an office in Williamsport, he married into the Grafius family, one of the city's earliest and most prominent. James Armstrong moved to Williamsport from Milton to practice the tanning trade but soon began studying law with Anthony, and later married Sarah Hepburn, daughter of Judge William Hepburn. William Packer, born in Center County, was orphaned at an early age and at 13 was a printer's apprentice at the Sunbury *Public Inquirer.* He served with two other papers before coming to Williamsport at the age of 20 to study law with Joseph B. Anthony. Shortly after his arrival in 1827 Packer secured an interest in the Lycoming *Gazette,* establishing a partnership with Joseph Brandon. Packer married Mary Vanderbelt in 1829, thus associating himself with another of the city's most successful first generation families. Coryell, son of a Revolutionary War veteran, secured a rudimentry education in Buffalo Valley to the south where his parents owned a farm. He then served as a clerk and mail carrier in the area before working for General John Burrows of Montoursville, himself a former Revolutionary War veteran and mail carrier. Coryell seems to have been fairly successful at the time of his marriage. He wed Burrows' daughter Sarah in 1816 and first appears in Williamsport's tax books in 1818 as owner of a substantial house and other land in the city. Robert Faires was born in County Antrim, Northern Ireland, but accompanied his parents to Philadelphia as an infant. His father achieved some political prominence in his new home and became a city commissioner. But while the youth was in his teens his father purchased a farm in Montgomery County where his son worked. When the survey for the canal was being completed, the young man secured a job as an axman but within a few years rose to become chief engineer of the West Branch Extension. Faires married Mary Jane Campbell, who was daughter of the prominent local jurist Francis C. Campbell, and Jane Hepburn Campbell, sister of Andrew D. Hepburn. Judging from the experience of the second generation of Williamsporters, opportunity for improvement was easily obtainable.

Far left: *Major James Perkins came to Williamsport in 1845. Born in New Hampshire in 1803, he learned to be a millwright and a machinist before moving to Philadelphia in 1830 where he employed his trades. In Williamsport he not only bought the Big Water Mill but also built a steam-powered sawmill and the first log boom.*

Left: *Tunison Coryell was involved in many of the efforts to improve Williamsport and develop it as a center of commerce. He lobbied hard for the West Branch Canal, worked to see the Philadelphia and Erie Railroad completed, and urged the government to build a national road through his city. He was cashier of the West Branch Bank and a chief organizer and secretary of the Williamsport Gas Company. In his later years he took an interest in local history and published a book about Williamsport's earliest settlers. He died in 1881.*

These newcomers did not displace the families of the founders. The names Hepburn, Wallis, Piatt, Cummings, Vanderbelt, McLure, and others appear as stockholders on various local utilities and through marriage, continued the lines of the early settlers.

The average workman, however, did not always fare so well during these years because economic ties linking Williamsport to the national economy were not always for the better. The financial Panic of 1837 and the ensuing depression which delayed construction of local railroads seems to have reduced economic opportunity during the 1830s and 1840s. The burden seems to have fallen most heavily on residents who did not own land, because a full two-thirds of the poorer half of the population present in 1830 had disappeared from the tax rolls by 1840. This was natural in an age before unemployment insurance and workfare when the unemployed urban worker had no recourse but to pull up stakes and seek employment elsewhere.

Those who stayed saw Williamsport change substantially during the Age of Jackson. The isolated frontier community had been swept into the mainstream of the changes engulfing America. The abolitionism, temperance reform, political democratization, and religious growth of the age are all reflected in Williamsport's story. The optimism that gave birth to these changes encouraged private and public investment which prepared the city for its golden era. However, the changes of the previous 30 years were nothing compared to what lay ahead.

CHAPTER FOUR

Years of Growth: The City

Left: Smokestacks and steeples dominated Williamsport in the industrial era. This 1875 view from Vallamont takes in the city from St. Boniface Church in the east to the Herdic House and Philadelphia and Erie Railroad Station in the west. The large building in the left center is Williamsport Dickinson Seminary.

The bloody turmoil of the Civil War and the Industrial Revolution surrounding it shattered the traditional ways of life throughout America. The war abruptly ended slavery in the South and thrust the federal government into the lives of a people who had rarely felt its reach before. The Industrial Revolution, while increasing national wealth enormously, left a small number of entrepreneurs living in splendor while common laborers toiled long hours over dangerous equipment for minimal rewards. In both of these efforts, the experience of Williamsporters was a microcosm of the American people as a whole.

The firing on Fort Sumter in April 1861 shocked the residents of Williamsport. Although some had expressed sympathy for slaveholders who had found it difficult to secure the return of their fugitive slaves from some Northern states, most now agreed with the Lycoming *Gazette* when it demanded that the rebels "be forced to obey the laws, cost what they may, even to the last man and last cent of the North."

The community responded concretely to the crisis when President Abraham Lincoln issued his call for 75,000 volunteers for three months of service to crush the rebellion. For this call, Lycoming County sent three companies, two from Williamsport and one from Muncy, to join the 11th Regiment of Pennsylvania Volunteers, which was mustered into federal service at Harrisburg on April 24, 1861. The following July this regiment became one of the first to extend its service to three years, and it earned a distinguished reputation for its service with the Army of the Potomic, participating in battles including Antietam, Fredericksburg, Chancellorsville, Gettysburg, and the Virginia campaign of 1864-1865.

Williamsport was also noted for the Repasz Band, a local musical group which had been formed in 1831. It served as the regimental band for the 11th and later the 29th regiments of Pennsylvania Volunteers and played *The Star Spangled Banner* when Robert E. Lee surrendered to Ulysses S. Grant at Appomattox.

These men were joined by other volunteers as new units were formed, and, after March 1863, by men raised through the

Stretching upstream from Williamsport, log cribs looked like strange river forts. When spring's high water brought down the logs, the cribs marked the boundary of a giant storage facility, holding the logs against the south side of the river until they could be sorted and used. Courtesy, Ralph E. Menne

national draft. Williamsporters manned one or more entire companies in eight infantry regiments of Pennsylvania Volunteers, and helped fill the ranks of at least 12 additional infantry and six cavalry regiments. Approximately 9 percent of the county's 1860 population served in one way or another in the Union armies, a proportion comparable to that of the nation as a whole.

The large armies raised by these means naturally required an equal effort on the home front to support them, and in this too, Williamsport and Lycoming County contibuted their share. Troops traveling through Williamsport on the railroad were fed by the women of the town who set up serving tables on Fourth Street between Pine and Mulberry streets. The citizens of the town raised $3,000 for the benefit of local families whose men were with the army, and at least one landlord suspended the rent payments for such families. Ladies aid societies were formed in conjunction with the U.S. Sanitary Commission to provide troops in the field with food and clothing beyond their normal issue. Their efforts throughout the war undoubtedly did much to improve the conditions and raise the morale of the men.

The near unanimity with which the community went to war

Logs were marked to identify those of a particular owner.

Logs were marked before they were floated downstream to prove ownership and ease sorting. This display in the Lycoming County Historical Museum shows some of the marks and the tools used in making them. More than 1,700 log marks were registered by the Susquehanna Boom Company. Log rustlers were common; they simply sawed off the marks and applied their own. Courtesy, Lycoming County Historical Museum

in 1861 could not be expected to last the duration of such a long struggle, and particularly after the last threat of invasion ended in the summer of 1863, partisan politics resumed its course. Despite the efforts of Republicans to brand all Democrats as sympathizers with the South, the latter were able to mount several successful local campaigns and carried the county with a 57 percent majority in the 1864 presidential election. The county even had its own self-styled "peace organ," a local German newspaper called the West Branch *Beobachter* (Observer), but it avoided the bitter internal strife which plagued some Northern communities.

When the guns of the Civil War ceased, Williamsport could

Right: *Peter Herdic (1824-1888), one of the leading figures of Williamsport's industrial era, is shown in this 1860s portrait.*

Far right: *Mahlon Fisher was born and reared in New Jersey. Moving to Williamsport in 1855, he held interests in the lumber firms of Reading, Fisher, and Company and Teneyke, Emery, and Company, as well as the planing mill of Reading, Fisher, and Reading. He was president of the Susquehanna Boom Company.*

justly claim its fair share in the Union victory. To those veterans who had seen extended service, however, the community to which they returned was vastly different than the one they had left.

During the decade following Major James Perkins' construction of the first lumber boom on the Susquehanna, Williamsport's lumber industry grew steadily but slowly. The apparent reason was the limited capacity of the boom. Only certain species of trees could be cut during the summer and very few, if any, logs could be transported down the streams during the fall and winter. Therefore, the lumber industry depended upon the boom's capacity to store a sufficient number of logs to keep the mills working for most of the year. Unfortunately, Perkins' original boom could hold only enough logs to feed a few mills and was not strong enough to withstand a serious flood.

This situation was dramatically transformed shortly after Peter Herdic, Mahlon Fisher, and John G. Reading bought the Susquehanna Boom Company in 1857. The new owners quickly moved to expand their operation. Floods in 1860 and 1861 severely damaged the boom and washed much of the season's harvest downstream, but by 1862 the new owners had devised a strengthened boom employing sunken cribs to which a string of logs was attached by cables. This boom combined the strength and capacity necessary to hold greater numbers of logs and proved itself during the 1865 flood. Eventually the boom was expanded until it ran from the vicinity of the Maynard Street

bridge seven miles to Linden and was anchored to 252 sunken cribs each measuring 20 x 50 feet and 22 feet high. At that point, it could hold 300 million feet of lumber at one time.

The new boom came at just the right time. The Civil War, industrial expansion in the North, and Southern reconstruction created a tremendous demand for lumber, and the invention of new machinery to process the lumber and power the mills greatly increased production capacity. Williamsport and the nation were entering the industrial age.

Much of this change in Williamsport was due to the personal efforts of Peter Herdic. Born in Ft. Plains, New York, in 1824, Herdic was a man of boundless energy and ruthless determination. He came to Lycoming County in 1846 and for several years successfully operated a farm, shingle mill, and sawmill along Lycoming Creek. In 1853 he sold these interests

The Herdic House was part of Peter Herdic's development of the western part of the city. He persuaded the railroad to build its main depot adjoining his hotel and built the horse-drawn streetcar line shown in this picture to provide transportation to Market Street. The streetcar began the same day the hotel opened: September 25, 1865. Courtesy, James V. Brown Library

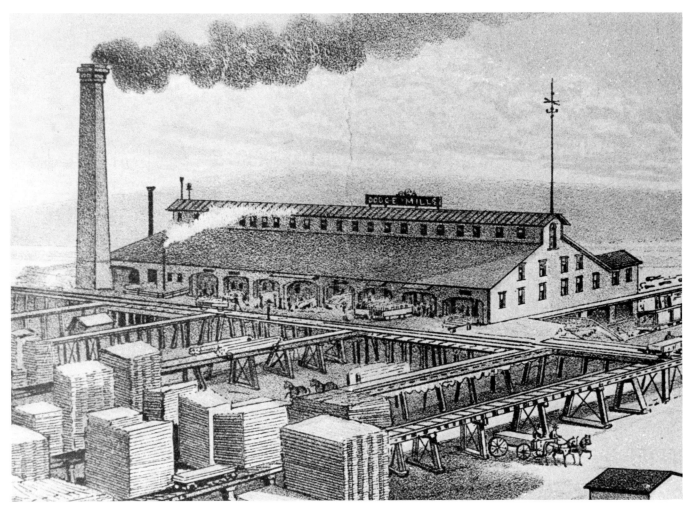

The Dodge Mills had the largest capacity of any Williamsport area lumber mill. In 1876, for example, Dodge processed 28 million board feet of lumber.

and moved to Williamsport. There he built a fortune and touched almost every aspect of the city's life. During his career, he wholly or partially owned almost every major business in the city, including several sawmills, a gasworks, a waterworks, several banks, a newspaper, the grandest hotel in town, the Herdic House, and enormous tracts of land. He actively participated in civic affairs, playing an instrumental role in making Williamsport a city, serving as mayor from 1869 to 1870, and bringing Newberry within its boundaries. He almost single-handedly created South Williamsport by convincing the Pennsylvania Railroad to run a spur along the south bank of the river and then selling lots he owned there to developers.

In all these activities, Herdic was more concerned with the ends he sought than with the means he employed to achieve them. His methods consequently raised more than a few eyebrows among his contemporaries. He was accused of buying his election as mayor. Money was passed freely in the saloons, and when the ballots were counted, his election had cost him

$15 per vote. But he was also a generous supporter of numerous local charities, contributing to the building of churches of all faiths in the city, including its first synagogue. He even sponsored an early form of public works projects to relieve the unemployment problem during the depression of the 1870s by building 800 dwellings in the city. In this effort, he overextended his resources and was forced into bankruptcy in 1878. However one balances his virtues and faults, he was instrumental in the development of Williamsport during the lumber years.

The heart of the lumber industry was of course the sawmills. From their humble beginnings, they grew to number more than 30. Larger mills, such as Guy W. Maynard and Company, B.C. Bowman and Company, and the Dodge Mills, were capable of cutting at least 100,000 feet of lumber in a single day. They were concentrated in five districts along the river, three in Williamsport itself and two on the south bank in South Williamsport and DuBoistown. Their combined record of production is still awesome, In 1862, the first year combined records were kept, 196,953 logs were processed into 37,853,621 board feet. For the next 20 years, production seldom fell below the 1862 figure and was often greater. Altogether, between 1862 and 1891, 31,606,557 logs were processed by the Williamsport mills into 5,545,298,406 board feet of lumber.

Those laboring in the mills found life was often harsh. They worked from 6 a.m. to 6 p.m. six days a week, earning only $1.50 a day and could hope for little improvement in their circumstances. The work was not only difficult, but dangerous and uncertain. Broken saws and flying bits of wood were common hazards. The mill districts were often ravaged by fires which destroyed entire mills and put many men out of work. Since mill hands were not paid for days they did not work, no matter what the reason, the threat of economic destitution was never far from their minds.

In 1872 these conditions pushed the mill workers to strike in what has become famous as the Sawdust War. The mill workers' central demand was a reduction of the workday to 10 hours with no reduction in pay. With the exception of Herdic, the mill owners rejected this demand and eventually had the governor send 400 militiamen to crush the strike. Four strike leaders, including Thomas H. Greevy, a distant relative of a later president judge of Lycoming County, were sentenced to prison. Peter Herdic intervened and persuaded the governor to pardon them. In any event, the strikers were defeated and organized labor in Williamsport suffered such a severe setback that it almost completely disappeared for the rest of the lumber era.

The lumber industry did more than simply provide jobs and wealth. It also served as a magnet to attract many other industries. In fact, of the 6,261 people employed in the city in 1886, only 2,000 worked in the sawmills. Many of these other industries were naturally related to lumber. The most important in terms of employment were: furniture manufacturing, employing 925 workers; metal products with 644 people producing many of the machines and tools used locally; planing mills with 425 workers; the tanning industry with 203 employees. Smaller manufacturers, which also relied on the lumber industry, produced match sticks, toothpicks, wooden toys, and charcoal. In addition, other industries were attracted to the area without regard for lumber. Of these, the most important was rubber manufacturing, which employed 252 people.

Industrial development extended Williamsport's importance as a manufacturing center well beyond the region of central Pennsylvania. Lumber and lumber products were not only sent all over the eastern United States but overseas. The metal industry sent its products equally far afield. The Valley Iron Works sold its products, which included both agricultural and industrial machinery, as far away as Japan and the Ottoman Empire. At the 1873 Vienna International Exhibition, a local firm displayed a steam powered brick-making machine.

This growth in manufacturing was also reflected in the expansion of rail and banking services. By 1886 Williamsport was connected to all major cities in the East by five railroads. Sixteen passenger trains stopped daily at its two stations. The number of banks and savings institutions increased from one before the Civil War to nine by 1890.

Finally, all of these activities led to an enormous expansion of the retail business which made Williamsport the commercial center of all North-Central Pennsylvania. By the mid-1880s the city could boast six hotels capable of housing more than 1,000 guests, 25 dry goods and millinery stores, 95 grocery stores, 13 boot and shoe stores, eight hardware and cutlery stores, 14 drugstores, eight bookstores, seven jewelry stores, and 13 livery stables. The most prominent mercantile establishment was L.L. Stearns, which moved from Jersey Shore in 1865.

The bustling business activity transformed the face of the community. Census figures provide the first indication of change: between 1860 and 1870, the city's population almost tripled from 5,664 to 16,030. The nationwide depression of the 1870s slowed the city's growth so that it only reached 18,934 by

Above: *E.A. Rowley and A.D. Hermance opened their woodworking machinery company in 1875. Growing rapidly, the establishment soon needed these impressive buildings to house it. The company made machinist's tools and all kinds of woodworking machinery for furniture factories and other wood-related businesses.*

Left: *This beautiful solid cherry sideboard was produced by the Mankey Decorative Works in the 1880s. Its Eastlake pattern was ebonized and ribbed with gilt. It represents the high quality of furniture produced in Williamsport. Courtesy, Lycoming County Historical Museum*

1880, but in the following decade it again climbed rapidly, reaching 27,132 in 1890. The national trend toward urbanization was also reflected in the region. In 1860 only 15 percent of the county's population lived in Williamsport, but by 1890 that rate had risen to 38 percent.

The political development of the community naturally reflected this growth. In 1866, largely as a result of the efforts of Peter Herdic, Williamsport was incorporated as a city. Major James M. Wood served as its first mayor. The following year Newberry was annexed to the city through the political slight of hand of Peter Herdic and Thomas Updegraff. A series of petitions regarding the future status of Newberry had been circulated when Herdic and Updegraff secured one or more of them. They clipped off the signatures which they then attached

to their own petition favoring annexation. The new petition was then sent to Harrisburg where it was approved before anyone in Newberry realized what had occurred.

In 1870 Williamsport was one of six cities under consideration as the state capital, and, while it was not chosen, its political influence in Harrisburg was so great that officials there came to refer to the city as "The Everlasting State of Williamsport." The growing political importance of the city was reflected in the construction of a new Lycoming County Court House in 1860 and the completion of a new U.S. Post Office and courthouse in 1891.

The growth of educational, religious, charitable, and cultural

Above left: The grocery department of L.L. Stearns is seen as it appeared in the 1870s. Stearns was one of the largest grocery and dry goods stores in the city. It occupied a building at the corner of Market and Third streets and had 16 employees. The store moved to its present location at Third and Pine streets, the former City Hotel, in 1889.

Above: *The Weightman Block at the corner of Campbell and West Fourth streets still stands as an outstanding example of a Victorian business building. Started by Peter Herdic using a design by architect Eber Culver, it was completed by Annie Weightman Walker. In 1890 it had "a bank, a furniture store, a druggist, a grocer, a meat market, a barber, and a hotel." When it was built it marked the extension of the commercial district from the "old town" at Market Square westward.*

institutions was also impressive. By the mid-1880s, the city had 3,793 students enrolled in 68 public schools. In addition, Dickinson Seminary had grown to number 200 students of both sexes, and a commercial college, established in 1865 to train young people for business, enrolled between 400 to 500 students. In March 1884 the first Sunday edition of the *Grit* appeared as the result of the efforts of Henry M. Wolf, J.M. Scott, and Dietrick Lamade. At the same time the city could boast 31 church structures serving every major Protestant denomination as well as citizens of the Roman Catholic and Jewish faiths. Among the more prominent ones built during this period were Beth Hashalom in 1871-1872, Trinity Episcopal in

Left: *Annunciation Roman Catholic Church, dedicated in 1889, still stands at the corner of Walnut and West Fourth streets in the middle of Millionaires Row. A great stone structure, it features a large marble altar and tiffany windows. This drawing, completed around the time of its construction in 1886, shows a high spire similar to the one on Trinity Episcopal Church. During the construction of the spire four workmen fell to their deaths. Father Garvey ordered the tower capped at that height and marked by a cross.*

Facing page, top: *Old Main of Williamsport Dickinson Seminary is seen as it looked in the 1870s industrial era. The west wing (left) was the original building. The east wing (right) was built next, and the two were finally joined by the six-story center unit. It was a private boarding school owned and operated by the Preachers' Aid Society of the Central Pennsylvania Conference of the Methodist Episcopal Church.*

Facing page, bottom right: *The interior of the Academy of Music is pictured as it appeared in an early 1870s advertisement. Prospective patrons were told "the seats are all numbered, and are all raised, so as to afford an entire view of the stage from any part of the house, which is lighted by a handsome chandelier, containing 60 burners." There were a number of dressing rooms for the actors, including a "special room for minstrels."*

Facing page, bottom left: *Dietrick Lamade was a German-born printer journeyman who settled in Williamsport and worked at his trade on an evening newspaper. When he became part owner of the Grit in 1884 he published it as an independent Sunday newspaper. Grit remained in the Lamade family until the early 1980s.*

Facing page: *The residence of James Gamble (top) is shown as it appeared in the early 1870s when he was serving as presiding judge of Lycoming County. The house, on East Fourth and Mulberry streets, had marble and tile trim in its interior as well as molded plaster decorations. At bottom is the Gamble house as it appeared in 1984. The house has retained much of its original beauty and style, including the window decorations and mansard roof. It has lost its cupola.*

1876, and Annuciation Roman Catholic in 1889.

Medical care expanded at an equally impressive rate. The Lycoming County Medical Society was organized in 1864 with only five members, but 20 years later the city had 40 physicians practicing within its limits. Significant for the times, four of the doctors were women. In 1873 the Williamsport Hospital was established with a nursing school attached, making the city the smallest in the nation to have a hospital. Located in a converted structure on Elmira Street, the hospital quickly outgrew this facility, moving in 1885 to another converted building on Pine Street. Following the 1889 flood, a new structure, complete with all the latest medical facilities, was constructed on Campbell Street north of Louisa Street. In addition, a Home for the Friendless, established in order to care for children and the aged and infirm, was established in 1872.

Finally, the citizens of Williamsport enhanced the city's cultural life with the construction of the Ulman Opera House in 1867 with a seating capacity of 1,000. This was replaced as the center of the city's cultural life only two years later with the construction of the Williamsport Academy of Music. In 1892 the Lycoming Opera House, with a seating capacity of 1,800, became the city's cultural center.

This building explosion naturally caused the plan of the city to be expanded. By the mid-1880s the city's business district (not counting the lumber mills) extended from Mulberry to William streets on Third Street, and from Market to William on Fourth Street. The number of dwellings increased five-fold between 1860 and 1890, from 1,036 to 5,536, and extended northward to the southern edge of what is today Brandon Park. The increased wealth in the city was reflected by the rise of the assessed value of property which climbed from just under two million dollars to more than eight million dollars in the same period.

The most impressive construction occurred on West Fourth Street, which became known as "Millionaires Row." Here the great lumber barons erected mansions derived from the Neo-Classical and Victorian styles, designed to flaunt their wealth and impress their neighbors. They spent as freely on the interiors as they did on the exteriors, filling their homes with grand staircases, polished wood, intricate mantle pieces, lush carpets, velvet curtains, and works of art. Undoubtedly the most impressive of these was the "Million Dollar House" built by Mahlon Fisher in 1867.

This was also the period in which many modern conveniences were established or greatly improved. A gas and water company had been established before the war, but only served the center

The Youngman estate was built as a summer home in the late 1860s by George Washington Youngman on what is now Round Hill Road. His winter residence was in downtown Williamsport on Pine Street. The estate featured a 24-room Italian Villa brick mansion with cupola, a tenant house, and a large barn.

of the city. When these services were slow to expand, Peter Herdic created new companies to provide gas and water service west of Campbell Street. Eventually the rival gas and water companies merged. Additional improvements followed at regular intervals. A horse-drawn street railroad was established in 1863, the paving of city streets was begun in 1864 although it was limited to the business area, telephone service was established in 1880, and electric lighting brightened the city in 1882. A more unusual service was provided by the Williamsport Steam Company in 1884. By laying five miles of pipe under city streets, it provided heat for businesses and homes up to one mile from its plant. Travel across the Susquehanna River was also improved by the construction of an improved bridge at Market Street. This bridge replaced the earlier one destroyed by the flood of 1865. Access was also aided by the construction of the Maynard Street bridge in 1878. Both bridges continued to charge tolls until 1891, much to the annoyance of South-Side residents.

This surge of growth in Williamsport obviously affected nearby communities although in different ways depending on their location. Montoursville was incorporated as a borough in 1862, South Williamsport in 1866, and DuBoistown in 1878, but the growth of all three was extremely small as Williamsport exerted a far greater draw to people seeking to settle in the immediate area. Lycoming County communities farther away grew at a far greater rate. Jersey Shore, for example, grew from 1,411 to 1,853 between 1880 and 1890, while Hughesville grew

Above: *This mansion was designed by Eber Culver for lumber baron Mahlon Fisher in 1867. It was built on Fourth Street across from the Herdic House and called the Million Dollar House because of what it cost Fisher to construct and furnish it. It was torn down in 1927 to make room for the Young Women's Christian Association. Courtesy, Lycoming County Historical Museum*

Right: *Peter Herdic's mansion in the 400 block of West Fourth Street was designed by Eber Culver in the Italian Villa Style. Built between 1854 and 1855 it was surrounded by lawns which were graced with fountains. Courtesy, James V. Brown Library*

from 899 to 1,358, and Montgomery from 406 to 770. Although all were dwarfed by Williamsport, the greater growth rate of the latter three indicates that Williamsport acted as a magnet, inhibiting the growth of adjacent communities.

These were glorious years for many Williamsporters, who saw their city's expansion and industrialization as part of a nationwide course to never ending opportunity, progress, and prosperity. Unfortunately, these changes also had their underside. One problem, highlighted by the Sawdust War, was changing employer-employee relationships and patterns of wealth. Early Williamsport society consisted largely of self-employed skilled workers and property was fairly evenly distributed. For example, in 1826 the wealthiest 10 percent of the population owned 30 percent of the property, while the poorest 30 percent owned 10 percent. By 1876 the pattern had changed drastically. In that year, most workers were unskilled laborers working for a relatively few factory owners. The distribution of wealth reflected this change. By 1876 the wealthiest 10 percent owned 61 percent of the wealth, while the poorest 30 percent owned only 3 percent. The Sawdust War reflected the tension this situation produced. While there were no further outbreaks of labor unrest for many years afterward, there was widespread speculation that some of the fires that swept through the mill districts after 1872 were started by workers, indicating at least that tensions were not wholly abated.

A far more serious problem, and the one that eventually doomed the lumber industry, was the lack of conservation. The resources of the vast forests seemed limitless to 19th century Americans who gave no thought to replacing what they had taken. So great was the devastation that one writer described it as "the war on the forests of Lycoming County," a phrase that contains far more truth than exaggeration. The debris from lumbering, limbs, stumps, tree tops, and abandoned logs was allowed to rot and became an ideal source of fuel for forest fires which became an all-too-common occurrence. The destruction of the forests also reduced the ability of the soil to hold water, which in turn increased flooding throughout the area. Land never before affected by high water was now regularly flooded, causing considerable damage to both industry and farming. The most visible result to the people of Williamsport was the great flood of 1889 which inundated much of the city, broke the boom, and carried some 300 million feet of lumber downstream. Although the damage to the West Branch Valley was enormous, much of the destruction was repaired relatively quickly. Unfortunately, the forests could not be replaced so easily.

Facing page, top: *The flood of 1889 crested at 33 feet, one inch, or more than 5 feet higher than the "great" flood of 1865. Every business in Williamsport was flooded, every bridge washed away or severely damaged. The log boom, a major key to the city's prosperity, broke and 200 million feet of lumber swept downstream. On June 1, Market Square was occupied by a single row boat and Market Street with its many food stalls was under water as far as the eye could see. Courtesy, James V. Brown Library*

Facing page, bottom: *When the flood waters receded the city faced a major cleaning task. This view of West Third and Elmira streets shows entire stacks of lumber resting in the middle of the street. Courtesy, Lycoming County Historical Museum, D. Vincent Smith Collection*

CHAPTER FIVE

Progress and Reform

Left: *This bustling circa 1910 street scene was taken on a summer day at Market Square. At right is an open trolley. At right center is the blur of an automobile, too fast for the camera's shutter. Courtesy, Lycoming County Historical Museum*

The late 19th and early 20th century was a time of renewal and modernization in Williamsport. During those years the city enlarged and diversified its industrial base. It modernized most of its urban services like water, sewer, urban transportation, and fire and police protection. The city attracted substantial numbers of immigrants, giving the community a more cosmopolitan and metropolitan flavor. At the same time, many people became increasingly aware of the social and political injustices that accompanied the Industrial Revolution.

Industrialization vastly increased the wealth of post-Civil War America, but much of it fell into the hands of a few. And these men, like Williamsport's Peter Herdic, often translated their riches into power and used that power in ways that seemed to threaten the American tradition of popular government.

Nationally, these concerns over the urban environment and attempts at social and political reform are often referred to as the Progressive Movement. Elements of that movement appeared in Williamsport but not until the city confronted the agonies surrounding the decline of the lumber industry.

In the mid-1880s a few far-sighted individuals realized that the prosperity based on lumber could not continue. The mountains in the region had been cut clean. Soon the resource that had brought Williamsport wealth and national prominence would be in such short supply that the city was in danger of reverting to the small Appalachian county seat and transportation depot that it had been before the Civil War. To encourage industrial diversification, a group of citizens led by Cyrus La Rue Munson, a wealthy lawyer and financier, and John F. Laedlein, a local realtor and insurance agent, organized The Board of Trade in 1885. Within two years the group issued the first pamphlet describing Williamsport's advantages, developed the first city atlas, and enticed several companies, including the Demorest Manufacturing Company, Williamsport Wire Rope Company, H. Diston Manufacturing, and the Royal Braid Company, to locate in Williamsport.

These successes were largely offset by the floods of 1889 and 1894 which broke the lumber boom and inundated old and new businesses alike. The destruction stalled Williamsport's economic

Above: *Williamsport built a new home for its expanding city government in the early 1890s. Designed by architect Eber Culver, built on the former Ross Park, City Hall or the Municipal Building was in use by 1895. The City Hall was expanded with a northeast wing in 1936 and placed on the National Register of Historic Places in 1976. Now the "Old City Hall" is home for various businesses and agencies, including the Williamsport-Lycoming Chamber of Commerce. Courtesy, James V. Brown Library*

life and slowed its population growth. The population which had increased 43.3 percent during the previous decade grew only 5.9 percent during the final 10 years of the century and the assessed property value of the town actually decreased by .4 percent.

This pattern of stagnation in a community for which rapid growth and economic development had become the norm produced another flurry of activity by The Board of Trade designed to revitalize the local economy. In 1900 a committee of 25 members assembled to propose changes in The Board. The Board acquired new offices in City Hall, launched a vigorous membership drive, and worked energetically to attract new industries to the area. All political factions in Williamsport pulled together in this effort. The president of the reorganized Board was J. Henry Cochran, the Democratic leader of the region. The vice president was Samuel N. Williams, the Republican mayor of the city, and the treasurer was James Mansel, the former Prohibitionist mayor.

The reorganized Board of Trade grew rapidly, achieving a total membership of 400 by 1903. This gave it the highest ratio of members to local businesses of any board in the country. The support and enthusiasm paid off quickly. In 1903 alone, seven firms employing 500 men settled in the region. Between 1899 and 1909 the number of manufacturing establishments in the city increased from 142 to 159, while the number of employees in these firms rose from 4,787 to 5,641. During this period the

Above: *Cyrus La Rue Munson was born in New York, and studied law at Yale College, and with the firm of Allen and Gamble in Williamsport. Admitted to the Lycoming County Bar in 1875, he became an outstanding business and civic leader as well as an attorney. He served as president of the Pennsylvania Bar, but was also president of the Savings Institution of Williamsport, of E. Keeler Company, and of the Manson Lumber Company. He was senior warden of Christ Episcopal Church and a chancellor of the Diocese of Harrisburg. Courtesy, Lycoming County Historical Museum*

Left: *The funeral train of President William B. McKinley drew a large crowd to the Pennsylvania Railroad Station when it passed through town September 16, 1901. Courtesy, James V. Brown Library*

average capital value per establishment increased from $60,993 to $88,491 and the value of the products rose from $9,726,000 to $15,348,000. Between 1900 and 1910 the city's population grew from 28,757 to 31,860, a healthy increase of 10.8 percent. The city was again growing and prospering.

In their attempt to attract industry The Board of Trade described Williamsport as a virtual Eden for prospective manufacturers. This placed substantial pressure on city government to provide the services to make this image a reality.

Between 1903 and 1906, the *Grit,* several mayors, and a number of local businessmen urged city government to modernize. The various groups noted that of 83.5 miles of city streets in Williamsport only 6.5 miles were paved. The

Right: The Imperial, *built in 1907, was the only automobile ever manufactured in Williamsport. Designed by C.P. VanFerls, a prototype was tested on April 2, 1907, and was said to have reached 60 miles per hour. The Imperial Motor Company built 24 cars, but the "Panic of 1907" tightened credit and the open-body construction hurt winter sales. Consequently, the company went into receivership in 1908. Courtesy, Williamsport* Sun-Gazette

Facing page, top: The Grit, *reorganized by Dietrick Lamade in 1884, was a particularly important force for improving community life in the years of progress and reform. The headquarters constructed on West Third Street in 1891 has retained much of its original beauty and grandeur. Courtesy, Grit Publishing Company*

Facing page, bottom: The First National Bank *of Williamsport celebrated its 50th Anniversary in 1913 by building a new home. The opening of the seven-story structure in 1914 was a major public event with thousands of people taking the elevator ride to the roof to see their city from above for the first time. Courtesy, Grit Publishing Company*

community had only 17 policemen. The police had to transport prisoners to city hall in a wheelbarrow because they lacked a police wagon. The city was also without a modern fire alarm or electric system. As a result many called for the establishment of a Board of Public Works run by men of skill and experience to keep streets, sidewalks, and sewers repaired and to establish a garbage collection system.

At the same time, two existing governmental institutions, the Board of Health and the Almshouse, also known as the "poor house," came under close scrutiny. Many citizens attacked the Board of Health because of its handling of a smallpox outbreak. The crisis began when Fred Leederman contracted the disease and was placed in quarantine as the law provided, but the house he was placed in was uninhabitable, the nursing care incompetent, and he escaped twice, dying of exposure on his second attempt. A short time later there were several smallpox deaths in the West End. A city-wide vaccination program prevented an epidemic, but many citizens, including the editors

Two small children stand in the middle of Park Avenue during its 1919 transition from a sometimes dusty, often muddy, rut-filled road to a paved thoroughfare. The view looks west toward Sawyer Park. The paving stones are stacked, ready for use. Courtesy, Grit Publishing Company

of the *Grit*, blamed the Board of Health's poor quarantine control for the later cases. The Almshouse came under attack when Mayor Seth Foresman called for its repair and expansion "because the crowded conditions ... became such a crying evil that public policy as well as common sentiment of humanity call loudly for improvements."

Of course it would take substantial amounts of money to complete all the projects various groups demanded. Money meant tax increases, which the people were reluctant to pay, and the politicians were reluctant to raise the necessary levies. Many argued that if assessments were made fairly the money would be available. Councilman Michael J. Winters represented these views when he stated, "many small properties are assessed for their full value and some of the valuable properties are not assessed for more than half what they would fetch at public sale." Following a similar call for assessment reform in 1907 by Mayor Foresman, the council established a committee to study the matter and subsequently passed a new assessment ordinance. Almost immediately the assessed value of property shot from

Digging sewers early in the 20th century was not only expensive for taxpayers, but it was also backbreaking work. Courtesy, Grit Publishing Company

nine to 15 million dollars, and tax receipts rose by 25 percent.

The city was now in a position to fulfull many of its institutional goals. During the next few years, 11,000 feet of sewer were laid and 359 sidewalks were repaired. Much of the remainder of the increased revenue was used to retire old debts. Order and organization came in other ways as well. For example, the city adopted a fire code controlling the storage of flammables widely used in industrial establishments.

While the city was working to upgrade its services, the privately-owned street railway was doing the same. The horse-drawn line in Center City was electrified in 1891 and the following year the city chartered six new traction companies including the Vallamont, Citizens, South Side, East End, West End, and Junction. Another line was opened to Montoursville in 1897. In 1905 the small single-truck cars began to be replaced with new double-truck cars. Under the one fare system a passenger could board a car in Newberry transfer at Market Square and travel to Vallamont for a nickle.

Some leaders, like Mayor Charles D. Wolfe, demanded additional improvements. Wolfe called for the appointment of fire and building inspectors, and for the development of regulations controlling the movement of electric current through

Above: *The Vallamont Traction Company stopped at this pavillion in the Vallamont section. Courtesy, Grit Publishing Company*

Left: *This view of Market Street Bridge in about 1910 is looking toward South Williamsport. The South Side Traction Company tracts were adjacent to the bridge. The city boat dock under the bridge was used by small craft as well as the Hiawatha. Courtesy, Lycoming County Historical Museum*

Above: *Saint Boniface Church was built in 1875 on Washington Boulevard and served primarily Williamsport's Roman Catholics of German tradition at the turn of the century. This picture was taken circa 1915. The building burned in a tragic fire on December 5, 1972, even as members of the parish were developing plans to celebrate 100 years of worship in it. Courtesy, Lycoming County Historical Museum*

city streets and buildings. He also argued for additional men and equipment for the police department and for the improvement of the city's sewers. Yet, most refused to support these programs.

The state changed Williamsport from the mayor-council form of government to a mayor and non-partisan commission form in 1913, and many local progressives hoped this would facilitate further reform. Instead, Williamsporters used the new mechanism to conduct business as usual. Even though more streets were paved and new storm and sanitary sewers were installed, taxes were cut, delaying many of the innovations demanded by local reform advocates.

By 1914 The Board of Trade added its voice to those of local progressives. It advocated tax reform, a broad range of public improvements, the establishment of a vocational training program in the high school, the establishment of a board of experts within The Board of Trade to give advice to local industries, and the acquisition of factory sites to provide an ideal environment for prospective new industries. Some Williamsporters, including Mayor Jonas Fischer, believed The Board had lost interest in attracting industry, and had become more concerned with improving the industrial environment for those already in the city. The Board disputed this criticism and worked to improve its image and secure its reformist goals. Some of these goals were achieved, but others were cut short as the nation's attention turned to war.

While Williamsport was modernizing, it was also becoming more cosmopolitan as it attracted significant numbers of migrants from central and eastern Europe. Though the largest numbers of immigrants continued to come from traditional areas

Left: *This new high school building was already under construction on the corner of West Third and Susquehanna streets when the Walnut Street high school burned. The Class of 1914 was graduated from the unfinished building. When Williamsport built yet another new high school in the early 1970s this building became the Klump Academic Center of Williamsport Area Community College. Courtesy, Lycoming County Historical Museum*

Facing page: *One of the spectacular fires in city history occurred on April 3, 1914, when the Williamsport High School, located on the corner of West Third and Walnut streets, burned. The fire started in a basement closet and destroyed the building and all student records. Courtesy, Lycoming County Historical Museum*

like Germany, England, and Ireland, more now began arriving from Italy, Russia, and Poland. By 1910 Williamsport contained 2,332 foreign-born people, approximately 7 percent of its total population. Another 18 percent had at least one parent born in Europe.

At this time, certain neighborhoods developed a distinct ethnic flavor. The Germans settled on "Dutch Hill" near Saint Boniface Church, the Gesang Verein Harmonia Society, and Stroehmann's Bakery. Germania Street was one of the lanes which was the home of many recent German immigrants. The Irish lived mainly on the numbered avenues and near Annuciation Church. The fact that Annuciation was founded in 1865 by the Reverend P.F. Sullivan, and that a large statue of Saint Patrick stands to the right of the altar, give testimony to the influence of the Irish in that part of the city.

The Italians settled in the areas circumscribed by Third, William, Canal, and Chatham streets. The Italian neighborhood

Above: *As new immigrants were arriving in Williamsport after 1900, old immigrant families were expanding. The Updegraff family came to the city very early in its history. Abraham Updegraff was a leading citizen in the years before the Civil War. This picture shows some of the family in about 1905. Levi, the black man, was a former slave whose freedom the family purchased. He is buried in the family plot. The woman in the front row directly in front of Levi was Laura Valeria Mahaffey, the grandmother of Mary Winner Stockwell, who is a business and civic leader in modern Williamsport. Courtesy, Mary Winner Stockwell*

Right: *Domenic Troisi is shown at top left shortly after he arrived in Williamsport in 1913. At top right, Domenic examines a coat in his 1935 tailor shop. Hand-tailored quality clothes was his trademark. Domenic and Bernardine Beiter were married at St. Boniface Church in 1920. At bottom they are seen joined by their family on the lawn of their home on their 45th wedding anniversary in 1965. Courtesy, the Troisi Family*

was known as "Little Hollywood." Tradition has it that the name originated because some of the Italian boys were so handsome they reminded people of movie stars. The Italians also founded their own church. Originally they worshipped at Annuciation, but in 1907 Father Domenico Landro, who established seven Italian churches in the Scranton Diocese, came to Williamsport to establish a congregation in Little Hollywood. In 1907 a group led by Father Landro, Americus Vannucci, Michael Chianelle, Peter Cillo, and Peter Nardi launched a fund raising effort to purchase two houses on the 200 block of Market Street which were converted into the First Church and rectory of Mater Dolorosa Parish.

The English were scattered around the city, but two other smaller ethnic neighborhoods did develop. Many of the Russian born, most of whom were of Jewish heritage, lived in the East End along Washington Street, Wyoming Avenue, and Elizabeth Street, but several families lived across town along Edwin and Lycoming streets. A Polish neighborhood was located around the intersection of Arch Street and Reach Road.

While ethnic neighborhoods existed, no firm pattern of ethnic segregation emerged. All of these neighborhoods had a mixture of ethnic groups though in certain areas one group predominated. A classic example of this existed on the 700 block of Poplar Street. The majority of people in the neighborhood were Pennsylvania born, but at 704 lived Louis Schneider and his wife Elizabeth who were German born; at 710 lived Italian-born Tony Rizzo and his wife Mary, while across the street at 711 in a boarding house lived Irish-born John Reedy.

Despite the ethnic mix, new immigrants, especially those from central and southern Europe, faced patterns of prejudice and discrimination. One first grade teacher separated the Jews and Italians and labeled them foreigners when class pictures were being taken. The 1928 *Williamsport City Directory* stated "The fact that Williamsport's foreign population is only about 6 percent of the total at once places it in a most unusual class. Since a very great majority of its people are of the real American type, it is easy to understand why Williamsport has achieved a reputation for hospitality and why those whom we have once welcomed are always anxious to return."

Although the new immigrants were facing some hostility, many residents worked to acculturate the immigrant and to improve the living standards of all the working class whose economic conditions were little better than they had been at the time of the Sawdust War.

Right: *The Knight family has operated a funeral home in Williamsport for four generations. This photograph shows Charles Knight (right) and a brother driving one of their funeral carriages, in about 1915. The view looks west on Memorial Avenue with the Holmes Silk Mill in the background. Courtesy, Knight Funeral Home*

Much of the economic exploitation of the blue collar worker in America during those years was justified by applying Darwinian evolutionary theory to social progress. The Social Darwinists argued that social progress came as a result of competition among the members of society. Many industrialists used this to justify long hours, dangerous working conditions, and low pay.

Nationally, many groups, including churches, the Socialist Party, and the newspapers, were appalled by the plight of the working class and rejected the Social Darwinian theory that was widely used to justify it. As early as the 1880s, churches began advocating the Social Gospel, which was based on the belief that there was a law higher than that of evolution, the law of love as expressed by God in the Bible. Through private benevolent activity, educational programs, and traditional

Mary Slaughter came to Williamsport after the Civil War. She not only cared for children and the elderly but she was also active in the temperance movement. She is seen here in about 1910.

devotional activity the churches sought to enhance the material as well as the spiritual existence of the workingman.

In Williamsport the local churches worked to secure Social Gospel ends in a variety of ways. An analysis of the benevolent giving by the various Presbyterian churches in town reveals that they allotted from 20 to 35 percent of their donations for such purposes between 1900 and 1915. In addition, the Second Presbyterian Church established a Mission Chapel on Hepburn Street near Front Street, and the Covenant Presbyterian Church established a neighborhood Bible reading class at this time.

The Hiawatha riverboat is pictured at its landing in Sylvan Dell Park, in about 1910.

Christ Episcopal Church helped establish an industrial school at Saint John's Chapel in South Williamsport in 1889 and it established a Deaf Mute Class in January 1899. Twenty-five churches joined to form the Williamsport Federation of Churches in 1912. Its committees reveal the type of work it valued. The committees included the home mission, Sunday observance, temperance, social purity, foreign missions, charity, social service, Bible study, community extension, boys work, and finance. The churches also pursued a variety of non-traditional projects to improve the quality of life for Williamsporters. For example, they began a private subscription drive to build the Brandon Park Bandshell in 1912. Although religious services and secular entertainment had long been held at the park, a shell was needed to provide decent acoustics for such occasions.

Residents also established numerous humanitarian enterprises independent of specific churches. Mary Slaughter, born a slave in Martinsburg, West, later moved to Williamsport with her husband where the couple served as caretakers for several local churches. Slaughter was well known for taking children of sick mothers into her home while they recovered. In 1897 she began a home for elderly black women which served the community until 1973. In 1975 the home was leveled and replaced by a low-income housing project for the elderly named in her honor.

While churches and private individuals were working to improve the quality of life for Williamsport's workers, the

D. Vincent Smith is one of the unsung historians of Williamsport and Lycoming County. For more than 50 years, beginning in 1892, he photographed the area, producing an unmatched and not yet compiled picture history. Here he is shown standing on a tractor-pulled wagon train in the Collomsville area. He toured the county on his bicycle, which is visible on top of the wagon. Courtesy, Lycoming County Historical Museum

Socialist Party was working toward similar goals. In the late 19th century, when people were working long hours for a few dollars a day, many began to argue that an undue portion of the wealth produced by industry was accruing to the entrepreneurial class and far too little was finding its way into the hands of the producing class, the machine operators. As a result, many began to argue for government ownership of such enterprises to secure a fair return for the workers. The Socialist movement, strong nationally, had a substantial following in Williamsport. The Socialist Party often had a member on the local city council and in 1917, when Mayor Jonas Fischer retired before the expiration of his term, the council offered the position to Socialist Willard G. Von Neida. Von Neida turned it down. Perhaps the clearest indication of the strength of the Socialist Party in Williamsport can be seen in the Presidential election of 1912. Socialist candidate Eugene V. Debs secured 6 percent of the vote nationally but received 15 percent of the votes cast in Williamsport. Indeed, Debs outpolled the Republican incumbent William Howard Taft by more than 100 votes in the city.

In an attempt to improve life for industrial workers, the press in America castigated all manner of corruption and exploitation, hoping to reestablish morality as the keystone of American life.

In September of 1912 the *Grit* ran stories titled "Little Slaves of the Glass Furnace," "Life Is Cheap in West Virginia Mines," and "Live by the Wages of Sin." These essays criticized child labor in the glass industry, the lack of safety regulations in the mines, and rampant prostitution in various areas of the nation. The paper also ran stories that encouraged humanitarian reform by praising work being done to reduce infant mortality and to educate the deaf and dumb.

Then, as today, working people found relaxation away from their jobs in a variety of ways. They shared in the city's centennial celebration in 1906, joining parades and viewing the displays at the specially-built Exhibition Hall. During the

Williamsport celebrated its centennial in 1906 in the midst of a prosperous decade. The Exposition Building, built on the corner of Pine and Fifth streets, was constructed specifically for the occasion. It later housed various businesses and remained in use in 1984. This photograph captures the original building but as the automobiles indicate is from a later date. Courtesy, the Grit Publishing Company

summers they engaged in numerous outdoor activities which culminated rather appropriately on Labor Day. On that holiday in 1912 there were motorcycle races at the County Fair Grounds, canoe races on the river at Sylvan Dell, and a 13-mile bike race from Jersey Shore to Newberry. For those who enjoyed hiking, the *Gazette and Bulletin* described an invigorating 12-hour-hike from Montoursville to Eagles Mere. After a bath and dinner, most of those completing the trek went dancing at the Forrest Inn.

By 1917 public and private groups had done much to improve life in Williamsport. During the next 25 years, wars and depression would test the human and economic resources of the city in many new ways.

CHAPTER SIX
World Wars and Depression

Left: *Some Williamsport veterans of World War I were at Camp Marks in Washington, D.C., in the summer of 1932 as part of the Bonus Army, seeking cash payment of their bonus. This truck carried two tons of food donated from the Williamsport area to help feed the vets who joined the protest in Washington. Courtesy, Grit Publishing Company*

The period from America's entry into World War I in April 1917 to the end of World War II in August 1945 was among the most dramatic in American history. Bounded on either side by massive struggles which demanded the fullest utilization of the nation's resources, its middle was marked by the slightly less turbulent, booming 1920s and depression-ridden 1930s. Like the rest of the nation, Williamsporters struggled with these challenges and, in the end, emerged victorious.

The American people who entered World War I did so with the realization that the oncoming struggle would require all their efforts. This was particularly true in the raising of troops. National Guard units would, of course, do their part, but the primary vehicle for recruitment was the national draft law signed on May 18, 1917, which became operational two months later. Williamsport's and Lycoming County's responses were immediate. The local National Guard unit, Battery D, 1st Pennsylvania Field Artillery, was called up on July 15. Redesignated Battery D, 107th Field Artillery, it sailed for France the following year and participated in the final American offensives of the war. Another local organization, the Repasz Band, which had seen service in the Civil War, also was recruited as a unit, redesignated as the Marine Band, and toured the country supporting recruiting and war bond drives.

Most men who served, whether as volunteers or as draftees, did not serve, however, with local units. A total of 3,170 Lycoming County men saw military service. Of these men, 1,296 were volunteers and 1,874 were draftees.

Efforts to mobilize the home front proceeded with equal rapidity. Immediately after war was declared, county officials established a Committee of Public Safety to coordinate all civil and military activity within the county. Eventually, this committee established more than 12 subcommittees to regulate every aspect of community life relating directly or indirectly to the war effort. Among the most important of these were finance, agriculture, plants and materials, fuel, transportation, and civic relief.

Many of the activities of these committees were concerned with conservation, for the United States not only had to supply

Left: *This huge crowd gave a rousing send-off to Battery D as its train moved out from the Market Street Railroad Station in the summer of 1917. Courtesy, Lycoming County Historical Museum*

Facing page, top: *These Navy recruits signed up during the first week after the United States entered World War I. They were sent off as apprentice seamen on April 10, 1917. The Army and Navy both had a record number of recruits from the Williamsport area that week. Courtesy, Grit Publishing Company*

Above: *Soldiers, sailors, marines, and a vast number of other paraders, 10,000 in all, passed under the Victory Arch during the Welcome Home celebration held June 18, 1919. The Arch stood at West Fourth and Hepburn streets. Courtesy, James V. Brown Library*

its own needs, but also quickly became a source of supplies for its allies. Williamsporters had to get used to "meatless" and "wheatless" days, reduction of the temperature in their homes to 65 degrees and, in the last months of the war, strict rationing of goods such as sugar. They also participated in raising money for the war effort through the sale of "Liberty Bonds." Civic organizations such as the Salvation Army, Red Cross, YMCA, and Knights of Columbus helped in the bond drives, as well as many local employers who established programs for their workers to buy bonds in installments.

The purpose of all these efforts was to support the national

Right: *The Curbstone Market was popular in the 1920s, symbolizing the continued strength of agriculture as an area industry. An 1876 ordinance provided for curbstone markets at various city locations, including both sides of Market Street from North Alley to Canal Street. This 1931 photograph shows Market Street north from Market Square. In that year the markets left the streets and moved into the Growers Association Market, a large market house erected at Market and Church streets. Courtesy, Grit Publishing Company*

Left: *A close look at the Curbstone Market in front of the White Kitchen Restaurant, on the west side of Market Street between Third and Fourth streets, was taken about 1920. Courtesy, James V. Brown Library*

war production effort, and in this Williamsport also played its part. The most notable local firms involved in this effort were the Lycoming Foundry and Machine Company (today Avco Lycoming) which produced more than 15,000 four-cylinder engines for army vehicles, and Williamsport Wire Rope Company (today part of Bethlehem Steel) which produced mine nets and cables. In an effort to secure additional contracts, The Board of Trade commissioned its president, Charles C. Krouse, in early 1918 to go to Washington as a representative of local industry. Eventually, the combination of a reduced labor force caused by the draft and increased war orders produced a labor shortage in the city. To help alleviate this, hundreds of women entered the work force, but the labor shortage persisted until the end of the war. By then, Williamsport had added the

manufacture of shell and shell cases, fragmentation bombs, powder bags, field desks, shoes, and uniforms to their production list.

The summer of 1918 produced another crisis: influenza. This worldwide epidemic, which eventually caused more deaths than the war itself, forced the city to close all schools, clubs, churches, and public places of entertainment, and significantly reduced war production for a brief period. At its height authorities estimated there were 1,000 cases in the city, with another 1,000 in the county. In the end, an estimated one person in every Williamsport home was stricken.

The end of the war brought the inevitable hopes for a better future but also problems of demobilization. The result was a depression lasting from 1919 to 1922, caused by the sudden end of war production and the increase in the labor force due to returning soldiers.

By 1922 the economy was again on the upswing as Williamsport, along with the rest of the nation, entered the "Roaring 20s." This term has special meaning for Williamsport, as the period ranks second in economic growth in the city's entire history, only behind the peak years of the lumber era. Equally significant is the fact that this growth was not dependent upon one industry as in the lumber years, but was now considerably diversified. The metal products industry producing engines and machinery had the largest number of workers, with 3,974 by 1929. Other industries such as leather and rubber, with 1,962 employees, and textiles with 1,335, were also of considerable importance. Surprisingly, the lumber industry continued to be an important source of employment, although its relative position in the local economy had declined considerably. In 1929 there were still six planing mills and seven furniture plants operating in the area with a total payroll of 1,553 people. Overall, the labor force of Williamsport and nearby communties in that year totaled 19,809, 54 percent of which were engaged in manufacturing.

Of the leading firms in the city, several achieved positions of national prominence during this period. The most important of them was the Lycoming Foundry and Machine Company, which changed its name to the Lycoming Mfg. Company in 1920. It produced a total of 57 different types of motors during this period, many of which it designed itself, and became a leading national manufacturer of automobile engines. Indeed, two of the classic automobiles of this period, the Cord and the Duesenberg, were powered by Lycoming engines. In 1928 the company entered the field of aircraft engine manufacture and the first

Right: *Public and private transportation vied for street space on West Third Street in front of the Lycoming County Court House in the pre-Depression summer of 1929. This was a time of transition in public transportation, from the trolleys on the left to the buses on the right. Courtesy, Lycoming County Historical Museum*

Above: *The expansion of the automobile industry created many other businesses, including gas stations. Local artist Larry Seaman created this drawing of the Sinclar Station which was located on the north side of East Third Street as it appeared in 1930. Gas was 16 cents per gallon. The car was a 1928 Studebaker. Courtesy, Larry Seaman*

plane with a Lycoming engine was test flown on April 5, 1929, laying the basis for the company's later fame. Other firms with national prominence were the J.K. Mosser Company, which had the largest leather sole cutting plant in the world; the Lycoming Rubber Company, which was the nation's leading producer of "Keds," and the C.A. Reed Company, which was one of the largest manufacturers of crepe paper and crepe paper novelties in the country.

One reason for this expansion was the continued easy access of Williamsport to the outside world. The city continued to be served by four railroads, although passenger service was reduced because of a decline in traffic. A major new route was opened in 1921 when the first paved highway, following the north shore of the river, reached the city line. In the 1920s paved roads were extended to the north and west, providing modern connections in all directions. Another modern transportation innovation reached the area in 1929, when the city bought a tract of land in Montoursville and built the Williamsport Airport.

One immediate result of the new roads was an attempt to revive the city's hotel business, which had declined steadily since the turn of the century. In 1920 a group of local leaders formed

Left: *Williamsport dedicated its airport on July 20, 1929. The large plane in the foreground was a Ford tri-motor and was one of the 75 planes at the airport that day. A crowd of 35,000 attended the ceremonies, including Amelia Earhart who flew in for the occasion. Courtesy, Grit Publishing Company*

Left: *The Fire Department's aerial ladder truck is shown here in 1921. The city had some high buildings and new ones were under construction in the early 1920s. The steel structure of one of them, the Lycoming Hotel, is visible in the background. Courtesy, James V. Brown Library*

Right: *Fred Lamade built the Family Theater on Pine Street south of Third Street in 1907. It was renamed the Majestic in 1917 and the Karlton in 1937. The Majestic showed the first silent movies in the area. A number of other entertainments came to this theater, including various vaudeville troupes. The photograph is from 1946. The theater was demolished in 1952. Courtesy, Lycoming County Historical Museum*

the Williamsport Hotels Company and began construction of the Lycoming Hotel, which was opened for business in June 1922. The Board of Trade also sought to take advantage of the new road connections by encouraging tourism through the publication of 50,000 pamphlets titled *The Beautiful Susquehanna Trail*. Although some new business was brought in by these efforts, the results failed to meet the expectations of the sponsors.

The overall expansion of business activity was reflected in the growing wealth and population of the city. The prosperity of the period helped produce better labor relations as local firms established programs such as insurance and pension plans, built plant cafeterias and athletic fields, and organized bands.

Williamsport's population had grown to 44,507 by 1929, an increase of more than 20 percent in only nine years. Real estate values had soared as higher wages enabled many more people to buy their own homes. In one year alone, two million dollars in building permits were issued in the city. Williamsporters were also quick to make the transition to motor vehicles. In 1924, for example, more than 4,000 vehicles were sold locally. By 1927 the city had 22 automobile dealers and repair shops, as well as an annual car show.

In 1929 the Williamsport Chamber of Commerce proudly reported that there were 10,350 dwellings in the city, 70 percent of which were paid for. In addition, public services had reached an all-time high. The public school system consisted of one high

Above: *The Susquehanna Canoe Club on the south side of the river above the Maynard Street Bridge was a popular recreation area. This large crowd was drawn by special late-summer water events in August 1930. Courtesy, Grit Publishing*

Top: *Frank E. Plankenhorn erected this stone entrance at the top of Packer Street in 1926 as one of three gateways to Grampian Hills, a new and elite residential area. The other gateways were to be at the tops of Franklin and Penn streets. The Depression and ill*

health brought Plankenhorn's dreams and his Grampian Hills Development Company to an end, forcing sale of the land. *Courtesy, Michael G. Roskin*

Above: *Sunset Park was located on Lycoming Creek east of Route 15 between Mill Lane and Roosevelt Avenue. It opened August 8, 1931, and featured many of the amusement rides which had formerly been at Memorial Park. An estimated 12,000 persons attended opening day to see a special balloon* ascension. *This photograph was taken during opening week from the rocky cliffs overlooking the park and shows Mill Lane and open fields in the background. Courtesy, Lycoming County Historical Museum, D. Vincent Smith Collection*

Facing page: *The Federal Surplus Commodities Corporation provided food for a special Christmas distribution in 1938 to persons on relief rolls in the county. The number of relief cases peaked earlier in 1938 at 4,500, representing approximately 22,000 people. The Pennsylvania Department of Public Assistance distributed the food. Courtesy, Grit Publishing Company*

Right: *The Depression inspired relief gardens. In 1934 this relief garden at the Consistory Plot on Packer Street was one of an estimated 2,500 in the city. A vegetable and canned goods show held in the Armory in August of that year was the first Relief Garden Show ever held in Pennsylvania. The Consistory Plot is now the Lycoming College Athletic Field. Courtesy, Grit Publishing Company*

school, three junior high schools, and 16 grade schools with 268 teachers and 8,664 students, supplemented by two parochial schools with an enrollment of 1,000 students. In 1929 the Williamsport Dickinson Seminary added a two-year college curriculum to its program and changed its name to the Williamsport Dickinson Seminary and Junior College. The Williamsport Hospital had expanded to 275 beds, of which 75 were set aside for those who were unable to pay. Recreational facilities abounded. There were 15 supervised playgrounds, three swimming pools, and numerous athletic fields for baseball, football, and soccer, in addition to facilities for tennis, basketball, and golf. There were seven theaters, eight hotels, and two local daily newspapers with a combined circulation of almost 43,000, plus the nationally-distributed *Grit* with a weekly circulation of more than 375,000.

Williamsport's hopes for continued growth were cruelly dashed by the Great Depression, which struck the nation with the Crash of 1929. Although the stock market crash had little immediate impact on the city, the sharp decline in commodity prices in the early spring of 1930 was quickly followed by the

The Civil Works Administration, which later became the Works Progress Administration, provided the money for many public works projects in Williamsport. This job on East Third Street east of Mulberry Street in the spring of 1934 involved removing the trolley tracks and repaving the street. Courtesy, Grit Publishing Company

curtailment of industrial production and inevitably by rising unemployment. The impact on Williamsport, as on the nation as a whole, was devastating. Between 1928 and 1933, for example, the Lycoming Mfg. Company reduced its payroll from 2,208 to 1,276; C.A. Reed from 771 to 541; and Williamsport Wire Rope Company from 443 to 201. The greatest single blow came in September 1932, when the U.S. Rubber Company, which had employed 1,162 people in 1928, closed its local plant. By 1933 the local unemployment rate soared to 25 percent. The situation was so bad that the Chamber of Commerce noted in its 1933 annual report that some were calling Williamsport "the hardest hit city in the state."

Efforts to relieve suffering caused by the Depression on the local level were not long in coming. In November 1930 a group of businessmen established the Central Emergency Relief Committee to distribute food and clothing to the needy unemployed. It secured funds from the contributions of local companies, organizations, individuals, and workers, many of whom donated 3 percent of their wages. It also held benefit performances and dances. The committee was able to provide $28,000 in goods between November 24, 1930, and April 11, 1931, to about 20 percent of the city's population. The committee attempted to provide temporary work for the unemployed, but, while it met with some success, results were

This swimming and life-saving class met at Mountain Beach in South Williamsport in the summer of 1935 under the sponsorship of the recreation division of the Federal Emergency Relief Administration. Courtesy, Grit Publishing Company

minimal in light of the situation.

While these efforts were a commendable reflection of civic concern, city leaders recognized that the only long-term solution to unemployment lay in attracting new business. Initially, the Williamsport Chamber of Commerce (which had changed its name from The Board of Trade in 1924) led the way in this effort. In May 1931 it hired Charles Krouse to act as its New York City agent to seek out firms that might be willing to move to Williamsport. When such companies were discovered, the Chamber sought to encourage the move by arranging for finanacial incentives such as assistance with moving expenses, local capital investment, a line of credit at a local bank, and rent-free facilities for a limited period. Unfortunately, it met with little initial success, largely because the Chamber's financial resources were in short supply and because many other cities throughout the nation were offering similar incentives. In March 1933 a group of prominent local businessmen, including George L. Stearns, III, and Thomas J. Rider, formed the "Committee of 100" with the expressed purpose of raising capital to encourage firms to move to Williamsport. Working together, the Chamber of Commerce and Committee of l00, which merged in April 1937 to form the Community Trade Association, brought 30 new firms with a total of 4,236 employees to the city by June 1941.

Much of this success was undoubtedly aided by a locally initiated and sponsored program of retraining, which eventually achieved national recognition and became known as the Williamsport Plan. Its origins lay in a 1930 survey conducted by the Employment Committee of the Chamber of Commerce, which revealed that while 75 percent of the unemployed in Williamsport were unskilled, 85 percent of those people had adequate educational background to become skilled or semi-skilled workers with the proper training. Moreover, the survey revealed that despite the high unemployment rate, there were shortages of skilled workers in many shops. The Williamsport Plan was designed to take the maximum advantage of the potential which this situation offered. Local firms were surveyed to determine exactly what type of skilled workers they required. Unemployed workers were then screened to determine their suitability for training in these skills, provided with the necessary training, and then placed with these firms. Much of the success of this plan was due to George H. Parkes, director of the vocational department at Williamsport High School, who actually designed the training program and put it into practice. Starting with virtually nothing, he salvaged equipment from local junkyards and obtained donations of unused equipment from local plants. By 1933 the school, known as the Williamsport Retraining School, had grown, and needed larger facilities, so a new building was constructed mostly by students, on West Third Street at Park Street. By 1940 it had trained and placed some 4,000 people, more than half of whom had been on relief rolls.

These efforts to restore prosperity were necessary for the long-term recovery of Williamsport, but they were of little help for many of its citizens who measured their survival in the short term. For these people, relief only came with the arrival of the presidency of Franklin D. Roosevelt and the New Deal. In particular, the Works Progress Administration, known as the WPA, not only provided necessary jobs for the unemployed, but also established many public works projects which benefited the entire community. Between July 1, 1935, and June 30, 1938, the WPA provided $5,343,170 in work relief for Lycoming County, of which more than 90 percent went for wages. At its peak, it provided employment for 3,637 persons in a wide range

Facing page: *Williamsporters gaze at the flood from the First Evangelical Church at the corner of Packer and Market streets in this March 16, 1936, photograph. The Susquehanna River, normally about 1,000 feet wide, expanded to about 7,000 feet. Courtesy, Lycoming County Historical Museum, D. Vincent Smith Collection*

of activities. New schools were built while others were rehabilitated or received additions, roads were paved and otherwise improved, and a runway and hanger were constructed at the airport in Montoursville.

Just as the first signs of recovery appeared, however, disaster struck again, this time in the form of a flood. The winter of 1935-1936 had been particularly severe, with temperatures close to zero for many weeks and heavy snowfalls in the mountains. Then in March the temperature suddenly turned warm and it began to rain heavily. During the night of March 18, the Susquehanna River crested at 33.9 feet. The results were devastating. Two thirds of the city, including most of the business and industrial districts, were inundated. At its height, the water swept through the city with such force that telephone

Left: *The flood waters were nearly 10 feet deep on William Street south of Third Street when fire erupted at the Wakenhut Building on March 18. The fire burned the entire block down to water level. Eighteen people were rescued from the buildings without loss of life. Fire equipment had been moved to Brandon Park to save it from the flood. Courtesy, Grit Publishing Company*

Left: *West Fourth Street is pictured looking east toward Pine Street during the flood of 1936. Almost every business in the city suffered damage. Courtesy, James V. Brown Library*

and telegraph lines were cut, railroad tracks were wiped out, and cars were overturned. Miraculously, only three people in the county lost their lives, undoubtedly a tribute to the early warnings and guidance of the community's civic leaders. As the waters receded, residents immediately began repairing the damage aided by local and federal relief agencies and began to study the possibility of constructing levees for protection against future floods.

By 1940 Williamsporters could thus feel that they had weathered the worst that nature and the economy could deal them. Yet, the cost was high. In fact, for the first time in its history, the population of Williamsport actually declined during this decade, from 45,729 in 1930 to 44,355 in 1940, a loss of almost 1,400 people, while during the same period the population of Lycoming County rose by only 200.

The Japanese attack on Pearl Harbor, which brought the United States into World War II, shocked the American people, uniting them in their resolve for total victory. Williamsport was involved in the struggle from the very beginning. One local serviceman stationed at Pearl Harbor, Joseph L. Lockard, observed the approaching Japanese planes on a primitive radar set, but his warnings were ignored by his superiors.

Williamsporters entered the war with the same determination and willingness to sacrifice that had marked their participation in the nation's earlier wars. Many young men served in the 109th Infantry Regiment of the 28th Infantry Division of the Pennsylvania National Guard. Following two years of training in the United States and Great Britian, the division landed in France shortly after D-Day and were among the first American troops to enter Paris in August 1944. In November they participated in the battle for Huertgen Forest where they suffered severe casualties in what many consider to be the most savage fighting the United States Army ever experienced in Europe. Afterwards they were transferred to a "quiet" sector of the front, the Ardennes. When the Germans attacked in what became known as the Battle of the Bulge, the division was shattered by an overwhelming superiority of numbers, but nonetheless helped slow the German tide until reinforcements arrived.

Meanwhile, Williamsporters at home were experiencing a degree of government control that greatly surpassed their earlier experiences. Rationing began within weeks of the start of the war. Automobile tires topped the list. In order to obtain new tires, it was necessary to receive approval from a county rationing board composed of four local citizens and, except for

The Lycoming engine, the R-680, 295 h.p., powered the twin engine Beech Trainer. These were being readied for delivery to army air force schools in August 1943. Courtesy, Grit Publishing Company

individuals who were in specified fields, such as physicians, this was extremely difficult. Moreover, the board decided early to publish the names of all individuals who received tires in the local newspapers to allay charges of favoritism. In May 1942 sugar rationing went into effect. In a three-day period, almost 45,000 families registered at city schools for their cards. The same month, gas rationing was announced, and non-essential vehicles were allotted two gallons per week. The following January pleasure driving was banned and local officials were given the unpopular task of checking the presence of cars at local amusement spots.

Williamsporters also contributed their share to war production and, because of the growing diversification of industry, did so in more ways than ever before. The largest private employer in the area remained the Lycoming Mfg. Company, which concentrated on building parts and engines for aircraft and tanks. At its peak, it turned out 600 engines a month, plus parts for planes such as the B-29 and P-51 Mustang.

Local industries employed many women during World War II. There were six times as many women at the Lycoming Division of the Aviation Corporation as there had been in World War I. Those pictured here in July 1943, include, from left, June Schauer, Florence Haines, Lois Livermore, Marie Allison, Shirley Miller, and Lois Messick. Courtesy, Grit Publishing Company

Other firms contributed in an enormous variety of ways, each designed to take advantage of their particular skills in civilian production. The Bethlehem Steel plant (formerly the Williamsport Wire Rope Company) made wire rope for submarine nets; Darling Valve and Manufacturing Company made 75mm and 105mm artillery shells, five-inch rockets, and steel valves for ships and landing craft; Sylvania Electric Products Company, Inc., produced radio tubes and radar equipment, and Holmes Silk Mill made parachutes. Williamsport Furniture Company made cots, lifeboats, bunk beds, and boxes for shipping artillery shells, while C.A. Reed made, among other things, small parachutes for fragmentation bombs. Even the lumber industry revived somewhat as 310 million board feet of finished goods were produced during the war years.

In short, Williamsport's contributions to the final victory were the result of a major community effort which left virtually no one untouched. It was a solid foundation on which to build what most were certain would be a better postwar world.

CHAPTER SEVEN
Regional Center

Left: *This aerial view of downtown Williamsport was taken on a late summer afternoon in 1983. The Canal Street area with its new Sheraton Motor Inn is at lower right. The Genetti Lycoming Hotel is at left center. The Academic Center and new gymnasium of Lycoming College dominate the right center part of the picture. Courtesy, Marlin D. Fausey and Michael G. Roskin*

Williamsport and Lycoming County are the regional centers of North-Central Pennsylvania. In one sense this has been true since their establishment, when the county comprised the entire north-central region of the state and the city served as its county seat. In the mid-19th century the rise of the lumber industry made the community the economic hub of the region as well. In another sense the role of the city and county as regional centers has developed since World War II when they became much more complete centers of social and economic life. Law and business continue to be important, but in recent years the city and county have become regional centers of education, health care, and the arts as well.

These developments occurred during a period of significant population changes. Between 1950 and 1980 the county grew from 101,249 to 118,416 residents. This represented a 17 percent growth rate, slightly more than the 13 percent rate the state experienced during the same period. Williamsport has not been so fortunate and suffered a dramatic population decline in the same period, a loss of 26 percent since 1950. The most recent census counted 33,401 inhabitants, down 4,517 or 11.9 percent since 1970. In fact, every Pennsylvania city but one lost population between 1970 and 1980. Many cities roughly comparable to Williamsport, like Wilkes-Barre, Altoona, and Johnstown, lost population at about the same rate. Such population exchanges between cities and their surrounding areas have been common in post-World War II America and have at least two clear causes: suburbanization and urban development.

The movement of people to the suburbs in search of space, lower taxes, or what they believed to be better living conditions began in the mid-1940s. By 1960 the city had lost significant numbers of citizens to the nearby areas of Loyalsock Township, Montoursville, Old Lycoming Township, and Woodward Township. Loyalsock Township grew so rapidly that it built its own junior-senior high school in 1956. All these suburbs have continued to grow since 1960, but the rate of growth has moderated except in the areas to the west of the city. New residents, drawn by available land, the new Industrial Park, and the new Williamsport Area High School, have continued to

Above: *By the 1970s housing construction had filled up most of the level areas of Loyalsock Township and was beginning to advance up the hills. Valley View Associates were in the process of building their apartment complex north of Four Mile Drive in the fall of 1971. Courtesy, Vannucci Foto*

pour into Woodward and Old Lycoming townships at substantial rates.

As suburbanization slowed in the 1960s, urban redevelopment and renewal picked up. Programs like the West Edwin Street Renewal Project involved the demolition of old structures and the construction of high-rise apartments. The West Edwin Street Project evolved into a series of renewal efforts, like the Homesteading Program, which offered low interest loans to save older homes by rehabilitation. Other efforts, like the Canal Street Urban Renewal project, resulted in substantial loss of housing, as homes were replaced by roads, parking lots, and businesses. People and institutions were uprooted and scattered to locations in and out of the city. The city began another renewal effort in 1981, the Main Street Project, aimed at revitalizing downtown buildings and enhancing both their appearance and commercial usefulness. These varied programs have had positive results but the city has not yet halted the exodus of its citizens.

Williamsport has been able to maintain and enhance its status as a regional center despite the loss of more than one-quarter of its population for several reasons. The city and its surrounding

Above, right: When people were moved by urban renewal or simply decided to settle in the suburbs they often took their religious institutions with them or created new ones. Congregation Ohev Shalom moved from West Edwin Street to Cherry Street in the early 1950s.

area has had an important resource in a large number of public spirited citizens, working as individuals or as part of small groups. These people have led, coaxed, pushed, and pulled their fellow citizens to support their visions of the future and their specific plans, like the dikes, the Keystone Shortway, and the establishment of new health care facilities. They have not always been successful. One of the ironies of the city's history since

1970 has been that areas of long-term strength, retail trade, and industry have declined.

Community leaders have united with or been joined in their efforts by formal organizations, particularly the Williamsport-Lycoming Chamber of Commerce and its predecessors, as well as one of its creations, the Industrial Properties Corporation. The area has also been blessed with financial resources large enough to launch new projects. Individual philanthropy and several private foundations have

Three leaders of the 1973 Lycoming United Fund are pictured here discussing goals. From left to right are Peyton D. McDonald, corporate division leader, Harold D. Hershberger, Jr., drive leader, and William Pickelner, assistant campaign chairman. The Fund passed its goal in October and raised $691,000 for community projects. Courtesy, Grit Publishing Company

been joined by one public agency, the Williamsport Foundation or Community Trust, and have poured many millions of dollars, from seed money to capital funds, into a great variety of efforts to enhance community life. The Foundation was created in 1916 with assets of $31, and is one of the 10 oldest community foundations in America. Since 1930 it has given $10.5 million to a variety of community causes, including $500,000 to Lycoming College for its Academic Center, $500,000 to Williamsport Hospital for Capital Funds, $300,000 to Hope Enterprises for its Rehabilitation Workshop, and $200,000 for the Center City Mall project. The Foundation's assets totaled $15 million in 1983.

If public-spirited citizens with vision are the key to the city's recent development, controling the Susquehanna River stands as

Above: *Although P.D. (Percy David) Mitchell was born in Virginia and educated in North Carolina, he gave his lifetime of community service to Williamsport. He came to the city in 1943 as director of the Bethune-Douglass Community Center. When he retired in 1976 he had touched and improved the lives of countless Williamsporters. In 1976 he was governor of Kiwanis in Pennsylvania. He received many honors, including a doctorate from Lycoming College in 1969 and the Grit Award for Meritorious Community Service in 1976. He died in 1981. Courtesy, Vannucci Foto*

Right: *Williamsport has attracted candidates for national political office. Lyndon Johnson visited in 1960 as the Democratic candidate for vice president and Jimmy Carter was in town in 1976 as the Democratic presidential candidate. Carter greeted people and spoke at the bandshell in Brandon Park. Courtesy, Michael G. Roskin*

their single most important success. Williamsport and its cross-river neighbor, South Williamsport, have grown and prospered at the discretion of the river. The thunderous sounds of the ice breaking up in the spring have not always been welcomed, for the spring thaws have often meant water in the streets, houses in the river, and the interruption of all transportation and business. Then in 1955, the dikes, aided by flood control dams on the watershed, tamed the mighty Susquehanna. The idea to use dikes had been raised over the years, but not until the disastrous 1936 flood were many people convinced that dikes were the only adequate answer. Attorney John C. Youngman, Sr., chaired the Flood Control Committee of the Community Trade Association, a predecessor of the

Left: If the 1936 flood persuaded residents to vote for the dikes, the 1946 flood reminded them how much they were needed. Lycoming Creek rose higher in 1946 than in 1936. It undermined the piers of the West Fourth Street Bridge and dropped the north side of the bridge six feet. Courtesy, Grit Publishing Company

Right: Most city residents have never seen the interior of the Hepburn Street Pumping Station although it is a vital part of the flood control system. Superintendent of the City Flood Control System, Otto R. Mueller, is holding a clipboard and talking to Mary Stull, secretary of Williamsport Civil Defense, Councilman Chester D. Wolfe, and Paul W. Reeder, director of Williamsport Civil Defense, in March 1957. Courtesy, Grit Publishing Company

Left: An early stage of dike construction in February 1947 shows stone and gravel fill pushed into the Susquehanna River channel to form a base for the dike. This view is west from the Market Street Bridge. The Reading Railroad Station is visible on the right. Courtesy, Grit Publishing Company

Williamsport-Lycoming Chamber of Commerce. His efforts reached a climax in April 1940, when the citizens of the city and South Williamsport voted for the dikes. Ground was broken in November of that year on the banks of Lycoming Creek near West Fourth Street, but war brought the project to a halt. Construction resumed in 1946 and took nine years and $15,250,000 to complete.

The wisdom of building the dikes became evident to every person living in Williamsport in June 1972, when Hurricane

Agnes struck the area. Rainfall on June 22 was a record 8.66 inches and the subsequent river crest reached a record 34.75 feet, yet downtown Williamsport remained free of water and served (in the unusual flood-time role) as the center of help for others. Some of those needing help lived in the typically flood-free northern parts of the city where entrances to conduits carrying streams under the city clogged. Grafius Run, for example, poured over Elmira and adjacent streets.

Up and down the river areas unprotected by dikes suffered heavy damage and whole sections of the county floodplain communities of Jersey Shore, Muncy, and Montgomery were

inundated. Agnes has been described as the greatest natural disaster in the history of Lycoming County, but it would have been immensely more destructive if the dikes had not kept the water away from the city.

The dikes promised Williamsport a future different from its past. They ended the cycles of destruction and reconstruction. They have not been, however, the only recent shaper of the city's life. Williamsporters have always been concerned with their routes to the world, from use of the river, to the development of the West Branch Canal, to the completion of very extensive railroad lines. As recently as 1940 the railroads' passenger and freight services seemed adequate for any future economic development. Perhaps no one projected then that within 40 years the passenger stations would have disappeared and the long freight docks would have been replaced by streets and

Left: *The old and new Market Street bridges stand side by side in August 1951, shortly before the new one opened and the old one was removed. The new bridge was much wider and met the demands of the vastly increased postwar use of private transportation. Courtesy, Grit Publishing Company*

Right: *Hurricane Agnes swept the Kenyon Avenue home of George Lepley from its foundation and deposited it, twisted and broken, two blocks away. Lepley not only retained his sense of humor but also vowed to rebuild on the same site. Courtesy, Grit Publishing Company*

housing projects. The last passenger train left the city on April 30, 1971. Long before this departure people with vision had worked to guarantee that the city and Lycoming County would be served by the most modern routes to the world: super highways.

The most important of these super highways is Interstate 80, providing Williamsport with easy, rapid access to points east and west. The manager of the Community Trade Association,

Charles E. Noyes, developed the idea for a Short Route to the 1939 New York World's Fair which directed travelers from Cleveland to New York City by way of Williamsport. The route proved popular and led to a plan, developed in 1952, for a toll road cutting across the northern tier of Pennsylvania, on the model of the Pennsylvania Turnpike which crosses the southern part of the state. Two years later an editor of the *Grit* Kenneth D. Rhone, coined the name, "Shortway", and in December 1954 the Keystone Shortway Association was organized. Williamsport businessman Z.H. Confair, later the state senator from Williamsport, served as president, and Noyes as executive director. This association built public and political support for the highway, which gradually changed in both location and designation. The planned road was moved from the northern tier to just south of Williamsport and from a toll road to a part of the Interstate System. On May 31, 1958, Governor George M. Leader broke ground for the new super highway in East Stroudsburg. Completed in 1970, the Keystone Shortway became a link in a major transcontinental route from New York City to San Francisco and an important element in Williamsport life. In the following decade the Susquehanna Beltway, designated Interstate 180, connected the river cities in Lycoming County with the Shortway. Williamsport has always been on the nation's roadmaps and it continues to have a favorable location on the most modern highways.

The regional status of Williamsport and Lycoming County since World War II has depended not only on the physical changes brought about by the dikes and highways, but also on developments in a variety of social and economic areas of life. The two areas of traditional strength have been law and business.

The legal system has grown in Williamsport with the expansion of court facilities and important changes in the county and federal judiciaries. Both county and federal governments built new homes in the 1970s. The Lycoming County Court House was built in 1971, and the United States Government erected a Federal Building in 1977. Opponents of these projects, led by the Williamsport Community Arts Council and the Lycoming County Historical Society, did not deny the need for new offices but argued for the preservation of historically important and artistically attractive structures. They failed to save the old courthouse but succeeded in preserving the old federal building, now remodeled and in use as city hall. The new buildings stand two blocks apart on West Third Street, and together testify to the important role of law in the area. The new courthouse has three courtrooms where there were once two, and since 1981 three judges where there were formerly two. The Federal Building, named the Herman T. Schneebeli Office Building in honor of Congressman Schneebeli, has new court facilities. Judge Malcolm Muir, judge of the United States District Court for the Middle District of Pennsylvania, has sat in Williamsport since the District Office opened in 1970, but he shared his time with Lewisburg until the construction of the new building. The new court space and expanded judicial services have played a significant role in the substantial increase in local and federal legal activity in the city.

The other area of traditional strength, business, has had troubled times. City retail trade has suffered from suburbanization and an apparent lack of vision and planning on the part of business and community leaders. As people

moved to the suburbs some retail businesses followed them,
setting up in shopping centers and malls. The malls began in
the 1960s and multiplied in the 1970s to the point of
threatening the very survival of downtown retail trade. Those
east of the city have been particularly strong and vigorous,
including Loyalsock Township's Loyal Plaza on its "Golden
Strip" and Hall Station's Crown American's Lycoming Mall. The
city lost W.T. Grant company to Loyal Plaza in 1971 and Sears,
Roebuck, and Company to Lycoming Mall in 1978. In addition,
a number of old downtown businesses closed, including Prior
and Salada Company (1896) and the Carroll House (1929). The
Grower's Market shut down in 1974 and Market Street became
strangely silent for the first time since the earliest days of
the city.

Dedication ceremonies for the new Federal Building were held in April 1978. The building was plagued by construction delays. Former Congressman Schneebeli jokingly accepted some responsibility for them, saying that the builders had to redesign the front to accommodate his long name. Schneebeli was flanked by federal and local officials, including Congressman Allen Ertel, seated third from the left, and Mayor Daniel P. Kirby, seated third from the right. Courtesy, Grit Publishing Company

By the mid-1970s city retailers and political leaders had
organized and had begun to fight hard to stem the outward
flow with a variety of promotions and projects. One of them,
the Center City Mall, dedicated in November 1976, created an
improved and attractive downtown setting. The project turned
Pine Street into a mall, planted trees throughout the downtown
area, and renewed enthusiasm for the city's retail business life,
but the future seems to promise a continued struggle for
downtown retailers. What the city lost, the county gained and
more, so that the area continues to be a regional retail center.

The industrial life of the city has also changed since 1945 but
not as dramatically as retail trade. Many of the city's largest
industries, like Avco and Bethlehem Steel, which had immersed
themselves in war production, successfully returned to civilian
work, but with much reduced labor forces. Other industries were

more war-related, like the Susquehanna Ordnance Depot. Although located outside the city, it employed a substantial number of city residents.

The postwar loss of jobs and some industries created a crisis that was met, in part, by the Industrial Properties Corporation, which developed an industrial park in 1956 on land on Reach Road in the west end of the city. The project began slowly with one tenant, the Steelex Corporation. During the years it attracted a number of industries which offered a new diversity in employment and production, and by 1984 it included 300 acres occupied by 30 industries which employed approximately 3,000 people.

Industrial growth has also taken place elsewhere in Lycoming County, particularly in the communities of Muncy and Jersey Shore, where industrial parks have been established since 1970. But industrial change and growth have not fully kept pace with population growth. Since the mid-1970s high unemployment, often more than 10 percent and above both the state and national averages, has plagued the area and demonstrated the need for new efforts to attract more industry. Such efforts have been initiated in recent years under the leadership of the

Left: *The interior of Alcan Cable Company is pictured here at its large facility in the Industrial Park in 1967. Miles and miles of cable await processing. Courtesy, Grit Publishing Company*

Williamsport-Lycoming Chamber of Commerce.

Education, health care, and the arts have joined law and business as important aspects of Williamsport life in the years since World War II. Change has taken place in all areas of learning, including public, private, higher, and special education. Public education has undergone massive reorganization, mandated by state legislation. The 1947 education act required jointures of schools in small boroughs and townships and the education legislation of 1961 ordered unification of jointures into larger school districts. In 1940 the county had almost 100 one-room schools. When Rose Valley and Beech Valley schools closed in 1967 it had none. In exchange for such centralization and the extensive busing of students, the students have broader curriculums, larger social environments, and more extensive extra-curricular activities.

From an administrative viewpoint, local control of education passed into the hands of eight school districts, the largest of which is the Williamsport Area School District. It has experimented with innovative educational settings, like the open school, and has remodeled or built many buildings, including a large high school. The high school, proposed in 1967, spawned one of the major political controversies of the postwar era. A taxpayers group, the Citizens Responsibility Committee, filed a lawsuit challenging the school board on the cost of the proposed school and the procedures used in acquiring the land. Judge Thomas Wood ruled for the school board and the taxpayers appealed, delaying construction. The school finally opened in January 1972.

Private education has existed alongside public education for many years in Williamsport, but it has flourished since 1968. The Roman Catholics opened St. Ann's, an elementary school, in Loyalsock Township that year and consolidated St. Joseph's and St. Mary's high schools into Bishop Neumann the following year. Protestant "Christian" schools have emerged, and two of them, the Williamsport Christian Schools of Emmanuel Baptist Church, which began in 1971, and Faith Tabernacle Christian Academy, organized in 1974, offer classes from kindergarten through high school. The West Branch School, the only non-religious private school in the area, opened in 1971 on the open school model, featuring independent study and a neighborhood school atmosphere with much parent involvement.

The truly dramatic growth in education has been at the college level. At the end of World War II Williamsport had one small liberal arts institution, Dickinson Junior College, enrolling

Left: *Students at the School of Hope presented Dr. and Mrs. Max C. Miller, who had been instrumental in founding the school, with a special Christmas decoration they created in 1967. The decoration, a partridge in a pear tree, was erected in the yard of the Miller home. Courtesy, Grit Publishing Company*

Right: *The Williamsport Area High School sits atop a ridge in the northwestern end of the city. Completed in 1972, at a cost of $15.6 million, it covers 9.87 acres and features a 1,600-seat auditorium, a large gymnasium and swimming pool, and a 6,000-seat stadium. Courtesy, Marlin D. Fausey and Michael G. Roskin*

about 230 students. In 1984 it boasted a four-year liberal arts school, Lycoming College, with 1,200 students, a two-year liberal arts, vocational and technical school, Williamsport Area Community College, with 3,675 students, and a School of Commerce with more than 100 students. Dickinson's transformation took place in 1947 under the able leadership of John W. Long, who had served as president of the junior college since 1921 and continued to lead the new college until 1955. Between 1948 and 1968, Lycoming built many new facilities, including a student center, eight new dormitories, and a new academic center, which featured a new library, a theater, a planetarium, a computer center, and a large auditorium. With a long tradition in the liberal arts and business, it has recently added computer science, mass communication, and nursing to its curriculum.

Williamsport Area Community College also grew out of an existing institution, the Williamsport Technical Institute. The Williamsport School Board created WTI in 1941 as a technical school separate from but related to its high school in order to provide technical training to high school and some post-high

school students. The Watsontown Plan, so named because it introduced Watsontown High School students into WTI's programs, began in 1945. Students from other community high schools soon followed. In 1965 the Pennsylvania Board of Education approved the transformation of the Technical Institute into a Community College and the new school opened in September of that year. Its first president, Kenneth E. Carl, had served as the last director of WTI. The college occupied the Technical Institute facilities in its early years. It expanded into the old Williamsport High School after the city vacated it. In the late 1970s, it embarked on an ambitious building program, which has thus far included new labs for its technical programs, a new library, and an Earth Science Center. It continues to offer a technical program to high school students from a number of surrounding school districts and runs an extensive adult evening education program, which enrolls about 4,500 students a year.

Education for children and adults with special disabilities has taken a great leap forward in Williamsport since the 1950s. Much of this has been mandated by state laws guaranteeing an education to all Pennsylvania citizens and has been facilitated by the creation of Intermediate Units. The one serving Williamsport and Lycoming County is Unit 17. The city, however, has had its own unique special education school since 1954, when the Lycoming Chapter of the Pennsylvania Association for Retarded Children founded the School of Hope to provide a school opportunity for children who could not attend public schools. The school merged with Enterprises for the Handicapped in 1974 to become Hope Enterprises, Inc. Hope runs several programs, including the school, renamed the Dr. Max C. Miller Training Center in 1981, and the Rehabilitation Workshop.

Health care has matched education in growth and development and has made Williamsport an important medical center. Williamsport Hospital grew dramatically in the decades after 1950 under the leadership of Daniel W. Hartman, Harry R. Gibson, and Clive R. Waxman. Beginning with a new V-shaped addition to the southern side of its main building in 1952, the hospital built a new home for its School of Nursing, a Rehabilitation Center, a Medical Center, and most recently a Core Services Building in 1974. Its major diagnostic tools include a CAT Scan and a Sonography Unit. It has established a variety of educational programs and continues to run "the oldest functioning nursing school in Pennsylvania."

Williamsport Hospital was the only medical facility in the city until 1951, when it was joined by Divine Providence Hospital. Mary Hills grew up in the city and became Mother Theresilla of the Sisters of Christian Charity. She dreamed of opening a home for the elderly in the city. The Sisters, with the help of Father Leo J. Post, pastor of St. Boniface Church, bought land in the northeastern corner of the city, raised funds, and built a hospital as their version of this dream. It no sooner opened its doors than it began to grow, adding a chapel, an auditorium, a convent, and in 1975 an East Wing, which contains emergency services and many of its special centers, including the region's Hemodialysis and Cancer Treatment centers. The Community Mental Health Center for Lycoming-Clinton Counties also makes its home in this medical complex. Williamsport and Divine Providence hospitals have many complimentary services which together have lifted Williamsport's medical care to regional status.

The arts have joined education and health care in their attainments. Williamsport has a remarkable tradition in the fields of music and theater. It boasts the oldest continuing band in the United States, the Repasz-Elks Band, as well as the Imperial Teteques, reborn in 1963 and named for the Williamsport Imperial Teteques, "the original all-Masonic music organization in the U.S." The Williamsport Symphony

Right: Dogwoods in bloom in Brandon Park create a wonderful sense of beauty for visitors.

Right: The campus of Lycoming College features a quadrangle surrounded by the Wertz Student Center, the Long Administration Building, the Clarke Building and Chapel, and dormitories. The large structure in the center foreground is the Academic Center, which was completed in 1968. The Athletic Stadium and fields are several blocks north of the main campus. Courtesy, Marlin D. Fausey and Michael G. Roskin

Left: *This courthouse served Lycoming County from 1860 until 1969. Designed by the well-known Pennsylvania architect Samuel Sloan, its stately form lives on in similarly designed courthouses in the nearby towns of Sunbury and Lock Haven. Courtesy, Ralph E. Menne*

Right: *Peter Herdic paid for the construction of this English Gothic church and then gave it to Trinity Episcopal Parish in 1876 for the sum of one dollar with the stipulation that the pews were to remain "forever free." It is built of Bald Eagle Mountain stone. Judge John Maynard presented the church with Westminster Chimes, the first church in the United States to have them.*

Left: *The current Lycoming County Court House is the third to occupy the traditional court site of Pine and West Third streets. Built at the cost of $3.5 million, it brought an expanding county government under one roof. County offices began to move in during December 1970, but official dedication ceremonies were not until May 1971. Courtesy, Ralph E. Menne*

Right: *Several prominent Williamsport families have owned the Emery House on West Fourth Street since it was built in 1889 by William Emery as a wedding present for his bride, Mary White Gamble. Although it has become an office building, its Romanesque style has been carefully maintained as has its stained glass and woodwork.*

Below: *Cornelius Woodward moved from New Orleans to Natchez and eventually to Williamsport where in 1803 he erected a four-room log house. He subsequently enlarged the home to 19 rooms, building it to reflect a Natchez-style architecture. Named Springside in 1849 by John Vanderbelt Woodward, it remained in the Woodward family until 1945. The spacious lawn is graced by a fountain which was once part of the Peter Herdic estate and is shadowed by a great copper beech tree planted by Cornelius' wife in 1802.*

Above: *This painting is one of more than 200 such compositions Severin Roesen is known to have created. Born in Germany in about 1816, he immigrated to the United States and lived in New York City for a time. He moved to Williamsport about 1859 where he lived until he died some 13 years later. In 1979 one of his paintings brought $50,000 at a New York City auction. Courtesy, Ralph E. Menne*

Right: *The Ulman Opera House, built on Market Square in 1867, was the first opera house in Williamsport. This painting captures it in its grandeur with its mansard roof intact. It has since been remodeled and is currently in use as the Market Square Office of Founders Federal Savings and Loan Association. Courtesy, Founders Federal Savings and Loan Association*

Top: *The* Hiawatha, *a project of the Williamsport-Lycoming Chamber of Commerce, made its maiden voyage in August 1982. It was named after a popular turn-of-the-century riverboat which sailed the Susquehanna between Williamsport and Sylvan Dell. Courtesy, Marlin D. Fausey*

Far left: *A corridor of fall colors and shadows graces Brandon Park. Courtesy, Michael G. Roskin*

Above: *Crowds pack the Howard J. Lamade Stadium during the Little League World Series in late August 1970. The Little League Baseball, Inc., complex is located in South Williamsport. The central part of the stadium was completed in 1959 in time for the World Series that year. The first and third base extensions were added in 1968. Courtesy, Ralph E. Menne*

Left: *Williamsport is seen at sunset from Bald Eagle Mountain. The city stretches for miles along the Susquehanna River and gives the impression of a large metropolitan area. Courtesy, Ralph E. Menne*

Orchestra, with Osborne Housel as conductor, played concerts for a 10-year span after its creation in 1948. The Susquehanna Valley Orchestra, formed in 1966, became a regional orchestra with Williamsport as one of its two concerts centers. In 1984 it was renamed the Williamsport Symphony Orchestra, the city serving as home base. Choral groups have added their voices to the music of the city. The oldest of these is the Gesang Verein Harmonia, founded by John Fischer in 1892. Thomas H. Shellenberger became director in 1975. Choral music in the city has been shaped since 1944 in large measure by Walter G. McIver. In that year he founded the Civic Choir, later the Civic Chorus. Two years later, as a faculty member of Lycoming College, he formed the Lycoming College Choir. The Civic Choir has had a distinguished life under McIver and his successors, Jay Stenger and Paul Ziegler, and has given many memorable performances, including *The Messiah* in 1948 and 1949, and *Amahl and the Night Visitors* in 1952 and 1953.

Theater, like music, has a distinguished history. In the 19th century performances were given by companies of traveling professional actors and singers at such places as the Ulman Opera House and the Lycoming Opera House. The theater of the mid-20th century has continued to include visiting professionals, but has been dominated by companies of local amateurs. The local groups include the Williamsport Players, organized in 1958, the Drama Workshop, founded in 1969, and the Community Theater League, created in 1976. Lycoming College's Arena Theater has offered summer as well as academic year dramatic productions since 1962. The city also has a Civic Ballet Company.

The arts are more than music and theater. Artists and craftsmen have created a wide variety of groups, including the Williamsport Chapter of the Pennsylvania Guild of Craftsmen in 1949, the Williamsport Creative Writers Forum in 1959, and the Bald Eagle Art League in 1972. Local artist Horace Hand, known for his Christmas Eve Church paintings published by the Williamsport *Sun-Gazette,* presided over the league until his death in 1977.

The arts have flourished because of local talent and widespread community support. They have been assisted by the Williamsport Community Arts Council, an organization proposed by the Williamsport Chamber of Commerce and carried out by Barnard Taylor and others. Its Festival of the Arts in 1960 has been followed by a variety of shows and performances, including a month-long festival in 1971. The October Festival of Arts, begun in 1973, has been the united effort of the Arts Council and the Art Department of the Williamsport Area School District, under the direction of June E. Baskin. Public celebrations in Williamsport invariably include the arts, further testimony to their importance in the life of the city.

Williamsport and Lycoming County have not only maintained their status as regional centers since 1945, but have enhanced it with significant developments in education, music, and the arts. Greater achievement in quality and quantity are doubtless attainable in every life area. City and county leaders have continued, for example, to be concerned with industrial growth and the survival of city retail trade. But even as these concerns exist, many of the same people have projected a new area of growth for the 1980s: recreation and tourism.

Williamsport has an impressive recreational tradition. Before the completion of the beltway, anyone who tried to travel near or in the city at the start of trout season in the spring, or buck season in the fall, faced incredible traffic congestion and learned the hard way that they were at the crossroads of a major sporting area. The city also had professional baseball teams for many of the years from 1940-1976, and a professional basketball team, the Williamsport Billies, from 1947-1964. These regional professional leagues were joined by Little League baseball beginning in 1939.

Carl E. Stotz was the founder and moving spirit of Little League. The first Little League World Series was held at Memorial Park in 1947. Little League has grown from 28 teams in seven leagues in Pennsylvania in 1946 to approximately 48,500 teams in about 6,900 leagues in many countries of the world in 1983. Every August the Williamsport area is the center of national sports attention as national television and tens of thousands of visitors come for the championship game.

While Little League has been and continues to be very important to the recreational and tourist life of the Williamsport area, it has not been able to lift it to the status of a regional recreation center. Community leaders have searched for additional recreational resources and believe they have found them in the Susquehanna River. The river has a long history of recreational use but in many ways it has disappeared from view for more than a generation. Canoe clubs, boat docks, and swimming beaches, once numerous, have declined dramatically. The dikes have kept the river in its channel but have also kept the people away. Indeed, until the completion of the beltway which elevated the roadbed the river was visible to city residents only from a bridge or a nearby hill. The plans of

Above: *Carl E. Stotz points to a baseball as his two nephews, Harold "Major" Gehron and Jimmy Gehron for whom he "invented" the game, listen. In the summer of 1938 Stotz experimented with a scaled-down baseball field suitable for young boys. The first Little League baseball game was played on a sandlot in Memorial Park outside the Bowman Field fence on June 6, 1939. Courtesy, Carl E. Stotz*

Below: *Susquehanna State Park is pictured in the mid-1960s before Hurricane Agnes virtually destroyed it. The park had been substantially refurbished in the early 1980s and has become home port for the riverboat, Hiawatha. Courtesy, Grit Publishing Company*

Right: *The new Hepburn Street Dam was under construction between 1983 and 1984. The project was funded by the Commonwealth of Pennsylvania.*

community leaders for the river have resulted in a new and stronger Hepburn Street Dam to guarantee a more stable and deeper pool upstream, the removal of the log boom cribs to open more of the "Long Reach" to boating, the construction of a new riverboat, the *Hiawatha,* to encourage use of the river and tourism, and the development of Susquehanna Park. The Susquehanna Boom Festival, begun by the Williamsport Jaycees in 1981, has highlighted the roles of lumber and the river in the area's life.

Michael Ross' early survey, the development of the canal and railroads, the building of the lumber boom, the development of a diversified industrial base at the turn of the century, and the building of the dikes and Shortway have brought a degree of growth and prosperity to Williamsport that is rare in the Appalachian region. This growth was made possible by the vigor, determination, and vision of its citizens. Today, Williamsport is at a crossroads. It is facing the decline of its retail trade and relatively high unemployment in its traditional industries. But again, the community seems determined to move forward. In 1982 the city adopted the motto, "A Proud Past and a Promising Future."

CHAPTER EIGHT
Partners in Progress
by Joseph P. Laver, Jr.

Left: *These automobiles, among them a score of new Auburns, were part of an 80-car "boost business caravan" which toured Williamsport and South Williamsport streets in the spring of 1932. They were all powered by Lycoming Mfg. Company engines. Two airplanes, also Lycoming engine powered, flew over the city during the caravan. Courtesy, Grit Publishing Company*

The collective histories of the companies and institutions included in this chapter are a microcosm of the Williamsport area's history. Some date back to the community's initial industrialization based on lumber; some are the fruits of various organized efforts to bolster Williamsport's economic base.

Early diversification began when new businesses were spawned to meet the various needs of the lumber industry. Quite often, in order to grow, these companies would branch out into nonlumber products. Wood-related industries, from toothpicks to furniture, sprang up, which in turn generated additional firms to supply such things as machinery, parts, and packaging. And the burgeoning population kept increasing the need for services and products.

Some of these needs were met by local people starting small ventures. Others were begun by newcomers investing their personal and financial equity in a new community. Many current local businesses and industries trace their roots to these companies.

All of them are part of Williamsport's continuing growth into a diversified, small metropolitan area in a rural setting. Agriculture has never dominated the region because of the limited amount of tillable land. The bituminous and anthracite coal deposits both just miss the area, and any gas or oil that might be present has been largely unmolested because of geologic and economic factors. The one natural resource that put Williamsport on the map—lumber—was overexploited, as was common practice.

Since starting as an "outpost" on the Susquehanna River, the Williamsport area has grown to nurture 186 manufacturing firms with more than 16,000 employees in 1984. There are over 2,000 businesses. Lycoming County has passed $275 million in annual payroll.

The organizations whose stories are detailed on the following pages have chosen to support this important literary and civic project. They illustrate the variety of ways in which individuals and their businesses have contributed to the growth and development of Williamsport and Lycoming County. The civic involvement of the area's businesses, learning institutions, and local government, in partnership with its citizens, has made it a first-class place to live and work.

WILLIAMSPORT-LYCOMING CHAMBER OF COMMERCE

For a century the Williamsport-Lycoming Chamber of Commerce has dedicated itself to improving the economy and the life-style of Williamsport and Lycoming County. During that time the Chamber has served as a catalyst for hundreds of ambitious community projects. Probably no other single organization has consistently provided so strong a commitment on behalf of the community's growth.

The Chamber's thrust has always been one of prompt adaptation to changing economic conditions. Originally known as the Board of Trade, this corporation of volunteer leaders and volunteer revenues was founded in 1885 in response to a fading lumber industry. A promotional pamphlet and city atlas were printed and a group of businessmen successfully marketed the area for the first time. New industries resulted.

This success spurred the Board of Trade and all Williamsport political factions to establish a Committee of 25 that spearheaded a $461,000 fund. By 1910 the committee had helped obtain 17 new industries, and the city was once again on the road to prosperity.

In 1921 a major effort was initiated to capitalize on the area's newly paved roads by promoting the "Beautiful Susquehanna Trail." Over 50,000 pieces of literature were distributed, and by 1929 an estimated $.5 million in tourist dollars had been generated.

The Board of Trade became the Williamsport Chamber of Commerce in 1924. Six years later the U.S. Rubber Company closed its doors and the Committee of 100, composed of business and civic leaders, and the Chamber of Commerce began a campaign to attract new industry. By 1941 they brought 30 new businesses into the

community. After World War II the Chamber-affiliated Industrial Properties Corporation helped establish the 300-acre Williamsport Industrial Park. A series of three more fund drives raised money for land purchase, utilities, and a third-mortgage revolving fund.

During its history the Chamber has grown significantly and now serves an impressive countywide constituency that includes more than 500 member firms throughout Lycoming County. In response to today's intense competition for jobs throughout the nation's Northeast, the Williamsport-Lycoming Chamber of Commerce has recently mounted a farsighted, multifaceted campaign for economic development.

Industrial development continues to be the backbone of the Chamber's economic-development programs. Through yet another

aggressive campaign to recruit new industry and to encourage the expansion of existing Lycoming County business, new industrial growth has visibly been generated for Williamsport and Lycoming County.

Because the heart of Pennsylvania's entire north-central region is the city of Williamsport, the Chamber is committed to reestablishing Williamsport as a prosperous economic center. Largely in response to a devastating fire in 1980 that tore through the central business district and damaged 12 businesses, the Chamber of Commerce formed the Greater Williamsport Partnership. A countywide committee of 18 business leaders invested well over $300,000 to recruit private investment projects for the downtown. Today there are a significant number of

restoration, reconstruction, and new commercial development ventures that are attributable to the partnership's efforts.

Expanding the county economy through the recruitment of business, convention, and leisure travelers is another high priority of the Chamber. And Chamber leaders are now marketing aggressively the existing travel attractions like the Little League Baseball Headquarters and International Museum, the world-renowned Shempp Toy Train Treasury, quaint specialty shops, outlet stores, and a recreational paradise heralded nationally by outdoor enthusiasts.

The development of major new attractions is also being accomplished. The *Hiawatha* is a new, old-fashioned simulated paddlewheeled excursion boat that plies the waters of the Susquehanna River. Rallying

around the riverboat's wholesome appeal and promise of adventure, hundreds of Lycoming Countians from all walks of life volunteered their services, donations, and spirited enthusiasm to help the Chamber launch the *Hiawatha* in 1982. Available for public and private charters, the *Hiawatha* promotes history, education, recreation, and the overall economy.

Lycoming County's newest attraction is an exciting excursion on one of the first passenger trains traveling through the picturesque Grand Canyon in over a quarter-century. Spearheaded by the Chamber, the biannual weekend railroading adventure tours through the scenic mountains of Pennsylvania and New York during spring's mountain laurel season and fall's foliage color peak. Stops along

the way encourage exploring the historic museums, shopping, and local attractions.

The Williamsport-Lycoming Chamber of Commerce is proud of its legacy of tradition. But progress is the promise of the future. As Lycoming County looks ahead, the Chamber and its business leadership will continue the forward-thinking momentum and vision that will ultimately play a major role in the region's ongoing pursuit of progress.

Chamber of Commerce volunteer business leadership directs today's ambitious course on behalf of Lycoming County's future growth and prosperity. From left to right are James P. Stopper, CPA, Rogers, Huber & Associates; Ralph A. Nardi, Jr., president, Canada Dry Bottling Company; William D. Davis, president, Commonwealth Bank & Trust Company, N.A.; Theodore H. Reich, president, Jersey Shore State Bank; Joseph Kramer, CPA, Phillips, Kramer & Hoffmann; and Richard H. Lundy, Jr., president, Lundy Construction Company.

WILLIAMSPORT SUN-GAZETTE

The *Williamsport Sun-Gazette* was founded at the dawn of the 19th century.

When publication began in 1801, Williamsport was a rough frontier village and the seat of the newly created Lycoming County. The United States of America was only 25 years old, and Thomas Jefferson —the nation's third President—was in the White House.

William F. Buyers, who at age 20 had just completed his apprenticeship as a printer, migrated from Sunbury and founded the *Lycoming Gazette* with a case of type and a hand-operated flat press. There were 131 residents in the community

Hand-lettered news bulletins once were daily fare outside the Sun-Gazette building in the days before radio and television. On May 10, 1915, the men below were reading details about the sinking of the Lusitania *by a German U-boat off Queenstown, Ireland.*

when he started his newspaper in a building situated somewhere in the present-day neighborhood of Penn Street and Washington Boulevard.

The *Gazette* name has been on the nameplate and masthead of a newspaper published in Williamsport continuously since that day in October 1801. And the business young Buyers began is the oldest enterprise of any kind in the West Branch Valley.

Today's *Sun-Gazette* is the twelfth-oldest newspaper in the nation, and the fourth-oldest in Pennsylvania.

The weekly *Lycoming Gazette* was converted to an afternoon daily newspaper in April 1867. It then acquired the *West Branch Bulletin,* which had been organized in 1860. The two were merged as the morning *Gazette and Bulletin* on November 22, 1869. It was published under that name until September 12,

1955, at which time it was consolidated with *The Williamsport Sun*—an afternoon daily that had been established on July 6, 1870, by Colonel Levi L. Tate. Both had been published by the Sun-Gazette Company since 1926 in the present plant on the northeast corner of West Fourth and Hepburn streets.

More than 30 other newspapers have opened and closed operations in Williamsport since 1801, including some that were merged into similar publications. There have been dozens of owners and editors who have made major contributions to the civic and commercial life of the community, men and women who have given readers the news of their area of north-central Pennsylvania, and of Williamsport the village to Williamsport the city.

The pages of the *Sun-Gazette* and its predecessors have been devoted to the news—local, state, national,

The old and the new are combined in the present-day Sun-Gazette building on the northeast corner of West Fourth and Hepburn streets.

and international—since the beginning. It has chronicled births and deaths, and the things people do in between.

The newspaper's emphasis has always been on the news of the day.

The Person family, which has the majority interest in the *Sun-Gazette*, has been a major factor in local journalism in the 100 years since Elmer E. Person arrived in Williamsport in 1884. The 19-year-old printer had just finished a five-year apprenticeship in Bloomsburg.

The newspaperman—grandfather of John E. Person, Jr., the current president of the Sun-Gazette Company—was one of the city's first journalists to become a

photographer as well as a reporter and copy editor. He was a printer and editorial employee on six different local newspapers before he became city editor of *The Sun* on January 1, 1900. He became editor of the newspaper in 1906 and served in that position until his death in 1912.

George E. Graff, formerly business manager of *The Sun,* then became editor. In 1919 he was succeeded by John E. Person, Sr., Elmer E. Person's son, who had started with the newspaper as a reporter under his father while still in high school. Early in 1926 the publication acquired the morning *Gazette and Bulletin* and moved its operations to *The Sun's* plant, which had been built at Fourth and Hepburn streets in 1910. It is still the home of the *Sun-Gazette.*

Person became president of the organization when Graff died in 1935. He took over during the Great Depression and directed the

newspaper's management for more than three decades. Upon his death in 1967 John E. Person, Jr., his son, assumed the presidency. Under the latter's leadership the *Sun-Gazette* switched from metal type to photocomposition, offset printing, and an electronic newsroom.

When the consolidation of the morning and afternoon newspapers was announced in 1955, *Sun-Gazette* readers were advised that it was done "to concentrate our entire effort and attention on one publication." The Sun-Gazette Company's single business interest is the publication of Williamsport's daily newspaper.

Elmer E. Person, who chose Williamsport as a place to live and work 100 years ago, believed in the community's promise for the future. So did his son. So does his grandson. And so, too, do his four great-grandsons associated with the *Sun-Gazette.*

KLINE & COMPANY

John R. Zurinsky went from ice cream to auto parts when he sold his Johnny-Z Restaurants in July 1979 and, with Richard A. Cashera, purchased one of Williamsport's oldest businesses, Kline & Company, located at 315 Hepburn Street.

The firm, whose original site was 18 Market Square, had been founded in 1873 as Kline and Keller; 107 years later Zurinsky became the sole proprietor, purchasing Cashera's share of the company in October 1980. An 1879 invoice of the growing enterprise lists hardware and cutlery as products for sale. An 1897 calendar has the address 15-19-21 Market Square and lists "Wholesale and Retail Dealers in Hardware, Stoves, Cutlery and Guns, Building Materials, Paints, Oils, Home Furnishings, Goods; Mill, Camp, and Mine Supplies; Railroad Contractors Equipment."

The firm became a corporation on March 21, 1898, headquartered in Trenton, New Jersey. James N. Kline was president, with 448 of 450 shares. By the end of 1914 the company had expanded to 13-15-17-19-21 East Third Street through to Willow Street, while a warehouse and barn on Bennett Street provided storage space. A 1916 copy of a bill of sale showed more expansion, adding "Tinners, Plumbers, Water, Steam, and Gas Fitters Goods." A 1921 calendar listed all the previous categories, plus "Sheet Metal, Tile Work, Sporting Goods, Automobile Accessories, and Bicycle Sundries."

After the August 1925 death of James N. Kline, his estate held the stock; J. Walton Bowman was named president. Before the 1929 stock

John R. Zurinsky acquired Kline & Company, 315 Hepburn Street, in 1979.

market crash, Kline & Company had 160 employees. However, on July 6, 1931, all retail departments began a "Sixty-Day Close Out Sale." The automotive and sporting goods jobbing departments continued to be profitable, and wholesale hardware sales remained stable. H. Merril Winner had by this time assumed the presidency of the organization.

In a series of ownership changes, Neyharts Hardware Company—owned by H. Merril Winner—became principal stockholder in 1932. Between 1935 and 1955 J.N. Kline and Harry M. Fessler held 99 percent of the stock. By 1958

William H. Evans, Lee R. Phillips, Harry H. King, and H.M. Fessler were the stockholders, with the latter serving as president. Three years later Fessler sold his interest to his partners, who subsequently sold to Zurinsky and Cashera.

In the 1930s the company had relocated to 335 West Third Street; in 1941 it moved to its present building, opened in 1929 as a car dealership. During World War II submarine nets were fabricated in the southern Quonset section. After the war and in the 1950s, the structure housed a Rambler dealership operated by building owner David Good.

Today Kline & Company utilizes 20,000 square feet, from which it sells thousands of parts and supplies annually to independent garages and service stations in the area. Auto parts, tools, garage equipment, and automotive products from 87 manufacturers are available wholesale and retail. The corporation also supplies Ford and GM dealerships within a 75-mile radius of Williamsport. Garage equipment repairs are included in the 95-percent wholesale, 5-percent retail business.

Since Zurinsky acquired the firm in 1979, its volume has doubled—and growth continues. In April 1984 Muncy Auto Parts was purchased; it is now operated under that name as a wholly owned subsidiary of Kline & Company.

Among Kline & Company's stock of auto supplies is this vast collection of pipes for all types of vehicles in the firm's 10,000-square-foot exhaust system warehouse.

ANCHOR/DARLING VALVE COMPANY

On August 29, 1859, the oil industry was born when Colonel Drake drilled the first successful well near Titusville, Pennsylvania. Though technological change was much slower then than we are accustomed to today, in just three decades the embryonic industry had grown to the point where new companies were being created primarily to serve its burgeoning needs. In 1888 one of them was the Darling Pump and Manufacturing Company, Inc., started in Williamsport because it was centrally located to the young oil fields.

Jonathan Louis Hough II, a clerk for the Pennsylvania Railroad, which had begun limited transportation of oil, and Ralph H. Thorne, a telegraph operator, started the company. Several members of the Darling family, who were Thorne's relatives, made a small investment in the enterprise based on their experience in oil.

The initial principal products were deep oil well pumps and supplies.

Within six years the first small plant was inadequate and a new site was purchased a short distance away along a Pennsylvania Railroad branch.

By the early 1900s the business had grown considerably and the two original partners split the responsibility; Hough was in charge of sales and accounting while Thorne directed manufacturing. C.W. Huling was secretary/accountant and A.G. Smith was sales manager. Harry Darling was plant superintendent.

The first fire hydrants were made in 1902 and were a gate type with a metal-to-metal shutoff. A hydrant with a frost jacket followed and then a compression type was designed by the company's Philadelphia sales agent.

As the valve and hydrant business increased, the firm

Anchor/Darling Valve Company in 1982.

gradually left the oil well supply business, except for the Darcova Valve and Pump Cups which were developed as an improvement over the leather cups in use early in the 20th century.

The original partners continued as active top management for nearly 30 years until J. Lewis Hough died in 1917. In 1918 the concern changed from a limited partnership to a corporation named Darling Valve and Manufacturing Company to more clearly identify the business. Robert Thorne became president, Marshall Hough, treasurer, and Huling, secretary.

In 1956 Darling entered the nuclear power field. Since then it has supplied a variety of valves ranging from the relatively straightforward needs of commercial demineralized cooling water services to the extremely sophisticated requirements of naval nuclear power components for primary loop service.

Growth and expansion required more capital, so on May 1, 1967, the estates of the founding families sold all their stock to the Philadelphia-based A.C. Forr Corporation. The firm had been founded in 1965 by Armin C. Frank, Jr., who became Darling president, and Robert A. Orr.

In 1969 the A.C. Forr Corporation acquired the Anchor Valve Company, located in San

Francisco, and in 1973 the valve companies combined the names to Anchor/Darling Valve Company with divisions in Hayward, California, and Williamsport, Pennsylvania.

Today Anchor/Darling Valve Company has grown to become one of the world's foremost suppliers of high-specification, custom-engineered valves for critical applications. It is headquartered in Radnor, Pennsylvania, and has its manufacturing facilities in Williamsport.

This carbon steel, air-motor-operated gate valve, as seen in Anchor/Darling's final assembly area, is one of many custom-engineered valves for use in such areas as radioactive, cryogenic, high-temperature, and high-pressure service throughout the world.

AVCO LYCOMING WILLIAMSPORT DIVISION

The financial crisis of 1907 spawned a Williamsport company that not only participated in the birth of the automobile age but also became a pioneer in the air age.

That year Demorest Manufacturing Company (a general engineering business founded in 1845, which had grown to manufacture bicycles, typewriters, sewing machines, duplicators, gas irons, and platen printing presses) went bankrupt. It was then reorganized as Lycoming Foundry and Machine Company, with A.H. Ahles as president. John A. McCormick, who became a vital ongoing figure in the enterprise's development, was secretary/treasurer.

On the advice of prominent industrialist Hugh Chalmers, McCormick spent the early months of 1909 negotiating contracts to make engines for firms that assembled automobiles. The first order came from Velie Motor Corporation of Illinois to manufacture four-cylinder units from Velie's design.

Within a year Lycoming Foundry and Machine Company was producing engines for Velie, Hatfield, Apple, and others. Garrett Cochran became president in 1915, and the versatile McCormick took on the added duties of general manager. At the same time, a large

expansion of the work force was initiated to produce the first Lycoming-designed motor for Dort automobiles.

The popularity of Lycoming engines continued to grow. In 1917 alone, 15,000 engines were built for Army trucks, ambulances, and other vehicles. They additionally powered the Martin-Perry delivery wagons, and Koehler one-ton and one-and-a-half-ton trucks.

Two years later 1,000 units were shipped to England—as well as U.S. sales to International Harvester, Federal, White, Republic, Stewart, Norwalk, Relay, Corbett, and Massey-Harris. Orders for 60,000 engines in 1919-1920 increased the work force to 2,000.

Small manufacturers of cars that joined the ranks of Lycoming-motor users included Dagmar and Roamer. Bradley-Ford used them in its hearses. Major customers in the southern United States were Piedmont Company in Virginia and Tulsa Company in Oklahoma for car engines; Southern Company in North Carolina for truck engines; and Texas Motors for both. Growth permitted boldness, and when Willys-Overland needed a large number of engine-block castings, Lycoming Foundry took the order and erected a large new facility to meet the added demand.

The reorganized and refinanced

organization became Lycoming Manufacturing Company in May 1920, with McCormick remaining as general manager. Frank A. Bender, who was to play an important role in Lycoming's expansion, was named chief engineer. Having joined the operation in 1911 as a blueprint boy, Bender subsequently designed a new four-cylinder engine. The unit, which went into production in 1922, was used in the Gardner, Bush, Auburn, and Elcar automobiles.

Yellow, Checker, and Henry cabs all used Lycoming power plants in 1924. The following year Bender was promoted to assistant general manager, and E.D. Herrick was promoted to chief engineer. An innovative Lycoming straight-eight-cylinder motor was first used in the 1925 Auburn; Elcar and Apperson used the same engine in 1926. A cooperative Bender/Herrick effort produced the firm's six-cylinder unit that became the standard engine in other models of the Auburn, Elcar, and Gardner. Other illustrious automobiles that were powered by Lycoming engines were Locomobile, Cord, Duesenberg, Kissell, Paige, Graham, and Mc-Farlan.

In the early 1920s the corporation also had begun serving the American commercial and residential market when it joined forces with the long-respected Williamsport Radiator Company, maker of the famous "Spencer Boilers." By the middle of the decade Lycoming Manufacturing Company employed

The Lycoming eight-cylinder engine assembly line. Engines were used in automobiles such as the Gardner, Elcar, and Auburn.

This 1936 Cord was powered by a Lycoming V-8 engine, which developed 115 horsepower at 3,500 r.p.m.

Stinson 0-49. Designated the L-1 by the U.S. Army, this aircraft was powered by the Lycoming R-680 radial engine.

Piper Mojave. Designed for high-altitude flight, this modern, pressurized general-aviation aircraft is powered by two Avco Lycoming T10-540-V2AD flat, opposed-cylinder engines.

2,500 persons with a $10,000 daily payroll to produce 57 different types of motors.

Errett L. Cord, president of Auburn Motors, in building a transportation empire acquired Lycoming Manufacturing Company in 1927. He assumed the chairmanship from J.B. Graham and named McCormick president. As that also was the year Charles A. Lindbergh made the first solo flight across the Atlantic, it was no coincidence that Cord decided that Auburn's new subsidiary should enter the aircraft-engine industry.

Designs were started in 1928 on new marine, aircraft, and industrial motors. Lycoming-powered boats had won many trophies and gold cups in important races in the 1920s, and continued to do so in the 1930s. As a marine-engine show-piece, Lycoming souped up an Auburn-6 to 180 horsepower, and created such a hit in 1936 that it was mass-produced. Customers for engines with 45 to 330 horsepower included Penn-Yan, Elco, Wheeler, and Horace Dodge.

The corporation also served the industrial and agricultural fields, developing improved liquid-cooled stationary engines whose farm applications included use in a John Deere combine. Throughout industry a four-cylinder, 30-horsepower Lycoming unit was used

primarily as a standby power plant for the generation of electricity.

Design work on the first Lycoming aircraft engine resulted in a conventional nine-cylinder radial engine with 680-cubic-inch displacement. The R-680 was an immediate success, and the first Lycoming-powered airplane flew at Williamsport in 1929. The engine soon powered the Beech-designed TravelAir and the Stinson Tri-motor used by Ludington Airline, National Airlines, and the Boston and Maine Airways—the earliest scheduled airlines in the United States. In addition to airline and personal aircraft of the period, the R-680 also powered several military trainers—including the well-known Stearman. During its period of manufacture, 25,000 of the engines were built.

In company boardrooms and private offices around the country, the many facets of the evolving air industry were prime topics of discussion; consequent decisions resulted in actions that would have immediate and long-range effects on Lycoming Manufacturing and Williamsport. The organization's future was effected in 1933, when Errett L. Cord gained control of Aviation Corporation and made it a subsidiary of Cord Corporation. Two years later he sold his controlling interest in Cord Corporation to Victor Emanuel, who immediately began to re-structure the Cord subsidiaries. By 1939 Aviation Corporation owned all former assets—including Aviation

Manufacturing Corporation and its subsidiary, Lycoming Manufacturing Company. In 1941 Aviation Manufacturing Corporation was dissolved, and Lycoming Manufacturing Company became a direct division of Aviation Corporation. The latter was renamed Avco Manufacturing Corporation in 1947, then Avco Corporation in 1959.

Meanwhile, in Williamsport, other important changes were taking place. Smith Engineering, a Lycoming Manufacturing Company subsidiary, in 1933 introduced the first mechanical, controllable propeller. (Over 84,000 eventually were produced.) The following year responsibility for automobile engines was largely removed from Williamsport to a Cord Corporation plant in Indiana. Also in 1934 W. Hubert Beal had become president of Lycoming Manufacturing Company—after having served as its sales manager since 1919, with the added duties of secretary since 1927. E.D. Herrick was promoted to general manager; three years later he was elected president.

In 1938, following up on its successful R-680 engine, the firm developed the flat, opposed-cylinder 0-145 aircraft engine. In the years that followed a complete series of four-, six-, and eight-cylinder engines, with up to 450 horsepower, was developed. They were used in aircraft produced by Piper, Beech, Ryan, and Taylorcraft, and became the standard for all leaders in the general-aviation aircraft industry. The company scored another coup in 1938 when Igor Sikorsky flew the first successful helicopter built in the United States. He used a four-cylinder, 75-horsepower Lycoming 0-145 engine.

The corporation's 12- and 24-cylinder, liquid-cooled engines were designed at 1,200 and 2,400 horsepower, respectively, prior to World War II. During that crisis the Williamsport facility became deeply involved in the research and development of larger units. Construction of a modern new laboratory began in 1943 to manufacture and test increasingly larger engines, including the XO-1230. By the end of the war Lycoming was experimenting with the world's largest piston engine with 36 cylinders at 5,000 horsepower—the famous XR-7755.

As the United States supported the Allies and then entered World War II, the firm played a vital role: Propellers for military aircraft were produced as well as thousands of engines in 30 versions. Its motors powered Vultee, Stinson, Curtiss-

Certified in 1983, the T10-540-V2AD is a modern opposed-cylinder Avco Lycoming piston engine which features low-drag cylinder heads, turbocharging, and intercooling for flight at altitudes above 20,000 feet.

Wright, Cessna, and Beechcraft training, liaison, and observation planes. The Stearman trainer, with a Lycoming engine, was used to train more pilots than any other aircraft during the war. The durable, reliable R-680 became known as "the old sewing machine that goes and goes and goes."

And "the best air-cooled engine on the market," according to Colonel Herrington, was the 0-435, 175-horsepower Lycoming Tank Unit used in the Marmon-Herrington tanks. Parts for the Packard-Merlin tank engines were also manufactured under subcontract.

In the ensuing years Avco Lycoming Williamsport has continued to develop and build engines for general aviation, including some of the best-known single- and twin-engine utility aircraft in the business. Subcontract work for other manufacturers has been also a continuous part of the company's activities and was particularly helpful in the late 1940s and through the 1950s when aircraft-engine demand was low. As an example, Hall Scott engines for buses were manufactured during most of 1946 in a program with ACF-Brill Motors.

The company's defense work, however, never completely stopped. Parts for the Wright Aeronautical and the Pratt & Whitney radial aircraft engines, then being used by the airlines and the military, were built under subcontract from 1947

until the late 1950s. By that time gas-turbine engines claimed the large aircraft engine market, and Dr. Anselm Franz began designing a Lycoming gas-turbine unit.

Several new endeavors began in Williamsport in 1948. The 0-290, four-cylinder opposed aircraft engine was adapted to use in ground power units, enabling it to start aircraft such as the mammoth B-36 bomber. Production continued into the 1950s, and over 15,000 units were manufactured. Connecting rods for the Ford Motor Company were also produced.

About this time as well, Lycoming's boiler-building unit—Spencer—reentered the residential market. In 1949 the two units were combined to form the Lycoming-Spencer Division of Avco Manufacturing Corporation.

When the Korean War erupted in 1950, the government stepped up its orders for small aircraft and helicopters. Within a few months the demand for Lycoming engines led to the founding of a new plant in Stratford, Connecticut, and the division's turbine operation was relocated there in 1952. That same year Floyd Bird moved to Williamsport as general manager, serving in that position until 1966.

As a part of the country's rearmament program in the 1950s,

Machining of crankcases for Avco Lycoming aircraft engines is accomplished by an automated, computerized flexible machining system installed during the late 1970s.

The Williamsport Lycoming Manufacturing Company plant in 1936.

This 1982 photo of the Avco Lycoming Williamsport Division facility shows many areas where the plant has been expanded to accommodate new machines and an increased production capability.

Lycoming Williamsport continued to build mobile auxiliary-power units and air-cooled Continental engines for medium tanks—which it had obtained the rights to produce at the beginning of the decade. The latter engine was manufactured under a government contract until 1955.

Under subcontract, in 1952 Lycoming initiated production of rotor components for the Piasecki H-21 helicopter. When the CH-46 Sea Knight helicopter was developed about 1960, the corporation obtained the subcontract to manufacture rotor components, which continue to be made in Williamsport in the 1980s.

Beginning in the late 1950s, geared supercharging was incorporated into Lycoming general-aviation engines to increase power output and provide for flight in the middle altitudes above 10,000 feet. Turbocharging, a more efficient method of compressing the thin air at high altitudes, was first used with Lycoming engines during the 1960s. The innovation utilized engine exhaust gases to turn the air compressor, and allow cruise flight at altitudes above 20,000 feet.

During the 1950s, 1960s, and 1970s Lycoming-powered aircraft continued in U.S. Army use. The Beech U-8 Seminole, a high-performance, all-weather courier that could easily be converted to an ambulance plane, and the Hughes Osage, a two-place helicopter used for pilot training,

are examples.

In addition to its military business, Lycoming Williamsport provided opposed-cylinder, air-cooled engines for both helicopters and an increasing number of fixed-wing, general-aviation airplanes. By 1963, when the Avco Lycoming Division was separated into Avco Lycoming Williamsport and Avco Lycoming Stratford divisions, the reciprocating engines made in Williamsport were being used by most major manufacturers of small aircraft. During the 1960s and 1970s, as general-aviation demands increased over previous decades, these reciprocating engines were utilized to power aircraft in countries around the world.

The Williamsport plant has undergone a continuous series of expansion and capability improvements. Under general managers John M. Ferris (1966-1974) and Peter J. Goodwin (1974-1983), major capital investments continued to enhance plant capability. A complete new connecting-rod line was installed and engine test cells were tied into a computer which could monitor and record all aspects of each engine test.

A flexible machining system (FMS) for the machining of crankcases was also procured. Installed in three phases, the computerized FMS will automatically control the material-handling and machining functions for every four- and six-cylinder crankcase used by Lycoming. The modernizing of equipment and tooling achieved more efficient production and the

capability of building 2,000 piston engines per month.

The rapid growth of general aviation and the demand for Lycoming power plants reached a peak in 1978, when 15,432 new and 1,063 remanufactured piston engines were shipped. In 1979 a further investment in plant capability upgraded and expanded the crankshaft line.

Late in 1980 the responsibility for the LT-101 gas-turbine engine was moved to Williamsport from Stratford, Connecticut. A $30.3-million plant expansion and upgrading of facilities was accomplished in 1981-1982. Production of the LT-101 began in June 1981.

Another milestone at Avco Lycoming Williamsport Division was reached in May 1982, when the 250,000th commercial piston-aircraft-engine was manufactured. That milestone is the latest of many that have been accomplished by thousands of dedicated employees who have put the proud name of Lycoming on hundreds of thousands of automotive, marine, stationary, and aviation engines throughout the world, and who will continue to build quality Lycoming products under the direction of Howard M. Knutson, who brought his experience with turbine engines and administration to the position of general manager in 1983.

143

PULLMAN POWER PRODUCTS CORPORATION

Pullman Power Products Corpora-tion, headquartered in Williams-port, serves the electric power-generating industry with 80 years of experience in the fabrication of pipe, the construction of mechanical and piping systems, and the design and construction of chimneys.

The company has developed welding and bending technology as well as quality-assurance methods for the piping-fabrication industry; erected nuclear and fossil generating units with a combined capacity of more than 24,000 megawatts; and designed and constructed the world's five tallest chimneys.

Pullman Power Products Corporation had its beginning in 1901, when Morris W. Kellogg founded a piping-fabrication business in Jersey City, New Jersey. A year later he added the con-struction of radial brick chimneys. Through the years his business expanded into other areas, such as the design of petroleum refineries and fertilizer plants. The M.W. Kellogg Company became a subsidiary of Pullman in 1944.

In 1977 the Power Piping and Chimney departments of the M.W.

An aerial view of the firm's world headquarters and pipe-fabrication facility in Williamsport.

Kellogg Company were established as a separate company of Pullman, Inc. Pullman Power Products became a corporation in 1980, and now—as a result of corporate mergers—is one of the Signal Companies. Williams-port is corporate headquarters for three lines of business involving 8,000 people: piping fabrication and mechanical construction, both in Williamsport; and chimney operations in Kansas City, Missouri.

The organization's association with Williamsport began on February 24, 1960, when the M.W. Kellogg Company purchased a site in the Industrial Park for a new piping-fabrication plant. Six months later, despite an unusually rainy summer, several firms in the city had met an "impossible" construction schedule, and piping fabrication began on September 6. The office building had been completed and put into use on August 1.

The $4-million facility was designed to be the most advanced plant ever built to manufacture high-temperature, high-pressure piping systems. As these systems are expected to operate on a 24-hour basis for 30 to 40 years, state-of-the-art technology and equipment were extremely important. Over 200 people were employed in the 240- by 110-foot headquarters building, and the 1,100-by 155-foot manufacturing and storage facility.

The first job in the plant had been started in New Jersey in 1958 and was transferred to Williamsport. The project involved fabricating all nuclear and non-nuclear piping,

A nuclear power generating plant in California. Pullman Power Products fabricated and erected the power piping.

A completed recirculation loop for a boiling-water nuclear reactor.

including the recirculating loop piping, for Con Edison's Indian Point No. One plant on the Hudson River in New York.

From 1960 to 1967 the plant manufactured main steam-propulsion piping for early nuclear Thresher class submarines. Concurrently, from the mid-1960s to the mid-1970s, electric-generating industry demands surged and fabrication of piping increased.

The Williamsport shop in 1969 became one of the first fabricators to qualify for and obtain the American Society of Mechanical Engineers code-symbol stamps for nuclear manufacture and installation. A fabricator must be certified by ASME in order to work on nuclear-generating plants in the United States. During the 1970s state-of-the-art equipment was installed, and quality-assurance programs were established at the Williamsport plant and at each nuclear-construction job site.

The Three Mile Island nuclear plant accident on March 28, 1979, had a major impact on Pullman Power Products: In April Westinghouse contracted the company to fabricate a system to interact with the existing core-decay heat-removal system to cool the reactor in the containment building. The task was to design details; requisition materials; purchase, expedite, and assemble system components (heat exchanger, valves,

The world's tallest chimney, at 1,250 feet, was built by Pullman Power Products for the International Nickel Company in Sudbury, Ontario, Canada.

and pumps); and fabricate piping, instrumentation, and support structures into complete assemblies that could be rapidly installed at the nuclear-power plant. The endeavor was completed in two weeks.

At that point Westinghouse ordered a second heat-removal system as a backup. It included a

motor-operated pump, surge tank, heat exchanger, and instrumentation rack, and also was completed in two weeks. Working around the clock, the company accomplished in one month a project that normally would have taken one year.

As a specialty mechanical contractor, PPP performs field erection of piping and mechanical equipment for fossil-fired and nuclear power-generating plants. In the past 16 years it has completed mechanical-construction contracts on 19 fossil units and 5 nuclear units. Eight additional nuclear units are under construction.

As the world's largest chimney builder, the firm has handled over 10,000 projects that include 4,000 new chimneys. It built the first chimney in North America using the slip-form method with concrete continuously poured 24 hours a day. The world's tallest chimney was constructed for International Nickel Company at Sudbury, Ontario, Canada, in 1970. In 60 working days 21,600 cubic feet of concrete were erected into a 1,250-foot column with a base diameter of 118 feet.

Pullman Power Products Corporation is committed to serving the electric power-generating industry through providing innovative, reliable, and quality design, fabrication, and construction services.

After being heated in a gas-fired furnace, heavy-walled pipe is bent on a hot table.

PMF INDUSTRIES, INC.

It all started in 1950, when Svensk Metallforadling (Swedish Metal Refining Co.) sent Birger H. Engzell as vice-president and general manager to Brooklyn, New York, to establish an American subsidiary, Steelex. The company manufactured specialty stainless steel products using the unique flow-turning method. At first Steelex produced cones for television tubes, but successful expansion into parts and components for jet engines, the food industry, and pulp and paper manufacturing created a need for more space in a better location.

In 1955 Engzell visited numerous sites in the eastern United States before narrowing the field to Pennsylvania, where "several cities competed considerably" for the company relocation. Williamsport interested Engzell "because of its cultural advantages, appealing living conditions, supply of skilled labor, availability of service industries, and because it is close to our raw materials."

The Industrial Development Bureau of the Chamber of Commerce, the Industrial Properties Corporation, and the Williamsport Foundation all worked to make the move possible. Four shovels of cornfield dirt were turned on Thanksgiving weekend 1955. The ceremony launched Williamsport's Industrial Park and the genesis of PMF Industries, Inc. Steelex opened for production the following spring.

In 1958 and 1960 the Swedish parent company placed Steelex on the market while it considered returning the subsidiary to Sweden. Engzell offered to purchase the firm. Because of the uncertainty and indecisiveness of the parent concern, Engzell resigned. Customers who wanted to retain their source of quality stainless and heat-resistant precision metal formings, and local interests who wanted to preserve

Birger H. Engzell founded PMF Industries, Inc., in 1961.

jobs, encouraged Engzell to stay in this area and begin his own enterprise. It all became a reality on March 1, 1961.

Five thousand square feet of space was leased from Williamsport Die and Machine Company at 910 Park Street. Mrs. Engzell, who assisted her husband with various tasks in getting the business started, suggested the name "Precision Metal Forming" since it so aptly described the company process.

The firm is located at 2601 Reach Road, Williamsport.

Business grew, and in the summer of 1964, with the help of the Pennsylvania Industrial Development Authority, construction began on an 18,000-square-foot building on a four-acre plot on Reach Road. The work force had grown to 35, and a dozen more employees were hired when the building was occupied in the spring of 1965.

Between 1968 and 1975 John T. Detwiler was a partner in the firm and served as vice-president. In early 1969 PMF purchased the equipment and remaining inventory of Steelex, which had by that time changed owners several times and was closing its operation. In order to accommodate the extra equipment, a 15,000-square-foot addition was built. In early 1973 a second addition of 12,880 square feet was completed to provide for two new large presses.

Today the family business continues under son-in-law Donald E. Alsted. Alsted returned to Williamsport in 1974 to learn the business. He assumed the duties of president and general manager upon the death of Birger Engzell in 1982.

Forty-two people are employed today at PMF, many of whom began their careers with Engzell at Steelex. PMF manufactures stainless steel hollow-cone, cylinder, and ogive shapes used in aircraft, food, filtration, and pulp and paper industries.

JERSEY SHORE STEEL COMPANY

In 1894 a boy of nine immigrated with his family to Syracuse, New York, from Germany. While still in his early teens, John A. Schultz, Sr., began working in a steel mill. When Sweet's Steel decided to relocate in 1903, John did not follow the popular advice of the day to, "Go west, young man," but instead went south with them to Williamsport. Nevertheless, in true Horatio Alger fashion, he rose from laborer, to superintendent, to president by 1933. When he resigned in 1938, he had 38 years' experience to use founding a new company.

Growing up with the steel industry, John recognized a need for a firm that would reroll used railroad rails into a high-grade steel. Jersey Shore Steel Company was created with John as its first president. Joining the venture were Sam C. Rebman as vice-president and general manager, and John E. Spotts as secretary/treasurer.

Jersey Shore Steel started production on July 5, 1938, in a building formerly occupied by the New York Central Erecting Shop. The sum of $56,500 had been raised by the Jersey Shore Industrial Committee to help finance the new industry, and confidence must have been high because a 40-year lease had been signed for the 130- by 750-foot building.

All equipment had been designed by Schultz, and much of it had been manufactured at the plant. With a furnace that heated to 2,600 degrees, and straightening and shearing machines, 60 men went to work making light-steel angles for the bedding industry; in addition, rails for the mining industry were fabricated from several tons of used rails.

After only 14 months of operation, more floor space and equipment were needed for finishing and storing the new light-steel rails

that had first been rolled on December 9, 1939, and now accounted for 50 percent of the company's production.

None of the production at that time involved war work. Principal products were light-steel angles and flats used by manufacturers of metal beds, bed springs, glider swings, and similar articles: steel mine ties and splice bars; porch furniture; and steel furniture.

On May 9, 1940, Sam C. Rebman, an original founder of the company, died at the age of 67. On February 17, 1941, John A. Schultz, Jr., roll designer and assistant to the general manager, was elected to succeed Rebman.

World War II had a major impact on the corporation. Gross income for 1940 was $277,000, which increased to $494,000 in 1941.

On August 13, 1943, John A. Schultz, Sr., died after a long illness. His sons, John Jr. and Charles M., and John E. Spotts, an original partner, took over operation of the plant. Two years later Spotts' share of the company was purchased by Jacob E. Eckel of Syracuse; upon his retirement in 1950, John and Charles assumed ownership.

Disaster struck the mill on Sunday, December 29, 1963, when a major fire erupted. By the end of the day the factory, which employed

about 225 people, was destroyed. In a remarkable industrial comeback, the steel mill was back in operation in a little over four months, resuming production on May 4, 1964.

In 1965 the facility was expanded to 1,000 by 130 feet. A new 250- by 200-foot warehouse was also erected.

Production has steadily increased since 1979 with the installation of new automatic cooling beds, which streamlined and boosted production capacity using sophisticated new equipment.

Charles M. Schultz died at the age of 63 on April 11, 1980. Current management includes John A. Schultz, Jr., president; John C. Schultz, executive vice-president; Peter D. Schultz, secretary; and Jay M. Dawson, treasurer.

Today, with 350 employees and sales offices in New York and San Francisco, Jersey Shore Steel Company supplies high-tensile-strength rail steel in specified lengths for such diverse uses as bedstead angles, crib frames, casket frames, electric fences, road barricades, folding tables, angle posts, shelving, stakes, scaffolds, and farm implements.

The headquarters of Jersey Shore Steel Company in South Avis.

THE WILLIAMSPORT HOSPITAL

The Williamsport Hospital represents over a century of caring.

Patient care in the early to mid-1800s in the community of Williamsport took place primarily in the home. Accidents, particularly relating to railroading, were treated in boardinghouse rooms, as the injured men were generally far removed from their homes. There was a need in the community for a hospital, in which persons could be fed and cared for in a clean environment.

Several accidents in 1872 led to a discussion in January 1873, by members of the Lycoming County Medical Society, concerning the necessity of a medical facility. The idea quickly created considerable interest throughout the city and comment in the local newspaper. As a result, on September 1, 1883, The Williamsport Hospital was incorporated.

Following incorporation, the newly elected board of managers found the initial enthusiasm for a hospital cooled when people were asked for money to purchase a building and beds. Four and one-half years passed before the facility could become a reality, at which time lumberman and former mayor James H. Perkins contributed half of the initial expense. A three-story brick building on Elmira Street, between Fourth and Edwin, was purchased.

The new hospital was in reality nothing more than a clean boardinghouse, intended for charity patients who had no suitable residence in Williamsport. Other patients still were treated in their homes. Physicians also felt there was a greater likelihood of being paid by treating patients in their homes. Consequently, during the first year of the hospital's existence, the 20 or so physicians in the community placed only nine patients in the hospital. In the second year there were only four.

At that point it was recognized that, in order to be successful, the institution needed someone with medical training to operate it. Dr. Jean Saylor (who had been active with the hospital) induced a college classmate, Dr. Rita B. Church, to come to Williamsport and run the hospital. Previously, a husband and

Dr. Rita B. Church, the first administrator of The Williamsport Hospital, was instrumental in organizing the School of Nursing in 1883.

wife had fed and bathed patients in return for free living quarters.

With the constant availability of a physician, hospital usage increased dramatically. A shortage of suitable women as nurses prompted Drs. Saylor and Church to organize a training course for the teaching of student nurses. At that time, there was only one other such school in Pennsylvania; it was part of the medical college in Philadelphia that the two doctors had attended. The first student, Alta J. King, graduated in 1884. As only one of two students could be used in the hospital, the school was limited to that number of students.

By 1884 a larger building was needed, and within two years a house on Pine Street near Fifth was purchased and occupied. While it was somewhat larger than the original facility, a nearby railroad and other distractions led officials to consider looking for a more appropriate location in 1888. The

Today The Williamsport Hospital provides the surrounding area with comprehensive care and quality educational opportunities in a variety of specialties.

June 1889 flood—which placed three feet of muddy water throughout the building—finally convinced the board of managers that a move was necessary.

A large tract of land, called the Old Oaks Park, in the vicinity of Louisa and Campbell streets and Rural Avenue was being opened for development. An entire city block was purchased, and a new facility was opened in 1891. The third hospital was actually three separate buildings connected by passageways. There was a central facility where surgery and treatments were performed, and in which the staff lived. On one side of the main building was a women's ward, and on the other a men's ward. There were also a few rooms for patients able to pay for their care.

The early years for the young hospital were formidable. More than half of its patients could not afford to pay, and acquiring money to keep it operating was difficult. A women's auxiliary played a major role in raising funds, and the state began to contribute toward the care of the indigent.

Increasing the use of the hospital necessitated finding adequate living space for the nurses. A patron, Mrs. Ida Hayes McCormick, solved the problem in 1900 by having a home for nurses constructed, which she gave to the hospital. As more beds were needed a second floor was erected on the two buildings housing patients, and a fourth floor was placed on the main structure. By 1907 the auxiliary had raised sufficient funds to pay for construction of a children's-ward building; in 1911 the will of Amanda Howard allowed for further construction of a facility to accommodate patients who could afford a private room.

The first of what comprises the hospital complex today was built in 1926. The seven-story structure represented the best expertise available for modern hospitals; and nearly 60 years later the North Building is still serving its original purpose of providing bed care, whereas the old hospital was obsolete in 1926 after only 35 years.

The post-World War II era has seen many changes and advances in the institution. First came additional bed space so that the old building could be eliminated, except for use as the School of Nursing. Then in 1961 the new nurses' residence and education hall was constructed, and a rehabilitation and physical-medicine center established. The success of the center led to the current five-story Rehabilitation Center, which was opened in 1970.

During the 1960s the hospital created a mental-health unit, and initiated the first intensive-care unit in Central Pennsylvania. Plans were also made at this time for a physicians' medical building.

In medicine, advances were being made in the treatment of heart patients; and the rapid strides in

The hospital moved to the Old Oaks Park section of Williamsport and opened in 1891. This third location is the site of today's medical complex.

medical science were prompting more and more physicians to specialize, which created a shortage of family practitioners. The problem became acute by the end of the decade, resulting in the development of the Family Practice Residency Program. The Williamsport Hospital was the first in the northern half of the state to organize such a program. By training young physicians in the practice of family medicine, the shortage in Lycoming County and other areas was alleviated.

The increasing use of radiology and nuclear medicine for diagnosis and treatment of outpatients, and the expanding role of laboratory services to meet the needs of patients, determined the need for a centralized medical support services facility. In 1974 the Core Services Building was completed and opened.

Today The Williamsport Hospital looks to the challenges of the future with the same enthusiasm that has characterized its past. Included in the plans for the 1980s is a major facilities-improvement program designed to meet the demands of today, tomorrow, and beyond.

The hospital staff, photographed at the former Hotel St. Charles, the second home of The Williamsport Hospital. Dr. Rita Church is standing in the next to top row, fourth from left.

DIVINE PROVIDENCE HOSPITAL

When Sister Mary Theresilla Hills, a native of Williamsport, reported the need for another hospital in her hometown to the Sisters of Christian Charity, plans were made in early 1945 to "provide a place where the sick and injured could be treated in accordance with the mercy and compassion of Christ, coupled with the best principles of medical practice."

Two campaigns were conducted to build Divine Providence Hospital, one in 1945-1946 and the other in 1948-1949. Excellent community and business support and involvement oversubscribed both goals. Ground was broken at 1100 Grampian Boulevard on June 27, 1948, and the hospital was dedicated on May 20, 1951. The 185-bed institution opened its doors on June 1, 1951, under the direction of Sister Emilene Wehner, S.C.C., administrator. On opening day, the entire staff totaled only 75 (although that number would eventually increase to almost 1,000 by 1984).

On January 7, 1954, the Divine Providence Hospital Auxiliary was founded. Since 1954 thousands of auxilians have volunteered numerous services to the hospital and its patients. Auxilians and other volunteers have played a vital role in the financial health of the institution and have provided extra service, care, and comfort to innumerable patients and their families.

Always striving to augment services to patients, the hospital expended over $200,000 in improvements in its first six years of operation. Additional land was purchased for future needs, and services and employees increased.

Construction of the first expansion of facilities began in 1958. The construction, costing over one million dollars, included a medical library, chapel, chaplain's quarters, convent, auditorium, and administrative offices. The laboratory, radiology, and dietary departments were expanded, and bed capacity was increased to 200.

A psychiatric inpatient unit was opened on the south wing of the third floor in the early 1960s. It was the first step toward the future comprehensive mental health program that Divine Providence Hospital would establish.

In May 1963 the intensive care unit was opened. The mid-1960s also saw the updating and renovating of the obstetric unit, laboratory, laundry, and pharmacy.

To keep up with patient needs and medical advances, another major renovation and expansion plan was developed in 1968. Friends raised $1,355,000, and ground was broken in November 1972. The construction, when completed three years later, doubled the size of the hospital and provided space for several community services.

Major construction included the Health Services Building, which was dedicated in July 1974 and housed doctors' offices, the outpatient pharmacy, and community health services. The latter was designed to meet the needs of families without a family physician. The new Health Services Building also housed the Community Mental Health Center, which was designated by the federal government to offer comprehensive services in Lycoming and Clinton counties.

Several regional services were begun in 1974, including the Francis V. Costello Dialysis Center with a hemodialysis treatment and training

Divine Providence Hospital strives to offer quality medical care to address the spiritual, emotional, and physical needs of its patients.

Divine Providence Hospital continues to live up to the doctrine on which it was founded: "provide a place where the sick and injured could be treated in accordance with the mercy and compassion of Christ, coupled with the best principles of medical practice."

unit on the third floor. The center serves patients from seven counties. The Cancer Treatment Center also opened in 1974 as a regional facility offering comprehensive radiation services and medical oncology.

In 1975 an addition to the main building was completed. Total bed capacity was increased to 225— including 21 additional beds for the inpatient mental health unit, and 4 for the intensive care unit. The new construction made possible the relocation of some departments and expansion and renovation of others, one of which was the rehabilitation services department. Instead of sharing space with other departments, the service obtained separate areas.

In 1975 an addition to the main building was completed. Among the renovations were refurbished nursery and obstetrical departments.

New facilities for the cardiology department included a specialized laboratory for diagnostic studies, evaluation of coronary artery disease, and temporary pacemaker insertion. Among other renovations were new facilities for the laboratory, emergency, radiology, central supply, and laundry departments; remodeled operating rooms and patient areas; and refurbished nursery and obstetrical departments. A Digestive Disease Center, another of the hospital's regional services, opened in 1976.

Divine Providence added 10 medical/surgical beds in 1981, establishing its current (1984) complement of 235 beds. Also in 1981, the Thomas J. Rider Building was completed as a third medical office building on the hospital's campus.

To provide mobile computerized tomographic scanning (CT scanning) services, the nonprofit North Central Mobile Scanning Services, Inc., was formed in 1981 by Divine Providence and two other area hospitals. North Central bought a CT scanner, housed in a 45-foot van, that cost $1.1 million. However, the group purchase helped to hold down expenses for each hospital, and offered rural communities a cost-effective, high-technology service. The success of the unit brought two more mobile scanners

and seven additional hospitals into the corporation in 1982.

Divine Providence Hospital's concern for the total health needs of the area has generated numerous community programs. These include free blood pressure screening clinics, industrial health programs, and seminars on selected health subjects.

In 1982 the institution implemented several programs and expanded others. One new program was LIFELINE, a system that allows the elderly, the handicapped, and the chronically ill to live independently in their own homes while having immediate access to the emergency department through an interconnected phone system. Also in 1982, the regional services of the Community Mental Health Center were expanded.

After several years of detailed planning and hard work on the part of many people within and outside Divine Providence, the hospital received governmental approval in July 1983 to proceed with a modernization and renovation program. The planned changes stem from significant increases in the number of services offered during the preceding decade. Expanded services, primarily outpatient in nature, included cancer treatment, CT scanning, ultrasound, cardiac rehabilitation, nuclear medicine, social service, and health screening and promotion. The modernization is designed to maximize efficiency of existing services whose needs have changed as outpatient volumes have dramatically increased.

"The project is part of our continuing effort to offer first-rate, comprehensive services to residents of north-central Pennsylvania," says Sister Emilene. "We will always strive to offer quality medical care that addresses the spiritual, emotional, and physical needs of all patients."

NORTHERN CENTRAL BANK

When Williamsport became a borough in 1806, there were no financial institutions to serve its banking needs. It was necessary to travel by horseback, stagecoach, or boat to Philadelphia or Baltimore to complete financial transactions. Often a messenger to one of these cities would buy supplies or pay bills for many Williamsport accounts.

By the 1830s the growing needs of the Williamsport community, as well as uncertain political and financial conditions at the national level, paved the way for a banking house in the area. In 1832 President Andrew Jackson eliminated the national banking system by vetoing the renewal of a charter for the Second United States Bank. He then gradually transferred government deposits to selected state-chartered institutions. This policy produced speculative situations in business and financial circles, resulting in the formation of many state-chartered banks.

The West Branch Bank was chartered in 1835 as the first banking house in Williamsport. The forerunner of Northern Central Bank, it occupied the old Eagle Hotel property in the city. John H. Cowden, a local businessman, was its first president. Shortly thereafter it moved to what is now part of L.L. Stearns and Sons.

As Williamsport continued to expand, the West Branch Bank also experienced rapid growth. Much of this growth could be attributed to the completion of the West Branch Canal, the advent of railroads, and the flourishing lumber industry.

With the enactment of the National Bank Act, the institution received a national charter in 1865 and became the West Branch National Bank. It was located at 309 Pine Street until 1917, at which time a handsome, white marble building

on the northwest corner of Fourth and Pine streets was completed. Today it serves as Northern Central Bank's main office and NCB Financial Corporation's corporate headquarters.

While the West Branch National Bank was growing, other financial institutions were developing that would play an important role in Northern Central Bank's history. In April 1871 the Lycoming County Savings Bank, a private financial institution, was organized with J.P. Finley as president; four years later it was converted into a national bank with the title Lycoming National Bank.

Another private bank—Cochran, Payne and McCormick—was organized in April 1887 with J. Henry Cochran (lumberman, industrialist, and state senator) as president. E.R. Payne was the only Williamsporter ever to own a seat on the New York Stock Exchange. Henry Clay McCormick, a lawyer, once was Pennsylvania's attorney general. In 1897 the firm's name was changed to Cochran, McCormick and Cochran, and in 1909 the bank

was transferred into the newly formed Northern Central Trust Company.

A most notable date in Northern Central Bank's history would have to be December 31, 1926, when the Lycoming Trust Company was formed. It began operations the next day as an amalgamation of the West Branch National Bank, then nearly a century old; the Lycoming National Bank; and the Northern Central Trust Company. James B. Graham was president of the combined banks. One other principal, Charles A. Schreyer, assistant secretary and trust officer, would later become president and chairman of Northern Central Bank and Trust Company.

The Susquehanna Trust and Safe Deposit Company was merged into the Lycoming Trust Company in 1930. Within a few years the branch offices previously maintained by West Branch National Bank,

---

West Branch National Bank, a forerunner of Northern Central Bank, under construction in 1916 at the corner of Fourth and Pine streets in Williamsport.

The same facility serves as the headquarters of NCB Financial Corporation as well as Northern Central Bank and its Center City consumer banking facility.

Susquehanna Trust and Safe Deposit Company, and Northern Central Trust Company (which had merged with Lycoming Trust Company in 1927) were all closed because of the financial strain on the newly formed bank.

The Bank Holiday in March 1933 gave financial institutions throughout the country many problems. In October the West Branch Trust Company was chartered to receive the liquid assets of Lycoming Trust Company, which had been placed on a restrictive operating basis by the Pennsylvania Department of Banking. In January 1934 the West Branch Bank & Trust Company was organized with assets of $4.5 million to succeed the West Branch Trust Company.

The next major event in Northern Central's history took place on November 4, 1963, when the West Branch Bank & Trust Company and the Bank of Newberry merged to form Northern Central Bank and Trust Company.

Charles A. Schreyer was chairman of the board and president, with Woodrow A. Knight serving as board vice-chairman and senior vice-president. Knight assumed the position of president in 1967, with Schreyer maintaining the chairmanship until 1972.

With expansion taking place in Loyalsock Township, the institution established a branch at the corner of River Avenue and Washington Boulevard. Opened in June 1966, this third bank office proved to be a successful venture.

Northern Central Bank and Trust Company shortened its name to Northern Central Bank in 1975. John B. McMurtrie became president that year, and in 1978 succeeded Knight as board chairman.

During the 1970s Northern Central embarked on an ambitious expansion program through seven mergers and the opening of two new offices. In order of merger, they included Milton Bank and Safe Deposit Company, Athens National Bank, First Citizens National Bank of Montgomery, Susquehanna Valley Bank in Sunbury, First National Bank of Dushore, Guaranty Trust and Safe Deposit Company in Shamokin, and the First National Bank of Millville. The new offices included the Southgate Plaza office in Milton, and the Lycoming Mall office in Muncy Township. In the early 1980s this merger trend continued, involving Lewisburg National Bank, The Farmers National Bank of Rome, and The State Bank of Avis.

As the financial industry entered a period of revolutionary change in the early 1980s, marked by less restrictive regulatory policy, directors and officers of Northern Central Bank recommended that its shareholders approve the establishment of a holding company

to take maximum advantage of broader opportunities for increased growth and profitability. In mid-1983 NCB Financial Corporation became a reality, with Northern Central Bank becoming a wholly owned subsidiary. This new entity could then consider an increasing number of nontraditional banking services under a more flexible capital structure and use more innovative and varied financial arrangements in mergers and acquisitions.

Shortly after its origination, NCB Financial Corporation became the parent organization of Tri-County National Bank of Middleburg. The holding company then consisted of two banks with 34 offices in nine counties, with total assets approximating $700 million.

Concurrent with the holding company formation, the bank significantly expanded its range of consumer services. The William Teller ATM network, which allows customers to do their banking 24 hours a day, became nationwide in scope by affiliating with the CashStream and CIRRUS ATM networks. The Discount Brokerage service offers investors the opportunity to buy and sell securities at a substantial cost reduction. The automobile-leasing program provides an alternative approach to traditional car purchasing. And a credit insurance subsidiary insures installment loan balances held by bank customers.

Further demonstrating its flexibility in responding to changes in the financial industry, in 1984 NCB Financial Corporation joined Mid-State Bancorp of Altoona to form Keystone Financial, Inc. This move strategically positions the new holding company and its bank subsidiaries to take full advantage of emerging trends in the financial industry, while meeting the ever-changing needs of its customers.

KEYSTONE FILLER & MFG. CO.

Father and son Elisha and Richard Gray formed Keystone Paint Company in 1877, after migrating to Muncy from Sharon, Ohio, to grind black slate located along the river and make it into paint at a mill up the Muncy Canal.

In 1882 Levi Hill and John F. Leinbach bought into the enterprise, which was incorporated the following year. Elisha was the first president, Richard served as treasurer, and Levi was made secretary. Richard became president a short time later. In 1888 Hill and Leinbach left Keystone and purchased interests in one of several rival companies, none of which survived the turn of the century.

That same year Keystone constructed a 40- by 50-foot building with a 20- by 30-foot engine room. Six hundred tons of black filler and 10,000 gallons of black lead paint were produced annually. Within a

The current facilities of Keystone Filler & Mfg. Co. after the 1982 expansion program, which added new factories and modern drying, screening, and grinding equipment.

The original building of Richard Gray's Keystone Paint Company was located at the junction of the Muncy and Pennsylvania canals. In 1888 the plant was moved to a new building constructed along the Reading Railroad adjacent to the depot to make it more convenient for shipping.

few years the plant was 200 feet long, but two-thirds of it blew down in a strong wind in 1896.

Following Richard Gray's death in 1900, the plant was acquired by A. DeLong and later by John L. Barbour. In 1934 it was sold to Cordeen C. Pfleegor, who incorporated it under Pennsylvania law as Keystone Filler & Mfg. Co. Although paint manufacturing had been discontinued, shale was being ground (until 1960), and paint fillers were still made. An anthracite-burning coal stoker was manufactured for a short period in Muncy.

In the late 1930s and early 1940s the owner's sons joined him in the business.

About 1938 Pfleegor developed a semianthracite coal filler, a lightweight product used in hard-rubber battery cases. During that time period as well, a grinding complex was put into a plant near Watsontown to produce finely ground filler for the record industry —which used red shale from that area. In the early 1950s the entire factory was purchased and made part of Keystone.

A fine-grinding plant was installed in 1951 in Muncy to produce materials on a custom basis. The machinery uses high-temperature, high-pressure steam, or compressed air to produce superfine materials.

Cordeen C. Pfleegor, Sr., died in 1957. His sons, Cordeen C. Jr. and Charles D., assumed management of the company. Both are still active in its operation.

Property and equipment expansion continued during the 1960s, due to increasing battery box-filler demands in the United States and Mexico. Although plastic battery cases introduced in the 1970s caused a decline in use of ground anthracite coal, it continues as a principal company product.

In the early 1970s Keystone began supplying metallurgical carbon products to the steel industry. This manufacture ranges from high-purity, selectively mixed anthracite coals to high-carbon metallurgical cokes, all available in different configurations.

A major expansion program was undertaken in 1982. New factories were erected, the Modecraft building was purchased, and modern drying, screening, and grinding equipment was acquired to be used by 75 employees.

SUSQUEHANNA SUPPLY COMPANY

Susquehanna Supply Company had its origins in 1903 as Susquehanna Stone Company, located in Dalmatia below Sunbury along the Susquehanna River. The enterprise was founded in 1906 by Joseph Cochran for the primary purpose of quarrying ballast stone for the railroads.

In an effort to increase its market volume, the firm in 1913 leased the former Lycoming Edison Electric Company property on Erie Avenue and Campbell Street in Williamsport. On that site it established a retail business in crushed stone and building supplies. Two years later the operation was taken over by the Susquehanna Supply Company, which was a partnership consisting of the stockholders of the Susquehanna Stone Company.

Susquehanna Supply Company, incorporated in Williamsport in 1920, expanded heavily into all phases of building supplies. Cochran died in 1926, and was succeeded as president by F. Ralph Lehman. The firm continued to flourish, and was prosperous at the onset of the Depression.

After the Depression the entire economic structure had changed, and the concern began looking for new areas of promise. This diversification led to the eventual phasing out of most building-supply lines, and to the concentration on ready-mix concrete. Only those building supplies that were related to the concrete business were retained.

Lehman died in 1969, and was succeeded in 1970 by Timothy J. Crotty. Under his leadership the company began an expansion into highway and bridge construction. The Agnes Flood of 1972 propelled the corporation heavily into that type of construction, due to a tremendous demand for postflood repairs to numerous roads, bridges,

and structures throughout the region. This concentration on heavy-construction projects continues today.

In 1976 Susquehanna Supply Company was the prime contractor for the Center City Mall. From 1977 to 1982 it was a prime contractor, subcontractor, and principal supplier of both structural and paving concrete as the final links of I-180 —the Susquehanna Beltway around Williamsport—were completed. The organization in 1983 executed the structural portion of the Hepburn Street Dam replacement. In 1984 it is undertaking bridge construction projects for the Commonwealth of Virginia.

Susquehanna Supply Company has also expanded into diverse and unique projects. Examples include the completion of a small boat harbor at the entrance of Cattaraguas Creek into Lake Erie near Dunkirk, New York, in 1982, as well as ongoing participation in the Environmental Protection

The Susquehanna Supply Company office and plant is located in Williamsport at the foot of Rose Street on the reclaimed former landfill site.

Agency's Superfund projects for hazardous-waste cleanup near Old Forge, Pennsylvania.

The ready-mix concrete operation, however, remains the backbone of the company. In 1983 the facility produced some 12,000 cubic yards of fly-ash concrete for the Pennsylvania Department of Environmental Resources. The utilization of this material represented the largest job to date in Lycoming County using fly ash—a by-product of energy production created at the nearby Pennsylvania Power & Light Company facility in Washingtonville. The concrete plant, which has full automation and recordation capabilities, is located on 10 acres of land at the foot of Rose Street. The relocation from Erie Avenue was made in 1977 as part of the Lycoming County Redevelopment Plan. This move not only released land in the West Edwin Street project, but also reclaimed part of the former city landfill as an industrial site.

Susquehanna Supply Company and its employees are proud to be part of the Chamber of Commerce's first 100 years, and look forward to continually greater accomplishments.

CONFAIR BOTTLING CO., INC./CENPRO, INC.

In December 1919 Charles Confair resigned his job as a foundry foreman. He also sold his house and grocery store, which his wife, Rena, tended during the day.

The couple then purchased the North Berwick Bottling Works, which was a building not much larger than a modern one-car garage. It contained a foot-power filler, a large wooden tub for washing bottles; some five-gallon wooden kegs used to mix syrup; and 100 cases of bottles. Also included was a house with no electricity or weatherboards—which was to be their home.

Charles did everything from production to delivery. Rena mixed syrups, kept the records, and washed bottles for her husband to fill. Deliveries were made in a half-ton Model T truck, or a horse-drawn bobsled during periods of deep snow.

Zehnder H. "Dick" Confair, age 13, helped in the plant and with deliveries when he was not in school. After graduating from the Wharton School of Business, he became his father's partner.

In 1929 Zehnder married Arlyne Hoyt, and they moved to Williamsport with their son, Richard, in 1933. The young entrepreneur sold his interest back to his father, then purchased the NuGrape Bottling Company of Race Street. Opening for business the day before the banks closed, the firm recorded first-day sales of five cases. Arlyne mixed syrup, did the office work, and sometimes drove a truck.

Both the Berwick and Williamsport plants sold flavored drinks under the Confair name, as well as such brands as Howdy and Moxie. In the late '30s franchises for Pepsi-Cola and Seven-Up were

Zehnder H. "Dick" Confair, founder of Confair Bottling Co.

obtained. Confair's Beverage Company (Berwick) was among the first 10 Seven-Up bottlers in the United States.

Zehnder built a new plant on Race Street in 1939 that was renamed Confair Bottling Co. He and his father also purchased the Pepsi-Cola plant in Elmira, New York, where a new plant was erected. The Pepsi franchise in Elmira was sold in 1946, after which Zehnder immediately formed the Seven-Up Bottling Company in that city.

Distribution warehouses for the Williamsport operation were established in Milesburg and Wellsboro in the late '40s. The two are still maintained today.

Richard Confair, son of the founder, is president of the firm today.

Zehnder's interest in public service through political activity led to his election to the state senate in 1957. He served until 1972, when his doctor advised him to remove himself from public office. His contributions to progress include the work that made him known as "Father of the Keystone Shortway" —Interstate 80, completed in 1970. Zehnder H. Confair died on January 25, 1982, after an extended illness.

In 1958, after graduation from Dartmouth and discharge from the Army, Richard—representing the third generation—joined the family business. He managed the Elmira Seven-Up plant for 11 years, then returned to Williamsport as president of Confair Bottling Co.

The Berwick and Williamsport companies merged with 15 other Pepsi-Cola bottlers from Pennsylvania, Maryland, and West Virginia to form Laurel Packaging, Inc., in Johnstown, Pennsylvania. This cooperative was established in 1968 to produce canned soft drinks, due to the inroads of cans as a part of the total product mix.

The Berwick production facility

Opened in 1976, Confair Bottling/Cenpro's modern plant at 1450 Dewey Avenue.

was closed in 1971. At that time Confair Beverage of Berwick and Confair Bottling Co. of Williamsport formed Cenpro, Inc. (a combination of the words "central production"), to do their bottling production in the Williamsport facility.

Cenpro subsequently produced for Seven-Up of Elmira, and later expanded production to include distribution to Pepsi and Seven-Up bottlers in neighboring mid-Atlantic states.

The Williamsport Race Street operation, however, could no longer accommodate the increasing case

production and growing number of employees. Consequently, in 1976 a new building was constructed at 1450 Dewey Avenue to be used for production, vending, office, and fleet maintenance. It was dedicated in 1977, and six years later production growth necessitated a 200,000-square-foot addition to this same facility. In order to allow expansion of the vending, marketing, and office areas, fleet maintenance was relocated to 1320 Dewey Avenue.

Cenpro, Inc., organized to produce for the stockholder companies, evolved into a separate entity with sales to outside customers nearing one million cases. In 1982 the firm joined a group of Pepsi-Cola bottlers to form a purchasing cooperative called Penn-Chesapeake Associates.

At the same time Confair Bottling Co., whose case sales were now in excess of one million per year, and a group of eight other Pepsi-Cola bottlers merged as Santa Fe Associates to acquire other Pepsi plants that were available. During the first two years of the group's existence, Pepsi plants were purchased in Johnstown, Pennsylvania; Petersburg, Virginia; Cumberland, Maryland; and Danville, Virginia.

While their business is somewhat seasonal, Confair Bottling Co., Inc., and Cenpro, Inc., have an average of 100 full- and part-time employees.

The Confair Bottling Co.'s Race Street plant, built in 1939.

HARTMAN AGENCY, INC.

The Hartman Agency, Inc., was founded by W. Howard Hartman in 1932, with the first office located at 152 West Fourth Street. Hartman, who started his enterprise with one secretary, represented Northern Fire Insurance Company and the American Casualty Insurance Company. As with so many of his generation, he closed his business and left for World War II in 1942. Upon his return in 1946 he reopened his insurance business, and expanded his horizons by including real estate sales.

In the early 1950s Hartman rented a portion of the second floor of 420 William Street from Walter Eck, and the agency prospered through the following decade. During that time the founder served terms as president of both the Lycoming County Real Estate Association and the Lycoming County Independent Insurance Agents' Association.

William R. Simons, Sr.—now president—joined the Hartman Agency in 1963, after working as an independent agent since 1955. (He began his insurance career in 1948 as an underwriter and auditor for Pennsylvania National Insurance Company and United States Fidelity and Guaranty Insurance Company.) In 1970 the firm was incorporated and purchased by Simons and his wife, Joyce. They had three employees.

In 1972 the William Street building was purchased by Mr. and Mrs. Simons from Walter Eck. The Chamber of Commerce was the first-floor tenant. In 1976 the Felix-Staib Insurance Agency of Williamsport was purchased and merged into the Hartman Agency, whose production had grown to over one million dollars in annual premiums.

Also, in 1976 Henry J. Stutz, now vice-president, joined the agency with 11 years' experience with PMA

Insurance Company in claims and sales. He developed a unique Workers' Compensation Program for the West Branch Manufacturers' Association, combining diverse manufacturers into a geographic group instead of one based on a specific industry group. This was the first such program in Pennsylvania. In 1978 Stutz became a shareholder in the Hartman Agency.

Terry L. Neubold, now treasurer, joined the firm in 1977. He had previously been with USF&G Company—since 1968—as underwriter, special agent, and casualty manager. Asked to join the Hartman Agency as office manager, he also became a shareholder in 1978. Neubold has developed a group legal liability insurance program for Little League Baseball, Inc. This plan made legal liability protection available to Little League coaches, umpires, and volunteers across the United States.

The expansion continued. In 1980 Lynn A. Sholley became an associate, and organized a branch office in Lewisburg now known as the Hartman-Sholley Agency. He had become a licensed insurance agent in 1975 at the age of 19, working part time while earning his degree from Susquehanna University. In a four-year span the young man reached the million-dollar-premium mark and became vice-president and a shareholder in the company. He now has four employees.

Larry Young was made a vice-president in 1980, when his firm, the McCormick Agency, merged with the Hartman Agency. The McCormick Agency, founded in 1917 by William C. McCormick, was purchased in 1947 by Franklin K. Baker. Young had joined Baker in 1965, after having gained experience with the Insurance Company of North America.

Following Baker's death in 1979, Young owned and operated the establishment with two employees until the merger, which brought together two of the area's oldest insurance organizations. The merger established the Hartman Agency as one of the leading independent insurance agencies in north-central Pennsylvania.

William R. Simons, Jr., a graduate of Shippensburg State College and the USF&G Insurance Agents School, became a member of the firm in 1978. A year later he was appointed manager of the Personal Division. In 1982 he was appointed vice-president of the Fauble Agency, Inc., in Bellefonte, Pennsylvania. Founded in 1929 by Francis X. Fauble, the company had been purchased by the shareholders of the Hartman Agency. It writes a million dollars a year in premiums and has three employees.

The Hartman Agency expanded into life, health, disability, and pension programs, including employee-benefit plans, in 1982. David J. Roche joined the agency to develop what was known as the Financial Services Division. His previous 10-year experience in sales and management with Metropolitan Life Insurance Company was combined with the existing property and casualty expertise within the firm to make the division a leader in this type of business. In 1984 the division was incorporated as Hartman Financial Services, Inc., with Roche as president. Together, the two corporations have given the agency the ability to fulfill virtually all the insurance needs of its clients.

Jeffrey W. Rauff joined the company to assume management of the Personal Lines Division in 1982. He had previous experience with the Rauff Agency, which was owned and operated by his father, Morton Rauff. His duties have since

William R. Simons, president.

Terry L. Neubold, treasurer.

expanded into the Commercial Division and many other management responsibilities. The property and casualty business owned by his father has been purchased and merged into the Hartman Agency.

In February 1983 the Hartman Agency took over the entire building at 420 William Street to accommodate its continued expansion. Then the computers came: the first in June, the second in July, the third in December. The goal is complete computerization by 1986, in order to interact with all Hartman affiliates and all major insurance carriers.

In December 1983 the agency was granted authority by USF&G Company to handle all claims for clients insured by USF&G. Only three agencies in the United States were granted such authority at that time. W. Kevin Hastings joined the firm to manage the division and brought with him six years' experience with General Adjustment Bureau, the largest independent insurance adjuster in the country.

The Hartman Agency represents most major stock companies, several mutual companies, and most major life insurance carriers. The agency is licensed in every state, as well as Puerto Rico and the Virgin Islands, and has written coverage in each of them. Over the past 52 years the Hartman Agency, Inc., has grown to be the largest independent insurance agency in north-central Pennsylvania. It employs 28 people who, together, have over 200 years of insurance experience.

Henry J. Stutz, vice-president.

Larry R. Young, vice-president.

FOUNDERS FEDERAL SAVINGS AND LOAN ASSOCIATION

The promotion of thrift and home ownership is the fundamental purpose of Founders Federal Savings and Loan Association, which was established on January 1, 1983, as a merger of First Federal Savings and Loan Association and Williamsport Federal Savings and Loan Association.

Its origins were rooted 63 years earlier, on December 19, 1919, when Peoples Building and Loan Association was incorporated. The office at 315 Pine Street, above the present Woolworth's, was open a few hours a week.

The organization grew, survived the Great Depression, and on February 16, 1933, secured federal insurance. A federal charter was issued on August 9, 1935, and the name was changed to First Federal Savings and Loan Association. Three days later officers elected were Howard S. Reese, president; F. Ralph Lehman, vice-president; Jesse S. Bell, secretary/manager; and Loretta W. Swank, treasurer.

James D. Wither was hired in 1937 as the institution's first full-time secretary and managing officer. In 1942 he was elected a director and became chairman in 1974, retaining that position when he retired in 1977.

The Founders Federal Savings and Loan Association's Market Square office.

The building at 2-4-6 East Third Street, purchased in 1944, was not occupied by the association until 1951. A $125,000, award-winning renovation was completed in 1969.

Robert G. Wharton, a staff member since 1962, was made a director in 1973, was named secretary/treasurer/managing officer in 1974, and five years later was appointed president and chief executive officer. He retired from active office in 1980, succeeded by Robert W. Klein.

Meanwhile, in 1934 Thomas J. Rider felt the Williamsport area needed a second savings and loan institution. Fifty investors raised $5,600 and applied for a federal charter and the name First Federal Savings and Loan Association, which was preempted by Peoples. Consequently, the title Williamsport Federal Savings and Loan Association was selected, and opened as such on May 1, 1935, at 442 William Street. The first officers were Harry L. Slack, president; Thomas J. Rider, vice-president; Fearns E. Bitler, treasurer; and Louis A. Wetzel, secretary/manager.

In 1955 the association moved to 434 William Street. The Housel Building at 135-137-141 West Fourth Street was purchased in 1965. After a $150,000 remodeling of the structure, Williamsport Federal moved into 137 in October of that

Founders Federal also has a facility located at 137 West Third Street.

year with five employees. W. Glenn Moon, who joined the organization in 1946, was the only employee until 1959. He was elected secretary/managing officer in 1960. In 1977 Moon was elected a director and president of Williamsport Federal. He is now chairman of the board, and Klein is president and chief executive officer of Founders Federal.

Many changes occurred during 1983, the first year of Founders Federal's merged operation. As well as the introduction of insured money-market and other types of accounts, consumer loans for autos, home repairs, college tuition, and personal requirements were offered. Savings-account holders received record-setting interest of over $6.3 million, and as of December 31 assets had increased $4.4 million in 1983 to $74.3 million.

The institution's customers are now served by 24 full-time employees in three Williamsport offices.

JOHN SAVOY & SON, INC.

In 1935 John D. Savoy traveled to Williamsport from New York City to set up and begin operations for the Chesterfield Furniture Company, which was relocating from the latter city. His intention was to remain until the plant was in operation and running smoothly. However, because of the beauty of the area and the friendliness of the people he met, he decided to remain; his family joined him in 1936.

Savoy and his sons, John A. and Albert, formed a small operation named Savoy's Machine Woodcarving Shop in 1946. They machined and hand-carved all the highly ornate parts of living room, bedroom, and family room furniture in such styles as French Provincial, Italian Provincial, English Tudor, and others. For almost three years they built the operation while working at other full-time employment. John D. Savoy remained at Chesterfield Furniture, and John A. Savoy worked at Bethlehem Steel Corporation.

The shop was moved in 1949 to a larger location known as the Majestic Garage, in downtown Williamsport behind the Keystone Theater; at the same time it was decided to expand the line to include furniture frames. The firm's growth by 1954 necessitated another move to a 10,000-square-foot building on Locust Street, known as the Eberhardt Planing Mill. In addition, the business name was changed to John Savoy & Son, Inc.

In 1958 the decision was made to include upholstered furniture in the product line, and a 2,500-square-foot building was rented at Fifth and Locust streets to house the operation.

Also that year, John A. became president when John D. retired and took the opportunity to fulfill a longtime dream. He returned to Budapest, Hungary, where he had been born and raised, to visit the family he had not seen in almost 40 years.

The business continued to grow, and it became apparent that both operations should be combined. In 1961 the move was made to a 48,000-square-foot facility at the present address at the corner of Charles and Howard streets in Montoursville.

A change of direction took place in 1963. John Savoy & Son, Inc., ceased manufacturing home furniture and entered the commercial-furniture field. The first large order received was from the Commonwealth of Pennsylvania: a contract to provide the furniture for all agencies of the state for a period of one year. It has held that contract continuously for over 20 years.

Between 1961 and 1968 a total of 14,000 square feet of floor space was added to enable the operation to continue its growth. John D. Savoy died in 1968. The following year the organization purchased a 30,000-square-foot building in Hughesville and began manufacturing case goods such as desks, credenzas, wardrobes, beds, and library furniture. This facility was known as Plant No. 2, and was used primarily as a test plant before any addition to the furniture line was made in Plant No. 1. By 1974 it was obvious that the trial period for the case goods was successful; consequently, approximately 15,000 square feet of floor space was added to Plant No. 1 and the two facilities were consolidated.

The company in 1978 decided to pursue military business, and was successful in obtaining contracts on all product lines. As a result, its sales, in addition to the commercial field, now include shipments to many military bases all over the world.

A 20,000-square-foot addition is under construction. At present, John Savoy & Son, Inc., employs 125 people—many of whom have been with the firm over 30 years. The annual payroll is approximately two million dollars.

The furniture manufacturing plant of John Savoy & Son, Inc., is located directly in front of the local airport in Montoursville. Construction for additional office space is under way, as shown at left.

BANK OF CENTRAL PENNSYLVANIA

This 1910 postcard depicts Broad Street, looking east, in Montoursville. The original First National Bank is on the left.

Paying five dollars a month rent for the Smith Building on the south side of Broad Street in Montoursville, First National Bank opened its doors on October 3, 1903, to serve the general banking needs of the community. C.E. Bennett was the first president and John H. Sherman was cashier of this establishment that was to evolve in 80 years to a $140-million institution.

For the first step of that development, the directors immediately constructed a building at 355 Broad Street—the present location of the customer service department and the safe deposit vault. Business grew, albeit slowly, and deposits had increased to $500,000 by October 1920.

That same year another bank was formed. In November the Peoples Bank of Montoursville opened for business in rented quarters on Broad Street in the David Wright storeroom. A new building (now the Montoursville Public Library) was erected on the corner of Broad and Washington streets and opened in 1921. Its first president was Charles V. Adams and J. Faries Sedam was cashier.

By December 1932 First National Bank of Montoursville had resources of approximately $850,000; The Peoples Bank recorded about $250,000.

Due to the economic conditions of the Depression years following the stock market crash of 1929, the two institutions agreed to merge, effective December 17, 1932, under the title First National Bank of Montoursville. Combined assets were over $1.1 million, with total capital of approximately $170,000. The officers of the merged bank were Charles V. Adams, chairman of the board; C.E. Bennett, president; Harrison W. App, cashier; and J. Faries Sedam, assistant cashier. The directors of each bank became the directors of the merged bank.

After Bennett resigned as president, Charles V. Adams was elected chairman of the board and president.

Total resources of First National Bank of Montoursville increased to $3.1 million by the end of 1944. As the economy improved and the city and surrounding area grew rapidly, the bank prospered.

Adjacent real estate along Broad Street was purchased and in 1965 a larger structure was built. Four teller drive-in units, two walk-up windows, and a large parking lot were installed.

On August 12, 1965, Adams retired as president, and C. Harry Forse was elected his successor. However, Adams continued as chairman of the board until his death in 1970.

Bank of South Williamsport had been organized in 1918, opening on the southeast corner of East Southern Avenue and Market Street in South Williamsport. Its first president was Charles W. Sones, followed by Harry S. Nolan. On December 31, 1973, it was consolidated with First National Bank of Montoursville (whose assets were by then approximately $33 million) into a new organization called Bank of Central Pennsylvania (BCP), with total resources of $48.7 million.

BCP began operations on January 1, 1974, with C. Harry Forse as president, and Emerson W. Knyrim as senior vice-president and trust officer. The South Williamsport office of BCP was modernized. With the acquisition of adjoining land, four teller drive-in units and a large parking lot were also provided.

A branch office was constructed

Bank of Central Pennsylvania, Montoursville.

Bank of Central Pennsylvania, Beltway.

Bank of Central Pennsylvania, South Williamsport.

in 1978 along Pennsylvania Route 87, at the Montoursville exit of Interstate 180. Half of the building was leased to Ideal Markets. The office, with two drive-in units, provides convenient banking for people in the Loyalsock Valley.

Forse retired as president on February 1, 1979, and became chairman of the board. Knyrim was named president. Vice-president and treasurer is George W. Ferlazzo, and vice-president and secretary, Rexford B. Hilton.

Bank of Central Pennsylvania and Grange National Bank of Lycoming County merged on December 31, 1980, which resulted in a bank with total resources of $115 million. The latter organization had been established in 1907, served by James K. Boaks as its first president. Other past presidents included Isaac Shaffer; Chester McConnell; Harry Keyte; William B. Seibert; Howard O. Shaffer, currently director and chairman of the regional board; and C. Paul McConnell.

Grange Bank operated in a facility at 32-42 North Main Street in Hughesville. After the merger with BCP, the building was

renovated and two drive-in teller units were added.

In 1982 BCP became a part of the "William Teller" Automatic Teller System. ATM units were installed at the South Williamsport and Beltway offices, and in the new Weis Market building in Montoursville. These three units, as well as 15 others, are now available for all BCP customers.

A new computer was installed at the Montoursville office, with Gerald M. Gordner as data-processing manager. The system is connected to BCP's four offices and the ATM stations.

A second floor was added to the Montoursville office. This new space plus the computer system make up the headquarters for the total BCP operation, which includes the Montoursville ground-floor customer facilities, and the Beltway, Hughesville, and South Williamsport offices. Assets at the beginning of 1984 were approximately $140 million, with

capital of about $10 million.

"People Serving People" is not only the motto, but also the everyday functioning of the staff offering customers a variety of services. The modern banking facilities provide 12 drive-in, three walk-up, and 18 William Teller units, along with 115 employees to give personal service to customers. Of its 89 full-time and 26 part-time staff members, Hughesville employs 12 and 6; Beltway, 4 and 3; South Williamsport, 17 and 7; and Montoursville, 56 and 10—all "People Serving People."

Bank of Central Pennsylvania, Hughsville. This was formerly the Grange National Bank of Lycoming County.

163

CANTEEN VENDING COMPANY, INC.

Fifteen dollars—in pennies and nickels—was the first week's return on Joseph N. Lytle's investment of $600 in September 1938. After working two years each in St. Joseph, Michigan, and Elmira, New York, the entrepreneur had moved to Punxsutawney, Pennsylvania, to originate an Automatic Canteen Corporation franchise. He continued serving six counties from that location until 1966.

Meanwhile, in 1936, Ed Harvey had started a similar Williamsport franchise at 379 West Third Street; his enterprise sold five-cent candy bars, one-cent sticks of gum, and one-cent portions of peanuts. Ralph Montgomery acquired the company in 1938, and two years later moved to the Triangle Building (now the Casale Building) on Schiffler Avenue. The operation was moved to its present location at 201 Maynard Street in October 1943. Although the 1946 flood submerged all the merchandise in eight feet of water, the firm was able to recover.

In April 1951 Lytle purchased the Williamsport franchise, which serves Lycoming, Clinton, Tioga, Northumberland, Columbia, Union, Montour, and part of Luzerne counties. During that decade coffee vendors and hot canned-food machines were introduced, which were soon followed by the addition of sandwiches, cold food, Jell-O, and dessert items. Coffee was still five cents.

While coin changers were first used in the early 1950s, 1961 saw the inauguration of dollar-bill changers. At that time as well, microwave ovens were added.

In October 1962 Lytle's son, Robert B., came into the business after his discharge from the Army. He started in sales, worked in management, and is now vice-president and secretary.

The dike kept the Agnes Flood,

in June 1972, from the building, but 277 vending machines were lost from Lock Haven to Danville. Undaunted, the company again survived to enter a new growth pattern.

A large warehouse was added in 1974. A Sunday morning fire in October 1978 destroyed the original facility; however, the warehouse's firewall saved it, and deliveries as usual were made on Monday. A year later a commissary was instituted on the first floor of the replacement building.

Today Canteen Vending Company, Inc., has 60 employees, including a staff of 10 in the commissary; a food-service manager; route-service people; machine-maintenance workers; office personnel; and cafeteria workers. Over 100 accounts in businesses and

These are some of the many delicious foods available from the vending machines of the Canteen Vending Company, Inc.

institutions have from one to multiple banks of machines. Serving them necessitates a fleet of 32 vehicles, which use 65,000 gallons of gas annually to drive over 520,000 miles.

Prodigious amounts of various foods are used, a substantial portion of which is bought locally. Milk, bread, produce, soft drinks, and other items are purchased in town; meat and eggs come from the Susquehanna Valley area.

Almost 10 million units a year are distributed through vending machines, plus the cafeteria requirements. The commissary alone prepares over 3,200 items daily that are sold through refrigerated vendors and snack bars.

Automatic Canteen Company of America was renamed Canteen Corporation, which is a subsidiary of Trans World Corporation. Canteen Vending Company, Inc., is now a franchise of Trans World Corporation.

WUNDIES INCORPORATED

Wundies—a manufacturer of children's and ladies' lingerie—was founded in 1947 by Jerry Banner, who sold the product from New York City, and by Harry Blum, who managed the factory employing approximately 50 people in space rented at 611 Rose Street. At that time the firm engaged in the production of ladies' sleepwear.

The first breakthrough in the business occurred in the mid-1950s with the popularity of little girls' bouffant slips, and accelerated further with the addition of children's underwear and sleepwear lines in 1961. During this time a small plant was established in Liberty, Pennsylvania, to augment the manufacture of underwear.

The company was sold to Duplan, a conglomerate now called Panex Industries, in 1968. Three years later a 100,000-square-foot building was constructed on West Third Street at the present location.

In 1973 an additional plant was opened in Wellsboro. At that time Blum retired, succeeded by Alan Daum as vice-president. Banner was named president of the organization, a position he continues to hold today.

In the past 10 years the company has enjoyed considerable success,

Wundies Incorporated occupies this 100,000-square-foot facility on West Third Street in Williamsport. Dawson Jones, photographer.

Over 1,100 people are employed in Wundies plants in Williamsport, Liberty, and Wellsboro. Dawson Jones, photographer.

due to several factors. Ladies' panties and sleepwear were introduced under the name "Kickaway®," and a new patented two-way stretch panty was marketed as "Lovepats®." Children's thermal underwear was added, while the sleepwear line was enlarged to include garments for infants and toddlers.

The most important factor in Wundies' growth has been the introduction of licensed products, which began in 1980 with the acquisition of the "Strawberry Shortcake®" trademark. The great

success of the apparel bearing that name led to the introduction of several other licensed items, including "Smurf®" and "Cabbage Patch Kids®." In the "Kickaway®" division such names as "Playmate®" and "Essence®" have contributed to significant increases in sales and profits.

Since its inception Wundies has been able to maintain a pattern of steady growth. There have been virtually no periods when the rise in employment has been interrupted. As the demands for its products have grown, additions to the existing plants have enlarged the total manufacturing space in Williamsport, Liberty, and Wellsboro to 257,000 square feet. Over 1,100 people are employed in these facilities.

The executive and sales offices are in New York City; a sales office is also maintained in Dallas, Texas. From these locations the company sells its lines to approximately 500 customers, consisting primarily of discount and national chain stores.

Wundies Incorporated sold over 55 million of its various garments in 1983, and looks forward to continued expansion in the future.

C.A. REED INCORPORATED

Postcards comprised the principal sales in the small retail store that C.A. Reed and two partners opened in downtown Williamsport on April 13, 1907, with a $135 investment. By 1915 the store had twice moved to larger rooms, reaching Reed's goal of being in the heart of the retail district. In the meantime he had become the largest postcard jobber in the United States, with several salesmen selling postcards and novelties.

That year sample nut-cups (souffle cups covered with crepe paper) made for the salesmen were readily accepted by the buyers. In 1916 nine women were making little crepe-paper novelties in the store basement. Eventually Reed persuaded Woolworth's buyer to try the favors in some stores. They were a big success, and by 1917 the favor business had to rent its own building. Then World War I erupted.

Split baskets for Easter candy were scarce, so Reed conceived the

idea of crepe-covered baskets with a fringed crepe-paper rope handle to replace the unavailable Japanese hinoka. Woolworth ordered 14,000 gross—creating problems of raising money, finding more factory space, getting materials, and planning production. Nonetheless, the order was completed for pre-Easter selling. Sales to all outlets continued to increase, and in 1920 an old building was purchased and converted into a three-story factory.

Reed was virtually begging his supplier to ship crepe paper in sufficient volume to keep his plant going. Several men in the Dennison organization—realizing the possibilities of Reed's business—suggested to him that if he wanted to make crepe paper, they would be glad to become affiliated with him. Eventually this happened. Three of these men, one of whom was Arad H. Stockwell, came to Williamsport in 1921, and a corporation was formed with a capitalization of $300,000. Stock was sold, and a modern 63,000-square-foot daylight building was erected. Machinery to fabricate crepe paper was installed, and in June 1922 about 100 factory workers and 8 office workers began the manufacturing of crepe paper and paper novelties on a much

C.A. Reed's initial venture was opened on April 13, 1907, at 20 West Fourth Street. It was from this small beginning that the present business evolved.

larger scale than anyone had previously attempted. Five salesmen covered Pennsylvania, New York, Maryland, and West Virginia with first-year sales of $415,000.

The company then installed a flatbed machine for embossing paper "club napkins," which became very popular. The rapid expansion of the business required reorganization and recapitalization in 1925. A 1926 addition to the plant increased floor space by 40,000 square feet, and machinery was installed to make table covers.

As napkins gained popularity, color in everything came into vogue. Simple one-color, border-design napkins were introduced. Before long, two rotary machines could not meet demand so additional machines were added periodically. When designs on napkins and table covers were introduced, the firm needed large printing machines. This necessitated additional space, and in 1930 a one-story, 10,240-square-foot addition was constructed.

During the Depression years the

C.A. Reed Incorporated executives and salesmen, January 1925. They are (left to right) Carl Ellingsworth, E.G. Knights, Mr. Loy, Earl Wilcox, Jack Jolly, Howard Hunt, A.H. Stockwell, Carl Plotz, Mr. Wilcox, C.A. Reed, Waldo Rich, Cy Waters, Harry Miller, J.D. Kennelly, Horace Hamilton, Howard Wise, and H.D. Pendergast.

company made slow, steady progress, and provided steady employment while expanding. In order to improve quality, a laboratory was established and a chemist was hired in 1931. Valuable research about crepe-paper making was done, and better equipment was developed to increase production and efficiency. An art department with six artists and a stylist was also instituted.

During this time an adjoining property of 3.5 acres was purchased. A building on it was remodeled into a 25,000-square-foot warehouse.

As a 1937 Pennsylvania law prohibited home production of C.A. Reed-type products, 800 home workers were transferred to the factory. New equipment and methods were developed, which improved operations and increased production.

Periodically production was increased by installing state-of-the-art machinery, by streamlining manufacturing processes, and by operating many departments 24 hours a day. When production

The officers of C.A. Reed Incorporated on March 23, 1984, consisted of (left to right) Brenton H. Fisher, Martin L. Gleason, Daniel H. Frantz, John W. Best, and Stephen D. Reed.

limits were reached, a two-story, 43,000-square-foot factory annex was erected in 1940.

Two years later facilities for making drinking cups were considerably increased and improved. New printing, cutting, and gluing equipment made cups with handles for hot drinks possible.

A one-acre warehouse was built. Then a 32,000-square-foot warehouse was constructed in 1955. A 41,000-square-foot building was erected in Hawthorne, California, to serve the West Coast.

Major marketing changes occurred in 1956, when the high-quality "Rembrandt" line was added; in 1957, when a new advertising program was introduced; and in 1959, when the "Futura" line was created for jobbers, with emphasis given to food and drug chains. A warehouse was added in Peoria, Illinois, in 1959 to serve the Midwest, and another in 1965 in Atlanta, Georgia, for the Southeast.

Westvaco Corporation purchased C.A. Reed Incorporated in 1968. It was made a division the following year.

A 100,000-square-foot distribution center was completed in Williamsport in 1971. A new, larger warehouse in Carson, California, replaced the Hawthorne facility; and

A sampling of the C.A. Reed product line in 1984, including paper plates, invitations, and crepe paper.

the Peoria and Atlanta warehouses were closed.

Today C.A. Reed Incorporated has about 340 employees in Williamsport who design and distribute 2,500 products—including matching paper, tableware, and accessories such as invitations, hats, cake decorations, loot bags, favors, toys, and centerpieces. They produce a wide variety of party goods, crepe paper, paper plates, napkins, cups, and table covers. The products cover all holidays: Valentine's Day, St. Patrick's Day, Easter, Halloween, Thanksgiving, Christmas, and New Year's Eve. A major area is birthday categories with royalty designs. Another 270 people sell and service C.A. Reed products nationwide.

On March 23, 1984, the Carman Group purchased the firm from Westvaco. Included in the group are investors from New York, Prudential Life Insurance, and C.A. Reed management.

Executives of the corporation include Martin L. Gleason, formerly division manager, who now serves as president; Stephen D. Reed, grandson of founder C.A. Reed, vice-president/marketing; John W. Best, vice-president/industrial relations; Brenton H. Fisher, vice-president/production; and Daniel H. Frantz, previously administrative manager, who holds the position of treasurer.

KOPPERS COMPANY, INC.

Koppers Company, Inc., was founded in 1912 by Heinrich Koppers, who designed and built the first by-product coke ovens. Today the firm, headquartered in Pittsburgh, employs about 14,000 people in 270 operating locations worldwide.

The Sprout-Waldron Division dates in history to 1866, when Lewis and Samuel Sprout began the manufacture of a horse-operated hayfork invented and patented by another brother, Ariel. Shortly after the introduction of the device, manufacturing facilities were established in Muncy, Pennsylvania, on the same site as the concern's current operations.

The enterprise assumed its present name after Lewis Sprout's son-in-law, John Waldron, was made an associate.

Charles Sprout, Lewis' son, designed a burrstone feed grinder in the early 1880s that enabled farmers to grind their own grain. This apparatus was the direct ancestor of many modern processing machines now manufactured by the organization.

Incorporated as Sprout, Waldron & Company on July 26, 1895, the firm expanded its line of milling equipment. It suffered two major fires and the deaths of several of its leaders, including John Waldron and Charles Sprout. The company rebuilt after each fire, expanding its facilities each time. Further expansion followed in the late 19th and early 20th centuries.

Shortly after World War I the commercial feed-milling industry— the production of feed for livestock —came into prominence, with Sprout, Waldron equipment supplying a significant portion of that market.

By 1950 Sprout, Waldron & Company had added innovative equipment and technology to its

capabilities, to serve the pulp, paper, and board industries.

During the 1970s the firm entered various overseas markets, establishing subsidiaries and client companies in Australia, Austria, France, South Africa, and the United Kingdom.

In October 1975 the Soars family (direct descendants of Lewis Sprout) sold Sprout, Waldron & Company to Koppers Company, Inc. The Sprout-Waldron Division has recently reentered the flour-milling industry on a worldwide basis, and has made international marketing and manufacturing agreements with such organizations as Golfetto of Italy and Kamyr of Sweden. With annual sales now in the $80- to $100-million range, the division employs about 1,000 personnel in and around Lycoming County.

The Koppers Susquehanna Plant of the Forest Products Division was built in Montgomery, Pennsylvania,

---

A late 19th-century Sprout, Waldron & Company vertical crusher.

in 1971 to supply pressure-creosoted materials to several eastern railroads that now form Conrail. One of the wood-preserving industry's most technologically advanced facilities, it has the capacity to annually treat 500 million board feet—more than 1.2 million railroad cross ties. Annual sales of the plant, which employs approximately 50 hourly and 10 salaried personnel during its peak production season, approximate $10 million.

Lycoming Silica Sand Company, a wholly owned subsidiary of Koppers since 1967, has operations in Pennsylvania and New York. Founded by the Joseph Heim family in 1916, the firm was the first aggregate company acquired by Koppers; it became the cornerstone for Koppers Construction Materials and Services.

Lycoming Silica Sand—with approximately 125 hourly and 25 salaried personnel—produces and sells approximately two million tons of crushed limestone, agricultural limestone, sand, gravel, and bituminous concrete each year.

GEORGE E. LOGUE, INC.

Starting with a backhoe he built in his basement, in 27 years George E. Logue's enterprise evolved into a construction company that reached 200 employees and $10.5 million in annual sales.

The Williamsport native attended local schools, and received an engineering degree from Penn State University in 1951. His first employment was with International Harvester in Chicago, where he worked three years at the proving ground. Desiring to return to Williamsport, Logue obtained a position with Sprout, Waldron & Company, remaining there for three years until he started his own business in 1957.

The entrepreneur's interest in Caterpillar tractors took serious form with his purchase of a new CAT933 in July 1957, when he was in business as an excavating contractor and a collector. From its humble beginning—digging ditches—the construction company grew into a multifaceted enterprise completing multimillion-dollar projects.

In 1968 a 68-acre tract of land along Route 220 at the west end of Williamsport was acquired and an asphalt plant was erected. In 1972 the asphalt plant and assets of the M.L. Smith Company in Loyalsock Township was purchased. With the only such facilities in the city, Logue built a substantial paving business—in addition to bridge and sewer construction in Central Pennsylvania.

Examples of the wide variety of projects include extension and rebuilding of the Williamsport Lycoming County Airport runway, reconstruction and widening of the Pleasant Gap-Center Hall road, laying of the West End and Erie Avenue storm sewers, construction of an eight-mile sanitary sewer in Carlisle, and constructing the Loyalsock Creek Barbours bridge. Among demolition endeavors were Old Main at Lycoming College, the County Court House, and the Campbell Street underpass removal and street reconstruction. During any paving season, residents encountered Logue projects throughout the Williamsport region.

Today the Caterpillar collection numbers 50, the construction company has been sold to Koppers Company, Inc. (in December 1983), and the manufacturing activities have taken center stage.

The remaining George E. Logue, Inc., is the manufacturing division that was established at 120 South Arch Street in Montoursville, when the old Carey McFall Building was purchased in June 1983. Logue designs and fabricates paving equipment to solve particular problems. Truck bodies are manufactured that incorporate numerous patented features and proprietary products—including a hydraulically operated, hinged tailgate for a dump truck that allows the operator to meter his dump. The tailgate can be also used as a hoist, and can fold out of the way to convert the dump body into a flatbed.

Logue's manufacturing business was inspired by the requests of his suppliers, customers, and associates. The company now produces limited runs of specialized items, such as sheet-metal cutting blades and hydraulic rock-splitters. His largest product has been a mechanical bomb-picker developed for the U.S. Navy. Research and development is being done on a radio-controlled grader with a single 12-function operating control that responds to actual hand movements. After eight months of operation there are 25 employees, and machinery is being shipped out regularly.

On land in Gamble Township settled by his grandfather Logue in 1884, the founder and his wife, Elizabeth, have raised 10 children. There are several buildings, which include a machine shop as well as a large structure that houses his collection of antique Caterpillar tractors and road machinery. The machine shop, equipped with the latest computerized technology, handles the manufacturing processes, and allows for creativity to develop into many diverse end products.

The George E. Logue, Inc., asphalt plant, construction equipment, and supplies site is located on Route 220.

KEELER/DORR-OLIVER

Like Williamsport, Keeler/ Dorr-Oliver has its roots in the lumber era. The lumber industry was rebuilding after the devastating spring-1860 and September-1861 floods—which had not only sent thousands of logs and finished boards downstream, but had severely damaged the Susquehanna Boom and sawmills.

After these floods the Boom was purchased by Peter Herdic, Mahlon Fisher, and John C. Reading, who vastly strengthened and enlarged the operation. The expansion of the sawmills and other lumber-related industries along Williamsport's river was able to accelerate at a great pace, spurred by the demand for lumber that was being used in the Northeast's industrial expansion and in the Civil War. These sawmills and other plants needed boilers. The enterprise that eventually became Keeler/Dorr-Oliver was established through the ambition of several men to make a profit meeting that need.

Though sketchy and ambiguous information made an exact sequence of events impossible to document, some picture of the company's beginnings can be constructed. Isaac Barton is credited with a long-term contribution to the survival and growth of the firm in its first 65 years. One old document states, "On October 1, 1864, Mr. Barton came to Williamsport and with the two Maitlands and Joseph Heathcote, an Englishman, opened a boiler shop on the west side of West Street. Showing business as well as mechanical qualifications, he was made superintendent of the plant originally known as the firm of J. Heathcote and Company."

The economic problems following the Civil War, and apparently unwise and conflicting business practices and philosophies, put the young organization in such drastic financial straits that it endured years of bankruptcy crises; ultimately, on January 22, 1879, it was sold to F.R. Weed/First National Bank and to others. On March 30, 1883, Emily Keeler and Eleanor Keeler Lehman purchased parts of the properties, the main plant in particular, for $5,300 from Weed. Eleanor, the company's bookkeeper, was Emily's daughter and Barton's niece; he had married Susan A. Keeler. Eleanor acquired other parcels in the ensuing years, as did other individuals involved.

On March 16, 1888, as stated on the bill of sale, "Eleanor Keeler Lehman, the only member of said firm of E. Keeler & Company," sold the firm to the E. Keeler Company for $35,000. Mrs. Emily Keeler had died, and all her heirs quit-claimed any rights to the property in favor of Eleanor.

Who set policy and actually ran the operation over any particular span of time cannot be precisely pinpointed. One stabilizing individual who seems to have kept the plant functioning and productive was Isaac Barton. He was physically active until 1914 when he was confined to his home, though he remained involved as vice-president until his death on May 25, 1929, at the age of 91.

The production history of the corporation is also vague at its beginning. The first boilers were constructed using very primitive methods: Burly men used 30-pound sledgehammers to pound steel plates into top-ended cylinders to which ends were attached to make the body of the boiler.

In 1888, when the firm incorporated, there were 35 men employed manufacturing steam boilers, tanks, engine supplies, and plate work. About 1890 a division was set up to install piping systems for use with Keeler boilers, as well as a mill-supply wholesale outlet.

By 1906 the E. Keeler Company had grown to employ 175 men in 10,000 square feet in several buildings. In addition to manufacturing boilers it installed complete power plants, did steam fitting, heavy pipe work, plus heating and ventilating contract work. The wholesale/jobbing division carried the largest stock of

This photo of Keeler personnel surrounding a long drum boiler was printed and distributed on postcards in 1914 to commemorate the firm's 50th anniversary.

mill and machinery supplies in the state outside of Pittsburgh and Philadelphia.

The federal government had become an extensive, continuing customer early in the firm's history. A large order in 1912 involved 12 water-tube boilers to operate in two permanent power plants on the Panama Canal. During World War I Keeler expanded to build boilers for government use and for firms producing war material. Wise investment of the profits, good management, and continued product development helped it to survive the heavy losses and operating deficits of the Depression.

During World War II Keeler manufactured boilers and furnaces for air force bases, training camps, depots, naval stations, and for many war-industry plants. In 1944 it received its largest single order up to that time when the U.S. Treasury Department placed a $2.5-million order for 80 easily transportable package boilers to produce 250 horsepower each in bombed-out cities desperately needing reliable power. The boilers were credited with helping to shorten the war and received a government citation. The Army Corps of Engineers diverted one Russia-bound boiler to help build an airstrip on Saipan, from which to bomb Tokyo.

In 1945 the wholesale-supply division was doing so well that it moved into a separate building at 335 West Third Street. That decade the success of the package-steam generators brought down costs but also reduced total sales volume. So success had to generate more innovations, which resulted in the D-Type boiler—a single-casing, pressure-fired unit that would account for half of Keeler's orders by 1971.

By its 100th anniversary in 1964, the corporation had operations in

five major buildings on 13 acres. The annual payroll exceeded $1.5 million for over 300 employees. The wholesale division had also grown to 22,500 square feet with 43 employees who sold equipment, tools, and supplies from a $500,000 inventory of 22,000 items.

In 1968 a $185,000 tube-bending shop was built at the east end of the boiler-manufacturing building. The same year the firm purchased the Faber Engineering Company of Norristown, Pennsylvania, which fabricated burners, and moved it to Williamsport. Keeler could then combine boilers and burners to provide new types of industrial burners in steam boilers, stills, kilns, and heaters.

The organization's concern for the environment and new sources of energy has produced new types of boilers. A 124,000-pound-per-hour generator operated entirely on wastewood was designed and built for the United States Plywood Corporation. A 125,000-PPH boiler built for Armstrong Cork Company fires on scrap linoleum and cork. A boiler that efficiently uses municipal refuse as fuel is also manufactured.

From a family business serving Williamsport sawmills, the enterprise evolved into a corporation selling quality products throughout the world. There are Keeler boilers in Canada, Australia, Europe, South America, Russia, China, Iceland, Ireland, Cuba, the Philippines, and

many other countries.

On February 23, 1982, the E. Keeler Company was acquired by Dorr-Oliver, which was founded over 75 years ago and is a wholly owned subsidiary of Standard Oil Company of Ohio. Stamford, Connecticut-based Dorr-Oliver, primarily a worldwide equipment manufacturer, specializing in the separation of solids from fluids for many of the processing industries, has several other manufacturing components.

The relationship began when Dorr-Oliver and Keeler cooperated in a Department of Energy project in the late 1970s in Shamokin to burn anthracite culm, a coal-preparation waste product, in a fluid-bed technology application. The project was so successful that Dorr-Oliver acquired Keeler.

The addition to the new product line of fluid-bed boilers, which should experience tremendous growth in the 1980s, has increased the firm's technical orientation and had required additional technical employees. A new engineering building, which houses 35 engineers and support people, has been constructed. In the future, new equipment and more people will be added to the manufacturing facility to accommodate this growth.

The shipping of an E. Keeler Co. boiler in 1890 prompted this celebration at the corner of Third and Washington streets.

CANADA DRY BOTTLING COMPANY, INC., OF WILLIAMSPORT

Since part of the A. Nardi & Sons produce business had been the distribution of Canada Dry beverages that were manufactured in New York State—packed in excelsior and shipped in wooden crates—two of the sons, Ralph A. Nardi, Sr., and Louis P. Nardi, obtained the franchise to bottle the drinks. On November 22, 1950, they established a new enterprise located at 517 Pine Street in a 5,000-square-foot building.

Ralph handled sales; Louis managed production; and their wives, Dorothy and Betty, shared the office work. Capacity was about 500 cases a day, and each of the 6,000 bottles had to be labeled one at a time by hand. Without modern forklifts, the heavy wooden crates and glass bottles had to be moved and stacked by hand. Within a year there were a dozen employees, one pickup truck, and two delivery trucks.

In 1952 the Hires franchise was acquired from Ray Thompson and moved to the Pine Street location. Hires remains the oldest brand of soft drink in the country. The 1950s also saw a steady growth in the pre-mix business for soda fountains.

Orange Crush brand was the next franchise to be acquired, in 1971, again from the Hires Company. A

The multifranchise Canada Dry Bottling Company, Inc., of Williamsport is in its 34th year of operation. Here one of the over 50 employees checks a variety of soft drinks ready for distribution.

year later the Thomas Boyle Bottling Works was purchased, and Royal Crown Cola and Squirt were produced at its Rose Street plant until the new plant was opened in 1973 at 2120 Marydale Avenue.

Dr Pepper, the second-oldest brand in the United States, was obtained in 1975. In the 1980s the firm became a jobber for Lipton Iced Tea, YOO-HOO Chocolate Drink, Hawaiian Punch, and Welch's brands.

In 1980 a distribution center was built in Lime Ridge (between Berwick and Bloomsburg) to service the Hazleton, Pottsville, and Shamokin areas.

Louis Nardi retired in 1969 and Ralph A. Nardi, Jr., purchased his share of the Canada Dry Bottling Company, Inc., of Williamsport. A year later the Canada Dry bottling plant in Hazleton closed, and distribution in the area was taken

over by the Williamsport firm. At that time Ralph Jr., who had been working for the parent Canada Dry Corp. in Philadelphia, returned to Williamsport to join his father.

In its 34th year Canada Dry Bottling Company, Inc., of Williamsport has evolved into a multifranchise company with over 50 employees, 37 vehicles, and facilities of 35,000 square feet. A population of close to one million people in 10,000 square miles spread over 14 counties is served. Many of the consumers obtain their beverages from the several hundred street vending machines owned and serviced by the company, and from restaurants that use its fountain syrup and pre-mix.

From this distribution center at 2120 Marydale Avenue, the Canada Dry Bottling Company, Inc., of Williamsport services markets in a 14-county area.

STROEHMANN BROTHERS COMPANY

Frederick G. Stroehmann, father of Carl F. and Harold J., learned the baking trade as a youth in Leun, Germany. In 1882, at the age of 16, he immigrated to Wheeling, West Virginia, where he found employment in a small local bakery. Five years later he married the owner's daughter, Louisa, and in 1892 they took over the family enterprise.

Fred and Louisa Stroehmann raised their family of three girls and two boys in a small apartment over the bakery. By this time the operation had expanded to include a small retail store, as well as a horse and wagon. Fred tended the store while Louisa went out on the wagon, selling and delivering bread daily to their wholesale customers.

Through hard work and perseverance the business prospered. By 1911 it had a three-story plant and its first wrapped and advertised loaf, "Mother Hubbard." In 1915 a plant was erected in Huntington, West Virginia, and four years later a bakery was acquired in Ashland, Kentucky. One of the sons, Carl, was put in charge of the Ashland Bakery in 1920, after graduating from Tufts University. In 1922 the family sold the business to W.B. Ward/United Bakeries.

In order to gain experience, Carl worked in a variety of capacities with several major bakeries until 1924. At that time Fred, Carl, and the other son, Harold Jr., purchased the Gramlich Bakery in Williamsport, Pennsylvania, and renamed it Stroehmann Brothers Company. Carl became the first general manager, and Harold the first sales manager.

Stroehmann Brothers built a successful business based on the principle of providing a quality product at a fair price. The company encouraged its salesmen to develop unique in-store displays,

and was willing to spend the money necessary to advertise its products. In harsh economic situations the firm met the competition's challenge by using strong, innovative sales techniques.

Acquisitions and new-plant openings followed through the years. In 1927 the purchase of the Schoeller Bakery in Norristown, Pennsylvania, provided entry into the Philadelphia market. With that facility the company was able to introduce a radically new product, sliced white bread. Stroehmann Brothers backed this product with aggressive advertising and heavy promotion—and soon owned the market.

During the Depression growth was slowed. People still needed bread, but bought the cheapest possible. Therefore, Stroehmann Brothers introduced another new product, a 39-cent angel food cake. This item proved so popular the bakery was never again "in the red."

As the years passed, the firm steadily expanded into new markets, and continued to acquire existing and construct new facilities. In 1931 it constructed a plant in Harrisburg, and moved the executive offices there. However, in February 1941 they were moved back to Williamsport.

Harold J. Stroehmann, Sr., died in 1953. In 1955 Carl Stroehmann retired, and Harold J. Stroehmann, Jr., was elected president of the

company. Within the next 10 years the firm's sales doubled, reaching $25 million.

In the 1960s an interesting character called "Grampa Stroehmann" was developed, and became the corporation's advertising spokesman. In 1983 Grampa Stroehmann became the official registered trademark for the Stroehmann Brothers Company.

Harold J. Stroehmann, Jr., died in 1978. Before his untimely demise, he had led the organization to become one of the strongest, most reputable bakeries on the East Coast.

Stroehmann Brothers Company was purchased in 1980 by George Weston Ltd. of Toronto, Canada. It has continued its pattern of steady growth: Additional acquisitions include Capital Bakery of Harrisburg, Pennsylvania; Firch Bakery of Erie, Pennsylvania, and Jamestown, New York; Keystone Bakery of West Bridgewater, Pennsylvania; and Hartford East Bakery of Hartford, Connecticut. In Hazleton a production facility, acquired from Spaulding, was completely renovated and opened in 1983.

Stroehmann Brothers Company, in its evolution, still upholds the traditional values that first brought it success.

Fred and Louisa Stroehmann, son Carl F., and two of their daughters stand in front of the original Wheeling, West Virginia, store.

FRITO-LAY, INC.

In San Antonio, Texas, in September 1932—during the Depression—a quiet, imaginative man named Elmer Doolin stopped in a small cafe for lunch. He discovered, and enjoyed immensely, a corn chip made from basic corn dough, masa, which has been used as a bread for centuries by the Mexicans. Intrigued, and intuitively sensing the product would have broad consumer appeal, Doolin purchased the recipe for these Fritos-brand corn chips, along with 19 retail accounts, and the manufacturing equipment—an old converted potato ricer! The total purchase price was $100. He set up his first Fritos plant in his mother's kitchen, and produced about 10 pounds of corn chips an hour. Sales totaled some $8 to $10 a day, earning profits of about $2.

Doolin's hunch was accurate, and sales began to grow. And as sales grew so did manufacturing challenges. Doolin found it necessary to develop his own manufacturing equipment, and soon replaced the humble potato ricer with a hand press that cut strips of dough. Within a year he moved his headquarters to the booming city of Dallas and opened manufacturing plants there, in Houston, and in Tulsa. By 1955 he had 11 plants and 12 franchise operations throughout the United States.

Coincidentally, young Herman Lay started a potato-chip business in Nashville the very year, 1932, that Doolin began his enterprise. Lay used his 1928 automobile as a delivery truck to distribute potato chips he purchased wholesale from an Atlanta firm. His distributorship —which included northern Tennessee and southern Kentucky —survived the Depression, and grew in its aftermath. First there were more routes, then more products. In 1936 Lay began to sell his own

Frito-Lay opened its Williamsport Industrial Park facility in 1971. Two years later an expansion, creating additional processing areas and warehouse space, almost doubled capacity.

brand-name popcorn, and by 1937 the Lay distributorship was a healthy, thriving business with 15 salesmen.

On October 2, 1939, the entrepreneur purchased the Atlanta and Memphis plants of Barrett Company, as well as its "Gardner's" brand name. The Lay Company continued to prosper, added products, expanded, moved its headquarters to Atlanta, and introduced a completely new

technique for potato-chip manufacture, the continuous-production line.

In 1945 the Frito Company awarded H.W. Lay & Company an exclusive franchise, to manufacture and distribute Fritos-brand corn chips in the Southeast, which was the beginning of a close affiliation that eventually led to a merger of the two organizations. Each firm continued its strong and rapid growth.

These successful snack-food operations merged to become Frito-Lay, Inc., in 1961, and a period of burgeoning growth began. Sales soared, more plants were opened, and new products multiplied. More jobs for employees with more opportunities were created. A distribution network spread out into every city in the country. The Frito-Lay name and trademark became bywords everywhere.

Another major step was taken in July 1965, when Frito-Lay merged with the Pepsi-Cola Company, a leader in a closely related field. Together they became PepsiCo, Inc. Today both organizations operate as separate divisions of the worldwide parent corporation, which does business in over 125 nations. Frito-Lay is one of 12 principal divisions and subsidiaries of PepsiCo.

Frito-Lay opened its Williamsport Industrial Park facility on January 11, 1971. Initially, 30 employees manufactured the first product, Funyuns onion-flavored snacks. In the following two weeks, 30 additional employees were added to make Doritos brand tortilla chips in regular, taco, and nacho cheese flavors. Three weeks later 20 more people were hired to produce Cheetos brand cheese-flavored snacks.

In 1973 a plant expansion, creating additional processing areas and warehouse space, almost doubled capacity. Funyuns manufacture became 11,500 pounds per day; 60,000 pounds of Doritos could be produced daily; and Cheetos could be made at the daily rate of 23,000 pounds.

A distribution center was established in 1975 to service the areas between West Virginia, Maine, north to New York, and as far west as Ohio. In 1976 a new office and maintenance facilities were built.

Presently, 125 production employees manufacture prodigious quantities of snacks—using enormous amounts of ingredients that include more than 900,000 gallons of vegetable oil; almost 13 million pounds of whole yellow corn; over 8 million pounds of cornmeal; 130 million packaging bags; and 5 million corrugated boxes, many of which are used several times.

The transport department of 40 drivers and support people handles 80,000 cases (40 trailers) per week—more than four million annually. About 25 management and clerical personnel coordinate deliveries, ensuring that the products are accurately and timely received by consumers in a 10-state area.

Frito-Lay acquired Grandma's Cookies in Beaverton, Oregon, in 1980. In order to widen the distribution area, the Pulaski, Tennessee, plant was expanded, and the Boise-Cascade building in Muncy Industrial Park was acquired, enlarged, and converted into a bakery for cookie production.

Various management people from Frito-Lay facilities in Florida, Indiana, and Oregon were assembled in Muncy to establish operations in the bakery. Production started on August 17, 1981, with 80 employees.

In early 1984 there were 450 employees making nine kinds of cookies, at the rate of 800,000 cookies an hour. The snacks are distributed from Muncy to the eastern and southern portions of the United States, and delivered as far west as Denver.

Frito-Lay hopes to increase its market share, in order to fully utilize the $26-million investment it has made at the 30-acre Muncy site. As market penetration increases and spreads, facilities and employment will expand. An addition under construction in 1984 will increase

the plant to approximately 145,000 square feet, and will provide more warehouse space for both shipping and receiving. A new cafeteria and lockers have been installed for the employees' welfare.

The Muncy and Williamsport operations are dynamic parts of the Frito-Lay division of PepsiCo, the 44th-largest industrial corporation in the United States. If Frito-Lay—the greatest profit contributor to PepsiCo—was taken as a separate company, it would rank in the top 200. The firm has increased its sales from $500 million in 1974 to an estimated $2.5 billion in 1984.

Herman Lay, who died in December 1982, was not only a strong believer in the free-enterprise system; he was a prime example of how hard work and persistence made it work. The founder of the enterprise that bears his name often remarked that, "Business doesn't move, it flies." He would be proud of Frito-Lay's continued soaring growth, and the important role it has in communities such as Muncy and Williamsport—and throughout the country.

One of Frito-Lay's 1,000 daily deliveries on its way to the firm's many satisfied customers.

INSOPORT INDUSTRIES, INC.

Insoport's roots go back to Sweden, where in the mid-1950s Crawford Door AB developed a steel sectional overhead door. To manufacture and market its product, a factory was built in Gothenburg, Sweden.

In the mid-1970s an insulated overhead door was developed. Initially the Thermacore insulated overhead door was built in Sweden; then in 1980, due to the success of this door, the decision was made to establish a factory in Williamsport. With the help of the Pennsylvania Industrial Development Authority and the Williamsport Area Industrial Development Corporation, the former Jim Walter property was acquired.

The new company was named

Insoport Industries, Inc., is the Williamsport branch of Overhead Door Corporation of Dallas, Texas. It is located at 3200 Reach Road.

Insoport Industries, Inc. The name Insoport is derived from the Swedish for insulated port or door. It is a company within the well-known Sonesson Group of Sweden. Sonesson's, whose chairman of the board is Anders Wall, began in 1982 as a wholesale distributor of engineered products; it is now one of the world's largest manufacturers of industrial overhead doors and the leading producer of industrial alkaline batteries.

An investment exceeding $15 million provided a 150,000-square-foot manufacturing plant for Insoport equipped with the ultimate in computerized state-of-the-art technology and equipment. Test production commenced in April 1981, and the first product was shipped the following August. Since then the unique insulated overhead doors have been shipped to all parts

of the Western Hemisphere.

Thirty people were employed the first year, and in three years that number has tripled. As marketing growth expands sales in an ever-increasingly energy-conscious world, the ultramodern plant—which can produce 80,000 Thermacore insulated doors a year—will steadily accelerate production and employment.

The process used to manufacture Thermacore doors is one of three such lines in the world. The original line is in Gothenburg, Sweden, and a new process line has just been completed in Holland. This line enables Insoport to manufacture the highest-quality insulated door in the industry, in the most efficient way.

On June 30, 1984, Overhead Door Corporation, located in Dallas, Texas, acquired 100-percent interest in Insoport Industries, Inc.

WWPA/SUMMIT ENTERPRISES

WWPA was conceived in 1946 when a group of local businessmen learned the FCC was going to allocate a Class-4 frequency to the area. Williamsport Broadcasting was formed with Harry J.W. Kiessling, president; William P. Wilson, treasurer; and stockholders George L. Stearns II, U.S. Congressman Alvin R. Bush, Carl F. Stroehmann, Ray L. Riley, Senator John C. Snowden, S. Dale Furst, and the Grit Publishing Company.

After three years of FCC hearings, WWPA was granted the 1340 frequency to operate a 250-watt AM station at 330 Government Place with the transmitter in South Williamsport. Area native Woodrow W. Ott, program director of WENY, Elmira, New York, joined the corporation as station manager.

Broadcasting began at 12:31 p.m. on Sunday, May 22, 1949. A CBS affiliate, Lycoming County's second station was middle of the road with a 6:30 a.m.-to-midnight schedule. Network favorites included "Arthur Godfrey," "Romance of Helen Trent," "Suspense," and "Lux Radio Theatre." Lowell Thomas brought world news to Williamsport. And Martin Jewelers made the first request for advertising time, 30 seconds before "The Jack Benny Show."

In addition to national programs and local news, WWPA strove to cover and support local programs and activities. "Sally Llson's Program," live from L.L. Stearns, was the first originating in Lycoming County about women's concerns. That year also brought the first of 35 continuous years of Penn State football broadcasts. Scholastic sports coverage was begun in football and basketball. The Eastern Baseball League Williamsport Grays and the Billies basketball games were covered live at home—and recreated by wire from the away games.

Summit Enterprises, Inc., acquired WWPA in March 1961. Ott became president, serving until his death in November 1975. His son, W. William Ott, was named president and general manager on January 19, 1976.

Sunday, February 13, 1977, saw four fires set in Williamsport. One totally destroyed Pine Street United Methodist Church. Another severely damaged the offices and studios of WWPA. For the remainder of the winter, the on-air staff operated from burned, damp studios; the office staff was housed at the Genetti Lycoming Hotel. An already-planned move to the old Growers' Market building at the foot of Market Street Bridge was accelerated, and the station moved into those quarters—where it remains today—on June 4, 1977.

Its daytime power increased to 1,000 watts in 1965, and WWPA now serves all of Lycoming County.

Penn State football games have been broadcast by WWPA since 1949.

Since the mid-1970s it has become a highly promotional station that gives away automobiles, trips to Hawaii and Bermuda, plus lots of America's favorite prize—cash.

From the beginning, community involvement has been WWPA's forte. It is recognized as a leader in this area and supports over 100 local organizations. In 1980 it played an integral part in establishing the "Fanny in the Susquehanny" annual charity inner tube float down the river. The event has grown to include over 20,000 floaters and spectators, and this helps support several local charities.

WWPA's success in the past can be attributed to such as John Archer, June Roland, Gordon Thomas, and Lee "Tom Cat" Moore—and will continue with the likes of Ken Sawyer and Gary Chrisman. News, sports, and information remain vital forces in future programming, which will be innovative, ambitious, and responsive to community needs.

GRUMMAN ALLIED INDUSTRIES, INC.

Grumman Allied Industries, Inc., a wholly owned subsidiary of Grumman Corporation, based in Long Island, New York, has two divisions, a vehicle division and a marine and energy division. They are engaged in the manufacture of commercial truck bodies, fire apparatus, yachts, canoes, and solar-energy units.

On May 22, 1972, Grumman Allied Industries opened the doors to a 100,000-square-foot manufacturing facility in Montgomery, Pennsylvania. Bob Somerville, at the time general manager of the Montgomery facility and currently president of Grumman Allied Industries, moved the production of motor homes from another Grumman Allied plant in Portsmouth, Rhode Island, and started production in this new facility. After one month of operation, and the hiring of 30 people, this area was hit by the Agnes Flood. The company released all of its employees to help the community and offered assistance to those who needed help.

Bill McLean, present general

The Grumman Kubvan is the country's first all-aluminum, front-wheel-drive, diesel-powered vehicle. Six of the minivans are produced daily.

manager of the plant, was appointed to that position in January 1973. Bill transferred from Grumman Aerospace, Long Island, after serving there for 28 years.

In September 1975 the area was once again hit by a flood. The company released 40 vehicles to employees, neighbors, civil defense units, and the fire department to aid in the evacuation of homes and businesses; all of the vehicles were returned in excellent condition.

In 12 years of operation this facility has been involved in many

product lines. Some of the products manufactured were 500 motor homes, 200 minibuses, many ambulances, and over 4,000 truck bodies. Current truck body production is 10 units per day.

The plant also functioned as the major structural repair facility during the reinforcement program for the Grumman Flexible 870 bus. During this program many instructors and students from the Williamsport Area Community College were employed. Over 1,500 units were completed at the Montgomery facility.

The latest addition to the vehicle product line is a minivan called the Kubvan—the first all-aluminum, front-wheel-drive, diesel-powered vehicle in the country. It is EPA-certified at 40.4 miles per gallon. This vehicle is being produced at the rate of six a day and is made specifically for commercial use.

Grumman Allied Industries, Inc., still has 18 of the original 30 employees at its Montgomery facility. The current work force measures 275 people. Grumman attributes its Montgomery plant's success to the attitude and resourcefulness of its employees, good community relations, and the firm's responsiveness to changes.

The ambulance, van, and motor home shown here are just three of the many commercial and recreational vehicles produced by Grumman Allied Industries, Inc.

GLYCO INC.

When Charles L. Huisking left his first and only job on January 1, 1910, to go into business for himself, his employer's parting words were, "My boy, you'll starve to death." It was a prophesy that never came true. Charles Huisking lived another 60 years; and when he died he left behind a rich heritage, which included the company known today as Glyco Inc.

Chas. L. Huisking & Co., Inc., began in 1910 as a drug-brokerage firm with two employees, one at $10 a week and the other, a stenographer, at $5 a week. Rent for the office was $27 a month. During World War I the enterprise built a solid reputation as a reliable supplier of drugs for the allied nations. After the war it became an importer and distributor, as well as an exporter.

Huisking continued to explore development of a manufacturing arm for his products. In 1958 he acquired Glyco Products, Inc., a small New York firm founded in 1927. Glyco had moved to Williamsport in 1952, after purchasing the former Keystone Tanning & Glue plant from Jaylen Corporation. Nine buildings and some smaller auxiliaries, with floor space of 145,000 square feet, occupied the 8.5-acre site. Another 28-acre tract adjacent to the plant was acquired from Pennsylvania Railroad.

A fatty acid manufacturing plant in Painesville, Ohio, was purchased in 1965, thus giving Glyco a source for the raw materials needed to manufacture its products in Williamsport.

In December 1961 Glyco was organized and incorporated under the laws of the Commonwealth of Pennsylvania, but continued to be operated as a wholly owned subsidiary of Chas. L. Huisking & Co., Inc.

Huisking accurately predicted the rapid growth of the drug, cosmetic, and food-additive industries—and structured the company and its products to serve these markets. Today Glyco products are sold in 18 markets, with the principal ones being the food, cosmetic, textile, and plastics industries. Most of Glyco's products are derivatives of natural ingredients and are found in the home in such everyday items as shampoo, chewing gum, ice cream, doughnuts, polyester, records, toys, and garden hose.

Glyco remains a privately owned company with executive offices in Norwalk, Connecticut. William W. Huisking, the entrepreneur's son, is chairman of the board. The corporation has grown and adapted to changing times and market conditions. It is a tribute to the business acumen of its founder that the Glyco of today is strong and healthy—although totally different from the organization he formed in 1910, when he was just 24 years old.

At its Williamsport site, Glyco employs between 150 and 200 people. Plant personnel work closely with local civil-defense, fire, and police departments to ensure the safety of Glyco's workers and its neighbors.

The company's research and development laboratories in Williamsport are staffed by highly qualified personnel and are provided the most sophisticated analytical equipment in order to assure Glyco's products are effective and meet government standards and specifications.

Glyco's growth and expansion at Williamsport reflect the corporation's commitment to the area, as well as its involvement as a responsible member of the business community.

Charles L. Huisking, who went to work at age 13, and founded the business at age 24 that eventually became Glyco Inc.

An aerial view of Glyco's Williamsport manufacturing plant. The research and development laboratories are on the left.

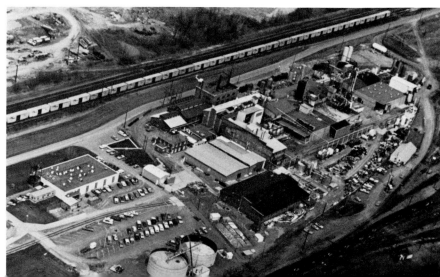

GRIT PUBLISHING COMPANY

In 1882 Dietrick Lamade, an assistant foreman at the Williamsport *Daily Sun and Banner,* began work on a Saturday afternoon supplement for the daily paper. Its name? *Grit.*

The supplement, however, found little favor beyond the city limits. In 1884 Lamade and two others purchased the foundering publication for a total of about $1,500. They then embarked on a long and fruitful endeavor.

That is not to say there were not difficulties. There were many. For example, there were eight changes in partnership in the first year alone.

Nevertheless, through some innovative marketing and plenty of hard work, Lamade and his staff turned things around. Through a gift giveaway, *Grit's* circulation was boosted from 4,000 to 14,000 in one six-month stretch.

After that, *Grit's* popularity grew steadily. Circulation reached 100,000 in 1900, 300,000 in 1916, and 500,000 in 1934.

Lamade died in 1938, but that didn't spell the end of *Grit's* success. His sons and their sons continued to run the business for decades.

In 1944 the paper was converted to a tabloid. The local edition went tabloid in 1946.

Grit Publishing Company was among the nation's leaders in pioneering offset printing. An ultramodern web offset press was installed in a new plant at the foot of Maynard Street in 1963.

That June, full-color pictures began appearing in the national edition. The first full-color front page of *Grit* featured the American flag.

The Lamade family's ownership of

Grit Publishing Company's West Third Street plant.

the firm ended in 1981 with the purchase of *Grit* by ADVO-System, Inc., of Hartford, Connecticut.

Two years later Stauffer Communications, Inc., of Topeka, Kansas, purchased Grit Publishing Company and ADVO Print, Inc. SCI already published a national tabloid called *Capper's Weekly.* When *Grit* joined Stauffer's national media division, the two publications offered a combined circulation of more than one million in small town and rural America.

Under SCI leadership, ADVO Print, Inc., was renamed Grit Printing Company. SCI leadership expanded the ability of the firm to further utilize its high-speed web press, as well as expand the capabilities and development of its commercial printing department.

The new leadership also enabled

Grit's marketing department to function independently in offering customers a book club, insurance packages and other consumer goods.

Finally, this restructuring divided the tabloid into two separate publications—the *Grit* and the *Sunday Grit.* The separation enabled each to better follow SCI's directive to become actively involved in the community.

The *Grit* is a vital part of the everyday lives of the citizens of the communities it serves—small-town and rural America. The *Sunday Grit* is deeply committed to the well-being of the communities it serves—14 counties in Central Pennsylvania.

Grit Publishing Company was among the nation's leaders in pioneering offset printing. An ultramodern web offset press was installed in the firm's plant on Maynard Street in 1963.

SHOP-VAC CORPORATION

The original Shop-Vac evolved from a need created by a product line of the Craftool Company, the parent of Shop-Vac Corporation.

That enterprise was founded by Martin Miller in 1953, to produce a line of craft machines for schools and the professions. His need for a vacuum-cleaning system that could be attached to the grinding and polishing equipment resulted in the development of the Shop-Vac. The inventor found it could be used for picking up dirt and debris around the shop, and thus designed the portable Shop-Vac. Martin Miller, who was previously an artist-craftsman and salesman, recognized the potential of the unit and went out to sell the concept.

The feasibility of a shop vacuum was not easy to convey, but over a period of years there was enough interest and sales generated to organize Shop-Vac Corporation to produce the equipment. Through a series of moves that started with a small factory in Brooklyn, New York, the company based its production in Wood-Ridge, New Jersey. A number of years later it expanded to a new location in Hackensack, New Jersey.

In 1969 Shop-Vac relocated and consolidated all its manufacturing operations into a modern plant in the Williamsport Industrial Park. The facility later doubled in size to its current quarter-million square feet, and today is the world corporate headquarters of the company.

The firm subsequently extended into California, Canada, England, Ireland, France, and Germany. It expanded its operation to include modern motor-manufacturing and plastic-modeling facilities.

Shop-Vac purchased the Goblin brand of vacuums, which had evolved from the first vacuum made in England. It is one of the oldest,

best-known names in its field in that country.

Today Shop-Vac Corporation is a multinational enterprise operating in 10 locations in six countries, and shipping to almost every country in the western world. It was awarded the coveted Army/Navy "E" Award by the United States government in 1982, in recognition of its performance and excellence in export.

From the organization's small beginnings to its present international scope, the founder has been personally involved in every aspect of the growth and development of the business. Martin Miller is chairman of the board; his sons, Jonathan and Matthew, are the presidents of the North American Group and the European Group, respectively.

For over 30 years Shop-Vac has been a leader in vacuum-cleaner technical innovation and market development—offering quality products that provide excellent value, produced with a manufacturing technology second to none. It fabricates a broad range of heavy-duty consumer vacuum cleaners, plus a complete line of industrial and commercial units.

Pioneering the industry with the

Shop-Vac Corporation's international headquarters and manufacturing facilities are located in the Williamsport Industrial Park.

first low-cost, consumer-oriented wet/dry vacuum, the firm is the world's largest manufacturer of that product.

Shop-Vac Corporation is one of the few local companies to have its world headquarters in Williamsport, Pennsylvania.

Shop-Vac founder Martin Miller (center), chairman of the board; Matthew Miller (left), president of the European Group; and Jonathan Miller (right), president of the North American Group.

LAMCO COMMUNICATIONS INC.

Communications has always been Lamco's business. For most of its corporate life, information was through the printed word. Today, however, the communication is through sights and sounds—television and radio. Lamco Communications Inc. is an old company with a new name.

The firm traces its origins to a weekly newspaper called *Grit,* which first appeared in Williamsport on December 16, 1882. However, after little more than a year, the paper verged on collapse.

Dietrick Lamade, a German immigrant who had worked as a printer since he was 13, saw possibilities in *Grit* and purchased it. While the paper initially was sold only in and around Williamsport, Lamade's leadership and efforts resulted in its circulation expanding far beyond the West Branch Valley. Copies began to reach many states.

The newspaper incorporated on June 1, 1892, as Grit Publishing Company. Due to its growth, a four-story office building and printing plant were constructed at Third and William streets, and by the turn of the century *Grit's* circulation passed the 100,000 mark. Soon afterward the paper became available in every state, thereby making it a national publication.

In 1936 leadership of the firm was turned over to Lamade's sons: George R. was named president, and Howard J., vice-president. Ralph R. Cranmer became president in 1962.

Pioneering in offset printing in the early 1960s, *Grit* attracted interest in the printing industry both in the United States and abroad.

The firm in 1977 acquired Appalachian Broadcasting Corporation in Bristol, Virginia, which operates station WCYB-TV, an NBC affiliate and the leading station in the Tri-City area of

Bristol-Kingston-Johnson City.

On March 31, 1981, the corporation sold its printing and publishing operations, as well as the name *Grit,* and changed its identity to Lamco Communications Inc. Three months later it acquired Pennsylvania Radio, Inc.—owner of radio stations WLYC and WILQ-FM, both with studios at 353 Pine Street.

Serving the greater Lycoming County area, WLYC and WILQ-FM offer their own special blend of entertainment and service features to the community. WLYC, 1050 AM, features the nationally syndicated adult-music format, Al Hamm's "Music of Your Life," which offers the nostalgic and contemporary standards from the 1940s through current favorites. WILQ, 105.1 FM, is the region's favorite radio station, broadcasting stereo country music 24 hours a day. As Lycoming County is in the heart of the rural

Dietrick Lamade, publisher of the Grit *from 1882 to 1938. By the turn of the century the newspaper had grown from a local to a national publication.*

Northeast, many of the tunes correspond to the life-styles of its citizenry.

WILQ and WLYC devote a great deal of time to meeting the needs of the community's residents. Promotion of projects, dedicated to enhancing life in Lycoming County, range from the *Hiawatha* boat ride

In 1936 the leadership of the company passed to Dietrick Lamade's sons. George R. (below) was named president and Howard J. (below right) became vice-president. Photos courtesy of Kaiden Kazanjian.

to the Lycoming County trash-collection campaign.

In March 1984 Lamco acquired Big River Broadcasting Company in Greenville, Mississippi—operator of WXVT-TV, a CBS affiliate serving the Mississippi Delta area.

During its years of producing a national newspaper or managing broadcast facilities, the corporation never lost interest in the city of its origin. Indeed, the company has been a vital part of Williamsport's progress through the years.

One of Lamco's proudest contributions is the 43-acre site it gave to Little League Baseball in 1959. The South Williamsport site is the international headquarters for that organization's worldwide program, as well as home for the annual Little League World Series. Little League proclaimed the stadium as Howard J. Lamade Field, in tribute to the benefactor who served on its board of directors for many years.

Another proud moment was in 1980 when Lycoming College named its new gymnasium for George R.

Lamade, longtime president and publisher. The honor was in recognition of the company's strong financial backing over a long period of time, and of his personal support of the college's long-range development.

Lamco executives have served on the boards of many civic organizations, among them Lycoming United Way, Williamsport-Lycoming Chamber of Commerce, The Williamsport Hospital, Divine Providence Hospital, Guthrie Medical Center, James V. Brown Library, YMCA, YWCA, Park Home, Salvation Army, Blind Association, the Williamsport Home for the Aged, American Red Cross, and The Repasz Band.

They have also served as school directors, college trustees, and board members of the Williamsport Foundation, the Lycoming Foundation, Lycoming Industrial Development Authority, and the Lycoming County Planning Commission. In addition, the civic-minded businessmen have chaired many capital development

drives for YWCA, YMCA, the library, and local hospitals.

Dietrick, George, Howard, J. Robert, and Howard Jr. have all been active in Freemasonry. Each has attained the honor of becoming a 33 Degree Mason.

Today, after 101 years of progress, Lamco looks to the future with eager anticipation to further growth and expansion. The closely held corporation maintains its headquarters in the Williamsport Building at 460 Market Street.

Officers of Lamco Communications Inc. are Andrew W. Stabler, Jr., president and general manager; James H. Lamade, vice-president and treasurer; Howard J. Lamade, Jr., vice-president and secretary; Robert J. Cunnion, Jr., vice-president; and Ruth S. Mitchell, assistant secretary.

The Lamco Communications Inc. board of directors includes (from left to right) Marshall R. Noecker, Ralph R. Cranmer, James H. Lamade, Andrew W. Stabler, Jr., Howard J. Lamade, Jr., J. Robert Lamade, and Robert J. Cunnion, Jr.

NEYHART'S/MARY LIB'S

When A.B. Neyhart and Emanuel Andrews opened their little hardware store on 145 West Third Street in 1870, no one would have imagined the enterprise would continue in the same location for 113 years. In 1905 Neyhart sold the business to two employees, W.R. Fisher and E.E. Cowdride.

H. Merrill Winner purchased the hardware store in 1920. His two brothers, William A. and Hiram F., joined him. The three men established a wholesale hardware business in conjunction with the retail operation. A short time later they expanded into major appliances on both the wholesale and retail levels. Copeland refrigerators and Maytag washers were the first large appliances sold.

The Maytag washer franchise for the area was acquired by purchasing the stock of a Harrisburg company in 1923. Wholesale/retail outlets were established in three locations. Two of the gasoline-powered washers were put on a truck, and two men would take them out and "blind" canvass the countryside. Neyhart's had 12 trucks at that time and sold 250 units a month, primarily by canvassing. The firm bought washers by the carload, and was Maytag's largest distributor.

In the early days of Winner ownership, Neyhart's went through a period of rapid diversification and acquisition. In 1926 it purchased a furniture company, and a short time later the entire stock of the Lewisburg Chair Company. During the next few years three local hardware stores were acquired.

As the business grew, several additions were built that enlarged the facility to 35,000 square feet of selling space for furniture, appliances, carpeting, floor covering, housewares, hardware, and gifts.

A new field was added in 1935 when a friend, James Foresman, saw bottled-gas operations in Florida. The industry was in its infancy, and the founder of Phillips Petroleum helped Winner establish the Rural Gas Company—one of the first bottled-gas companies in the country. They established dealerships all over Pennsylvania and New York. A distribution plant was built on Reach Road, which was later moved to Route 15 below South Williamsport to comply with a new city ordinance banning gas operations in the city.

The 1936 flood devastated Neyhart's. The building was flooded and the safe—with all the accounts receivable in it—floated away. However, for years afterward customers came in to pay the bills they owed. During the flood the Wanook Ice Cream Company next door exploded and burned to the waterline, taking Neyhart's with it. While Neyhart's was reconstructed

---

In 1920 H. Merrill Winner bought the hardware store that was the forerunner of Neyhart's diverse interests today.

Charles J. Stockwell, president of Neyhart's and the Rural Gas Company.

---

immediately, the new facility was flooded in 1948.

Even with its setbacks—two major floods, two disastrous fires, and the Depression—the venture survived and grew. The wholesale business was expanded into 17 counties, and sold Norge, Zenith, Fedders, Warm Morning Heaters, and other name brands to 27 dealers.

Winner died in January 1968, and his son-in-law, Charles Stockwell, joined Neyhart's as president. The company continued the retail and Rural Gas lines, and added a realty firm.

In March 1983 the Neyhart's Building was sold. Mary Lib's retail gift shop is now located across the street. The Rural Gas Company has 21 dealerships around Pennsylvania; the local facility is on Route 15 South, with offices at 301 Walnut Street.

HOPE ENTERPRISES, INC.

When Neil Armstrong first set foot on the moon, he said it was "one small step for man—one giant step for mankind." In 1952 a small group of people in Williamsport took the "one small step" for the mentally, physically, and socially handicapped. They formed an organization that six years later would open what was believed to be one of the first schools in the country for retarded children.

Mrs. Max C. Miller spearheaded the small group, comprised of volunteers who were concerned parents of retarded children, social workers, and teachers, which originated the Lycoming County Chapter of the Pennsylvania Association for Retarded Children. (In 1960 the name was changed to the Lycoming County Society for Retarded Children.) Meetings were held at various sites made available through community support, and the group moved from one location to another as the number of participants grew.

In 1958 the organization finally obtained a permanent home after the School of Hope was constructed at 1536 Catherine Street. Additions to the school were made in 1962 and 1974 in order to accommodate

the increased enrollment. In 1981 the building was renamed the Dr. Max C. Miller Training Center, in honor of one of the agency's pioneers.

Realizing the need for additional services for the handicapped, a newly formed organization, Enterprises for the Handicapped, purchased a building at 136 Catawissa Avenue in July 1971. This became the first sheltered workshop in the area. Only 12 individuals were served in the beginning; however, for the first time in their lives, these people received pay for performing work. Another giant step was taken.

Other giant steps followed that would have been unimaginable a few years earlier. In August 1973 the first group home was opened by the Lycoming County Society for Retarded Children at 713 Hepburn Street. It served eight adult women.

The Lycoming County Society for Retarded Children, and Enterprises for the Handicapped merged to form Hope Enterprises, Inc., in 1974. The new agency has grown into a large organization with a staff of approximately 175, and almost 500 individuals are served annually in a number of different programs in Lycoming, Clinton, and Tioga counties. In 1975 a center was opened in Renovo to provide sheltered employment and work activities for handicapped individuals in that area. Five years later the Tioga County Partners in Progress in Wellsboro merged with Hope Enterprises.

Residential Services continued to

expand. It now serves over 120 individuals in 20 residence homes and apartments.

The Industrial Division provides sheltered employment and vocational services for more than 150 individuals daily. In addition to subcontract work, Hope Enterprises manufactures its own proprietary products, provides custodial services for the Federal Building and other facilities, operates the laundry at Divine Providence Hospital, and operates Photo Licensing Centers in Lock Haven and Wellsboro.

Merle S. Arnold, president, has administered Hope Enterprises since 1969. James K. Gates II is currently chairman of the board of directors.

This historical review is sponsored in recognition, and in honor, of those individuals and organizations that have inspired and nurtured the development of services to the handicapped through Hope Enterprises.

CHAIRMEN OF HOPE ENTERPRISES
FROM 1952 TO 1984

Mrs. Frank J. Toohey	Marvin H. Staiman
Mrs. Henry Hessert	David L. Stroehmann
Philip N. Pulizzi	Robert B. Lenhart
Bernard Levinson	John T. Detwiler
Dr. Max C. Miller	Alfred J. Economu
James K. Gates II	

The board of directors of the Lycoming County Chapter of the Pennsylvania Association for Retarded Children in 1958 consisted of (left to right) Rabbi Emanuel Kramer, Relda Hazzard, Olga Ladika, Mrs. Meyer Levine, Oscar Horn, William Wilkinson, Dr. Max C. Miller, and Bernard Levinson.

The original School of Hope building was constructed in 1958 with additions made in 1962 and 1974. The school was renamed Dr. Max C. Miller Training Center in 1981 in honor of one of the agency's pioneers.

LITTLE LEAGUE BASEBALL®

Little Leaguers are found in all corners of the globe, playing baseball and softball during the active summer months. For over 2.5 million participants, the words "Little League" are magical, as magical as its humble beginning in Williamsport in 1939.

Organized baseball was previously the domain of teenagers and adults, while children, who had always been mesmerized by the sport, fended for themselves on corner lots or wherever space would permit. As a result, a group of concerned parents and other adults decided to do something about the lack of organized sports for youth. Little League Baseball would be the vehicle for a program to promote the attributes of fair play, good sportsmanship, and a desire to excel through friendly competition. The seed had been planted from which a giant in the world of sports would emerge.

The Little League program that summer of 1939 consisted of three teams. Its founders were able to convince several local businesses of the benefits of an organized baseball program for youth, thereby giving the endeavor its first sponsors—still the backbone of Little League operations today. During that initial year, a $35 donation bought uniforms for all three teams.

The community effort was an instant success. Word spread, and the following year neighboring Jersey Shore founded its first Little League. Growth was stymied by World War II; however, by 1946 there were 12 such programs—all in Pennsylvania.

The following year Little League expanded into New Jersey. Rapid growth continued. Within a year there were 95 leagues in six states; by 1949, 13 states had 198 leagues. In 1951 a group was organized in British Columbia, Canada, the first

outside the United States. A year later a league from Montreal became the first foreign entry in the Little League World Series.

Since its origination in 1947, the Little League World Series has been considered the most noted event of the entire Little League schedule. The first tournament was won by the Maynard Little League of Williamsport, which played against one New Jersey and 10 Pennsylvania teams.

That same year a search for a safe, rubber-cleated baseball shoe led to an association with U.S. Rubber Company. Company officials developed a safe baseball shoe for youngsters, establishing Little League as a leader in sports safety. In further recognition of the value of the organization, U.S. Rubber Company became its national sponsor. This entailed underwriting the World Series, defraying most of the cost of maintaining the headquarters, conducting clinics, and providing teaching and training aids for the thousands of adult volunteers in the program.

By 1955 Little League was found in every state, as well as in England, Germany, Venezuela, and Mexico. It is currently played in 25 countries and territorial possessions throughout the world.

The Little League Foundation became the sole sponsor of the program in 1956. This assured the

Eight teams from around the world participate in the Little League World Series every August.

continuity and support of Little League for generations of participants yet to come.

Monterrey, Mexico, in 1957 was the first foreign winner of the Little League World Series, and the first team to attain consecutive titles when they won again the following year. The World Series continues to bring together teams from four regions in the United States (East, West, Central, and South), as well as four foreign regional winners representing Canada, Latin America, Europe, and the Far East—making it the only true World Series event in all of baseball. Having been televised 22 consecutive years by ABC Sports, it is an international celebration

The Little League headquarters building handles administrative work for leagues around the world.

where ballplayers 11 and 12 years old transcend cultural and language barriers during a week of friendly competition.

The initial Little League program, for ballplayers 8 to 12 years old, soon found its graduates clamoring for a similar plan for older age groups. In 1961 Senior League Baseball was created for youngsters 13 to 15 years old, and in 1968 Big League Baseball was organized for ages 16 to 18.

In response to the desires of many girls to participate in organized sports, Little League and Senior Little League Softball programs were instituted in 1974. With the 1980 season, Big League Softball became available for the large number of graduates of the new Little League Softball divisions.

The organization has grown to include instructional Tee Ball for children aged 6 to 10 years, and a separate Junior League Baseball program for 13-year-old players.

As the entire Little League movement has grown, so has the administration in order to accommodate the 2.5 million youths now playing every year. The largest youth sports program in the world today, it requires several offices to maintain close and efficient contact with its thousands of affiliate leagues.

The international headquarters remains in Williamsport, while regional and state centers have been constructed in St. Petersburg, Florida; Waco, Texas; San Bernardino, California; and Lisle, Illinois. Little League complexes will soon be constructed in Indianapolis, Indiana; and in the Town of Newburgh, New York.

Little League has been honored by being the only youth sports organization to be chartered by the federal government. In 1959 President Dwight D. Eisenhower proclaimed the first "Little League Baseball Week" the second week in June, now celebrated every year by members throughout the country.

Over 450 Major League Baseball players and countless leaders in politics, business, and industry are Little League graduates. All that identifies the association—its growth, endorsements, and achievements since 1939—is memorialized in the Peter J. McGovern Little League Museum at the headquarters complex in Williamsport.

McGovern was Little League's first full-time president, as well as its chairman of the board from 1956 to 1983. It was during his tenure, and through his farsighted leadership, that Little League Baseball achieved unprecedented growth and unequaled prestige in the arena of youth sports.

The new Little League Museum is a popular attraction for baseball enthusiasts of all ages.

Now involving over 2.5 million participants each year, Little League Baseball was founded in Williamsport in 1939.

RALPH S. ALBERTS COMPANY, INC.

The Ralph S. Alberts Company, Inc., is a job shop that manufactures molds, prototypes, parts, and tooling in all types of plastics for many and varied industries. It specializes in injection molding, vacuum forming, fiberglass lay-ups, epoxy and urethane tooling, as well as molding and casting of rigid or flexible urethane-foam parts.

The firm had its origin in 1962 when Ralph S. Alberts, then a manufacturers' representative for eight plastics companies, saw a need for plastic tooling and fixtures among industries that he visited. Piper Aircraft had such a need, and supported his ideas with an interest in purchasing such parts. With this encouragement, Alberts began experimenting in a small workshop in the basement of his home.

His first customer was Gentex Corporation in Carbondale, Pennsylvania. Tooling and fixtures for aircraft and tank helmets used by the armed services were developed and manufactured.

A corporation was formed and was moved to its present location at 97 Eck Circle in 1967. The business is based on the idea of making dimensionally stable molds and parts without the high cost of machining. When prototyping with plastic, modifications can be made to molds economically before more expensive high-production molds are made.

Although the company has had steady growth, two major expansions have occurred. In 1970 RCA Corporation became a steady customer for parts and fixtures for its equipment-development division in several of its plants. This created new types of experimental work and provided exposure to other large industries.

In 1978 a different aspect of the

Epoxy molds are used for short-run, injection-molded parts.

operation developed when Hershey Park approached the organization to manufacture replacement parts for amusement-park rides. Now molded foam-rail padding, seats, side cushions and headrests, semirigid urethane steering wheels, and urethane coatings produced by the company can be seen in amusement parks throughout Pennsylvania, New York, New Jersey, Virginia, and Maryland. Some large ride manufacturers have now become customers.

A retail product, the Down's Fly Box, has been developed and manufactured recently. This new item has proven to be very popular among fishermen, and has warranted an article in *Flyfisherman's Magazine.*

Individually molded parts produce an assembly used as a checking fixture for an industrial customer.

In 22 years the Ralph S. Alberts Company, Inc., has expanded to a 4,200-plus-square-foot facility housing highly technical machinery. With its founder as president, the firm has 12 skilled employees managed by Ed Alberts and Mike Downs. The precision products they create reflect the corporation's motto, "Pride in Workmanship—Today and Tomorrow," which helps account for its steady growth.

A comment by Ed Alberts about the new amusement-park venture reflects this philosophy: "We've had fun because most of the work we do is behind the scenes; we do work and it leaves here and we never see it again. Now we have something the public can see. It's unique and we are proud of it."

A seat for an amusement-park ride is molded with the latest and most modern equipment available.

DATA PAPERS, INC.

Continuous rows of corn gave way to continuous forms in November 1969 when Data Papers, Inc., opened its printing plant on what was once part of Bryfogle's farm.

Founder Joe E. Hume had been director of marketing and sales for a Paramus, New Jersey, business-forms firm. He and a group of investors, primarily from the Williamsport area, felt that there was a definite need for a manufacturer of high-quality custom continuous forms strategically located to serve the mid-Atlantic area. The Muncy location would serve a circle of customers within a 300-mile radius, an area containing about one-third of the nation's population at the time.

Production in the new 20,000-square-foot printing plant, the first building in the Muncy Industrial Park, started with two major pieces of machinery. The five employees drew $870 for the first weekly payroll. Today there are 12 major pieces of machinery in a 40,000-square-foot building. The 110 employees, in three locations, receive an annual payroll of approximately two million dollars.

In the spring of 1977 Data Papers, Inc., purchased Paper Power, Inc. The Buffalo firm—which manufactures multipart, snap-out forms—serves the same general market as the parent organization.

Keystone Business Forms Company, located on the second floor of the Vannucci Building at 318 West Fourth Street in Williamsport, was formed in 1968. The subsidiary is a retail distributor to end users of continuous and other business forms in a 12-county area.

In order to open a new market, in the fall of 1983 Data Papers

purchased a six-color Harris offset press. Extensive marketing research had indicated a growing market for custom promotional printing used by the direct-mail industry. Demand was so great that early in 1984 a second six-color press was ordered.

Over the years the company has won numerous awards from associations and suppliers, and in 1980 was named Manufacturer of the Year by the National Business Forms Association. Data Papers president Joe Hume has been active in the association, serving as associate vice-president and on the board of directors and its executive committee.

Early in the summer of 1984 Data Papers, Inc., opened a new plant in Forest City, North Carolina. It serves a 300-mile circle of customers in such cities as Richmond, Virginia; Savannah and Columbus, Georgia; Huntsville, Alabama; Nashville, Tennessee; Louisville, Kentucky; Cincinnati, Ohio; and Morgantown, West Virginia.

For 14 years the corporation's continuous growth has been one of the stabilizing factors in Williamsport's business community. Employment has increased steadily, without any layoffs, as Data Papers, Inc., has become well known and respected in the continuous-forms industry.

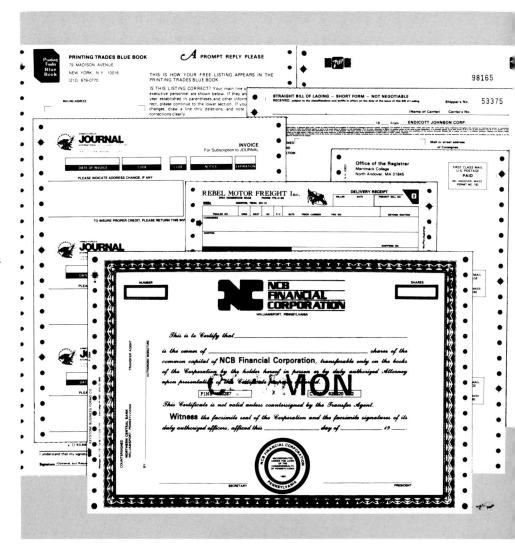

Computer forms produced by Data Papers, Inc.

KEYSTONE FRICTION HINGE COMPANY

By 1862 the rebuilt, expanded, and greatly strengthened Susquehanna Boom—after being severely damaged by the 1860 and 1861 floods—which gave great impetus to industries that processed and used lumber, also created a demand for numerous kindred supply, service, and manufacturing enterprises. One man to get an early start in the lumber-related business was a German immigrant named George Luppert, who in the 1860s founded the Keystone Furniture Company.

Valentine Charles Luppert, his son, worked as a designer and wood-carver in the factory. His work in designing dressers and washstands created a need for a hinge that would hold a mirror in a fixed position between upright standards. To achieve this he riveted two pieces of metal, which were bent at right angles, tightly together. The patented invention was known as the Luppert friction hinge, due to the tightly riveted parts held together by friction.

Thomas Duer, a Baltimore jobber who had married a Gibson woman from Williamsport, visited the community frequently. He saw the friction hinge, and requested permission to market it. The item became so popular that the demand was more than could be produced in the furniture factory's basement.

In 1905 the Keystone Friction Hinge Company was originated, and a building was constructed a few hundred feet upriver from the furniture factory. As the new venture grew, the problem of skilled help became of prime importance. There were two plants in the area that had begun manufacturing metal items, the Bicycle Plant and Demorest Manufacturing Company. From the Demorest plant Luppert secured two excellent tool-and-die men—Ernest Orchard, who was

made plant manager, and Ernest Featherstone, who became the toolroom foreman.

The sons of these two machinists —both of whom had emigrated from England, arriving in Williamsport about 1909—learned the toolmaking trade in Keystone's apprentice program. Jim Orchard spent his working life at Keystone, while Hugh Orchard went with Sylvania. Charles and Art Featherstone went to Sylvania after finishing their apprenticeships.

The firm prospered through World War I and into the 1920s. During this period V.C. Luppert formed the Imperial Band Instrument Works; the Park, Keystone, and Rialto theaters; and the Keystone Food Products Company.

When the Great Depression struck, Luppert lost almost everything except the hinge company. That enterprise was saved by 10 prominent citizens who each put up $10,000 to satisfy creditors. They were James Graham, Robert Thorne, John McCormick, Senator Charles Sones, W.L. King, Irv Gleason, L.R. Gleason, Clarence Shope, Dietrick L. Lamade, and George Graf. With their help it was possible to avoid bankruptcy, and by 1939 the debts had been satisfied and all benefactors were paid.

The 1936 flood inundated the lower areas, and put the water level at three feet on the machine floor; in addition to extensive water damage to the equipment and raw materials, there was considerable deterioration of the building.

In June 1939 Grantham Taggart joined Keystone Friction Hinge Company as sales manager, and two years later became general manager. With the advent of World War II, he enlisted in the service. While Taggart was in Europe Luppert died, and the company was sold to

Dr. E. Lloyd Rothfuss and George Spotts as a partnership.

After the war's end Taggart returned, Lamont Seitzer joined the organization in production, and Miles C. MacGill was hired as comptroller. Also in 1946 another flood descended upon the plant, with water again reaching the three-foot level on the machine floor. The same adverse results were experienced as in 1936, as well as further problems with the deterioration of the building. Fortunately, the construction of dikes in the early 1950s put an end to the flooding problems.

Dr. Rothfuss acquired Spotts' interest in 1950, and operated the business as a sole proprietorship until 1965. During this period Keystone Friction Hinge Company grew modestly and continued to operate in the old plant, which had five separate levels with a series of ramps as the only means of moving

---

Valentine C. Luppert, son of the founder of the Keystone Furniture Company, invented the Luppert friction hinge which led to the Keystone Friction Hinge Company being established in South Williamsport.

One of the many styles of hinges manufactured at Keystone Friction Hinge Company.

materials from one level to another.

In 1965 Taggart, Seitzer, and MacGill purchased the firm from Dr. Rothfuss. They incorporated with Taggart as president, MacGill as vice-president and treasurer, and Seitzer as secretary.

It was immediately determined that new facilities and equipment were essential to Keystone Friction Hinge Company's prosperity. With the help of the Pennsylvania Industrial Development Authority, a new structure, on one level, was

erected at 520 Matthews Boulevard in South Williamsport. This proved to be a big boost, and business began to improve.

Edward J. Hannan joined the organization in 1970 as vice-president of engineering and sales. The product line changed more to custom work, with emphasis upon quality and service. Sales mounted rapidly, and the financial condition became quite satisfactory.

The firm was purchased in 1965 by longtime employees Miles C. MacGill, who became vice-president/treasurer; Grantham Taggart, president; and Lamont A. Seitzer, secretary.

In July 1977 Lamont Seitzer, Jr., and Creighton MacGill were taken into the corporation. They are sons of two of the principals. In May 1979 Seitzer left Keystone Friction Hinge Company to join a larger organization.

The facilities have been expanded —with additions built in '72, '74, '79, and '83. A contract has been signed for yet another addition. Upon its completion in September 1984, the plant will have a total area of 51,252 square feet. There will be over 70 employees.

Only two shareholders who are members of the board are not active in the daily operation of the plant. Herbert Liebman of Long Island, New York, an original stockholder in the new organization, is a jobber whose company has done business with Keystone since the 1920s. Thomas Humphries, who represents the firm in upper Illinois and Wisconsin, rounds out the corporate group. Previously associated with American Cabinet Hardware Company, and with many contacts in the industry, he has been most helpful in the growth of the concern.

Keystone Friction Hinge Company started with four or five people working in the furniture firm's basement. During the Korean War the maximum payroll of 82 was reached, and the corporation had $400,000 to $500,000 in annual sales. Today there are 67 employees and sales exceed $4 million a year.

In recent years efficiency in equipment and facilities has been stressed to make Keystone Friction Hinge Company as competitive as possible in the world market. An effort has been made to keep employment constant, and there have been practically no layoffs— 25 percent of the personnel have been with the firm over 20 years and 50 percent over 10 years.

CANDOR, YOUNGMAN, GIBSON & GAULT

Addison Candor

The law firm of Candor, Youngman, Gibson & Gault had its beginning

C. LaRue Munson

when Addison Candor and C. (Cyrus) LaRue Munson went into partnership on October 1, 1875, at 46 Pine Street.

Addison Candor was born in Lewistown, Pennsylvania, in 1852. He earned his A.B. from Princeton in 1873, and subsequently read law at the office of Allen and Gamble —the most prominent law firm in Williamsport at the time. He was admitted to the Bar in 1875. Upon the death in 1900 of Lycoming County Judge John J. Metzger, the governor tendered the judgeship to Candor; however, he refused it and Max L. Mitchell was appointed.

Born in Bradford, New York, in 1854, C. LaRue Munson graduated from Episcopal Academy in 1871. The young man received his L.L.B. from Yale Law School in 1875, where he was a guest lecturer on legal practices for a number of years. President of the Pennsylvania Bar Association in 1902, Munson died 20 years later in China.

Both founders had sons who joined the organization after graduation from law school. Edgar Munson was awarded an A.B. from Yale in 1904 and an L.L.B. from Yale Law School in 1907. The latter year he was also admitted to the Bar. Prior to his death in 1930, Edgar Munson served as president of E. Keeler Company, vice-president of Williamsport Wire Rope Company, and was a trustee of The Savings Institution.

John Grafius Candor graduated in 1902 with an A.B. from Princeton and in 1905 with an L.L.B. from the University of Pennsylvania Law School. In addition to his position as president of The Williamsport Hospital, he was a member of the board of directors of the West Branch Bank and The Savings Institution.

John C. Youngman, Sr., who earned a B.S. in economics from the

Edgar Munson

John G. Candor

John C. Youngman, Sr.

University of Pennsylvania Wharton School in 1924, obtained his L.L.B. from Harvard Law School in 1927. Between 1932 and 1935 he served as district attorney of Lycoming County, and in 1943 formed a partnership with John G. Candor and Harry R. Gibson in the firm of Candor, Youngman and Gibson. Active in community affairs, Youngman was instrumental in procuring dikes for the Williamsport area and in the formation of the Williamsport Sanitation Authority. Now nestor of the Bar, he has practiced law for 57 years.

Receiving a B.S. from Lafayette College in 1928, Harry R. Gibson three years later was awarded an L.L.B. from Columbia University. The young attorney began his career in New York City with the firm of Robert H. Montgomery Law Offices, remaining there a year before returning to Williamsport. He has practiced law for 53 years and has been active in community affairs—notably as president of The Williamsport Hospital and as a director of the Northern Central Bank.

John C. Gault attained his A.B. from Bucknell University in 1939 and his L.L.B. from Dickinson Law School in 1942. A member of the FBI during World War II, he became a partner in the firm in 1948. Gault has served in the community with the Boy Scouts, as a trustee of The Savings Institution, and as a director of Commonwealth Bank and Trust Company, N.A.

John C. Youngman, Jr., was awarded a B.S. at Yale University in 1956, and earned an L.L.B. from Harvard Law School in 1959—at which time he joined the law firm. He also has been active in civic affairs, including serving as school director for 10 years, and leading the fight for fluoridation of the city's water supply.

John C. Gault

Harry R. Gibson

John C. Youngman, Jr.

ALCAN CABLE

Alcan Cable had its beginning on May 1, 1939, when Central Cable Corporation began production in the former Susquehanna Silk Mill on Washington Avenue in Jersey Shore, Pennsylvania. The three Detwiler founders, David Roy, president; John G., treasurer; and William F. Jr., decided to specialize in manufacturing copper cables for utilities.

Jersey Shore was selected by the trio because of its ready access to a rapidly expanding market for the product. Pennsylvania had no other manufacturer of insulated wire and cable at the time.

The operation began with 50 to 60 young women operating braiding machines, which applied cotton to the wire. Then an asphalt coating, followed by one of wax, was applied.

An important factor in the growth of the company was the increasing impact of the Rural Electrification Administration, which spread electrical transmission lines into the countryside—using miles of cable. After John G. Detwiler became president in 1946, a major expansion step was taken with the opening of another plant at Freeport, Illinois, to serve the Midwest.

New materials and processes were constantly evolving. When aluminum became a rival to copper in 1950, bare and weatherproof aluminum cable were added to the line.

Plastic cable covering emerged in late 1952, and a few months later the first neoprene continuous vulcanizing line was installed. A third plant was opened at Tucker, Georgia, in 1961, and expanded in 1964.

Central Cable Corporation became a wholly owned subsidiary of Alcan Aluminium Limited of Montreal, Canada, in 1963.

A fabrication plant was constructed in 1964 on a 25-acre site in Williamsport's Industrial Park to house a large new wire mill. Growth was rapid, and from 1966 to 1967 a total of seven bays were added to

In 1964 Alcan Cable Company constructed a 250- by 400-foot fabrication plant on a 25-acre site in Williamsport's Industrial Park. As shown here, after several additions the facility now houses over 276,000 square feet of manufacturing space.

the building to provide more manufacturing and warehouse space on the east end of the facility.

The company's name was changed to Alcan Cable on January 1, 1966. Later that year construction of a modern wire-fabricating plant was started at Sunset/Whitney, California.

Also during 1966 plans were begun to build a high-speed rolling mill in a new addition to the

Alcan Cable's Jersey Shore plant.

Williamsport plant. The unique 80,000-ton-capacity Swedish rolling mill began producing a high-quality wire rod, the initial ingredient for manufacturing aluminum cable, in 1968; it is still one of the fastest methods used in the United States.

In 1968 a new research and development building became operational, in order to develop better and more sophisticated cable coverings. Another structure was built in 1971 for use as the division office, until the division headquarters office later moved to Atlanta.

The need for covered storage was met in 1972, with the erection of an inflatable warehouse adjacent to the plant. The current larger version was installed in 1978.

By 1984 the Alcan Cable facility in Williamsport had over 276,000 square feet of manufacturing space —including the 80,000-ton rod mill, a 15,000-ton cable plant, two research and development buildings, and the "Bubble Building" warehouse. Its 279 employees operate the plant 24 hours a day, seven days a week, producing cable and aluminum rods known and used internationally.

EUREKA PAPER BOX COMPANY, INC.

Eureka Paper Box Company, Inc., was founded in 1915 by Christian Stanton Knaur, John Lupert, and John Candor. The firm—located on Bridge Street, in the southern end of the Lowery Building—employed seven people making folding cartons: cake, candy, and food boxes; and other product containers. About three years later Knaur acquired Lupert's and Candor's interests in the enterprise. From the beginning annual sales ranged between $40,000 and $50,000, and the growing firm soon needed more space.

In 1925 it was moved to a 5,100-square-foot plant at 401 Eureka Place near Penn and Canal streets where 12 people were employed. A 13,000-square-foot section was added in 1933, at which time there were 23 employees. Sales escalated to $450,000 annually by 1950, and in 1952 a 5,600-square-foot office section was constructed.

Until 1962 printing was done on letterpress with cylinder and platen cutters. Brightwood folders folded the cut pieces. The plant then changed to offset printing. Between 1952 and 1968 Eureka had a steady uphill growth that saw annual sales reach $969,000.

A warehouse addition was built in 1968; however, a year later the 28,000 square feet were converted to production space for high-speed offset presses. More economical rolls of paper, instead of pre-cut sheets,

began to be purchased in 1972. A new high-speed cutter produced 2,400 sheets per hour. Since 1968 annual sales have accelerated to three million dollars, and employees have stabilized between 50 to 62, including 10 office personnel.

In order to expand the market area, two companies were purchased by Eureka. On July 14, 1976, Tri-State Paper Box in Middletown, New York, was acquired. On December 6, 1979, Schiefer Packaging, Inc., in Syracuse, New York, was bought. While both plants make the same type of products as Williamsport, Middletown produces corrugated boxes, as well.

Although the customer base for each plant is a 300-mile radius, there are other customers throughout the United States, such as Stroehmann, Sylvania, San Giorgio, Johnson & Johnson, Purex, and Tastycake.

Founder Christian Stanton Knaur was active in his company until his death in 1946. His son, Christian Mowry Knaur, was vice-president from 1935 to 1946, then served as

Still located on Eureka Place, Eureka Paper Box Company, Inc., now occupies this expanded facility.

president for two years. He was then succeeded by his son, Raymond Mowry Knaur, who was president from 1948 to 1961. Perry Knaur, Raymond's brother, then served as president while Raymond was chairman of the board from 1961 to 1969. Raymond and Perry retired in 1969. Maude O. Knaur, Raymond's aunt—who had served as secretary/treasurer since 1946—also retired in 1969. Richard Wagner joined the firm at that point as secretary/treasurer. Richard M. Knaur, Raymond's son, became president and chairman of the board. In 1970 Charles Simek joined the firm as an officer.

Eureka Paper Box has grown as an extended family business, and many employees have been with the company for over 40 years.

The year was 1935 and the company's 23 employees pose in front of the 401 Eureka Place location.

WOOLRICH, INC.

John Rich left England in 1811 for a better, freer life in the United States. Nineteen years and several attempts later, he finally established a business that not only survives 154 years later, but is internationally known for quality products that are preeminent in their field.

In 1830 John Rich and an associate started making woolen fabrics and blankets with a few machines operated by a half-dozen helpers using water power in a small building located on Plum Run in Clinton County. Since then the company has grown and diversified through eight wars and numerous periods of business prosperity and recession, under the active management of seven generations of the Rich family and their associates.

Rich and his son in 1845 relocated the firm to its present location, known as Woolrich, to obtain more water for power and textile finishing. The founder and his associates cut the timber and molded the bricks to erect an 80- by 45-foot, three-story facility. In the ensuing 139 years several additional buildings have been constructed— adjoining and dwarfing the original one.

In 1852 the second generation came into the company when Rich's son, John F., became a partner. From 1857 to 1864 the firm's name was John Rich and Son.

Following his father's retirement in 1864 and his younger brother's death in 1868, John F. Rich owned and operated the company until 1877. That year he took two of his sons, John and Michael B., into partnership under the name John F. Rich and Sons.

When John F. Rich died in 1888, his third son, W.F., became a partner in the company, which was renamed John Rich and Brothers in 1891.

Jennie Rich, John Rich's widow, became a partner upon his death in

The evolution of Woolrich, Inc., is depicted in this montage. John Rich (center) founded the firm in 1830, and the first woolen mill (center, left) at Woolrich is surrounded by examples of the company's products through the years. Montage created by The Advertising Bunch.

1895. Robert F. Rich, son of Michael B. Rich, became a partner in 1906. Ellery C. Tobias became a partner in 1910 upon the death of Jennie Rich.

John B. Rich, second son of Michael B. Rich, became a partner in 1919; John Woods Rich, son of the late John Rich, in 1923; and Fleming B. Rich, son of W.F. Rich, in 1927.

After 100 years as a co-partnership, on January 1, 1930, the company was incorporated as Woolrich Woolen Mills. Michael B. Rich was the firm's first president for seven months until his death, at which time William Fleming Rich became president until 1943.

Several reasons for incorporating were stated by Robert F. Rich: "To give our foremen and employees who have been in our employ for

five years the privilege of purchasing stock, and for better and more up-to-date business" to handle the size of the company and volume of sales. Two sewing plants and the woolen mill together employed 206 people plus salesmen.

In 1830, under John Rich's direction, the company began to provide durable, warm fabrics to be made into jackets, coats, and pants for those who worked outdoors, particularly the lumbermen. Yarns, coverlets, blankets, and flannel cloth were made, and socks were added later. By the turn of the century Woolrich started to manufacture and sell woolen garments. As the local lumbering employment dropped around 1910, garments for hunters and fishermen were designed and produced. By 1922 the famous Buffalo shirt was selling so well that a plant in Avis was built just to make wool shirts.

As the product line increased, sales coverage spread over the entire United States, including Alaska. By the end of its first century Woolrich was producing a diversified line of woolen outer wear.

The physical growth of the plant kept pace with the growth of products and sales. Through the years new facilities were constructed, in addition to acquisitions and expansions.

During world wars I and II Woolrich supplied blankets and coats for the Army; in 1983 it had a $2.1-million contract to make 130,000 Army blankets. It also had outfitted Admiral Richard E. Byrd's expeditions to the Antarctic in 1939, 1940, and 1941.

In 1948 the firm purchased Hall Brothers' sewing plant in Howard and leased it to Pearce Woolen Mills (an affiliate) to make wool shirts and boys' coats with Pearce labels, and caps and sportswear for the Woolrich line.

The oldest blanket company in the country, Pearce Woolen Mills (founded in 1805) was sold to Woolrich in 1928. From 1958 to 1960 manufacturing at the Latrobe plant was gradually closed out, and Pearce blankets are now made and merchandised in Woolrich.

In 1968 Roswell Brayton, Sr., became president, succeeding John Woods Rich, who had served since 1964. Robert Fleming Rich had preceded him since 1959, when Ellery Channing Tobias had retired after serving since 1943.

In July 1969 Woolrich began doing business with Bob Lamphere, president of Down Products Corporation. In 1972 a joint agreement established a down-insulated-apparel operation in Alliance, Nebraska, and a Denver distribution center. In October 1973 the firm, also doing business as Woolrich, Inc., acquired Down Products by an exchange of stock. It leased a plant in Seattle, two in Denver, and one in Broomfield. Woolrich has since purchased the Delaware plant in Denver. A new Broomfield plant, including offices for headquarters, was constructed to replace the leased one. The four facilities compose the firm's Western Division.

An outstanding accomplishment of the corporation's expansion and modernization program was the new 15,000-square-foot Outlet Store, built in 1979 at Woolrich. It has attracted shoppers from many states and even foreign visitors. Its success led to opening an Outlet Store in the Broomfield Sewing Plant, as well as the latest Outlet Store in Colorado Springs.

A feature in the Woolrich Outlet Store is the Outdoor Hall of Fame, established during its 150th anniversary in 1980. First inductees were Lowell Thomas, author, traveler, and newscaster; Leon Gorman, president of L.L. Bean;

James Whitaker, internationally recognized mountain climber; and Dr. Laurence Gould, polar explorer.

Woolrich, Inc., in 1984 operated in four states—with over 1,700 employees in Pennsylvania, and approximately 300 in the Western Division. Annual sales exceed $121 million. The modern woolen mill in Woolrich annually uses four million pounds of primarily American-raised wool to produce three million yards of fabric. While woolen fabric is still most important in the firm's garments, a wide variety of other fabrics are used each year in marketing over five million garments.

A very significant part of

A 1979 addition to Woolrich's operation was this 19,000-square-foot Outlet Store in Woolrich.

Woolrich's history has been the active role the Riches and other members of the business have taken for seven generations in community affairs, including religion, education, charities, hospitals, and politics. Every major drive for a new hospital, YMCA, Salvation Army, United Fund, Boy Scouts, and other community endeavors has been actively supported in time and money by members of Woolrich and donations from the company itself. Woolrich has especially been a strong supporter of Lycoming College during their mutual history.

In the words of president Roswell Brayton: "We are proud to be a part of the American free-enterprise system, and we believe in our democratic political institutions that have made Woolrich possible."

MARATHON CAREY-MCFALL COMPANY

In 1864 Dr. Elias R. Carey, a surgeon who served in the Civil War, ended his association with the medical profession due to religious beliefs. He established his own enterprise to manufacture lamps for horse-drawn carriages. The small firm of Carey & Company prospered, and in 1889 Edward Reukauf, Sr., became a partner. In the early 1900s the automobile was slowly replacing the horse and buggy. It soon became evident that carriage lamps, like horse-drawn carriages, would become just a pleasant memory and a collector's item.

Edward Reukauf, Jr., joined Carey & Company in 1906. He eventually was named president of the firm and served until 1956. It was at this time that Carey & Company started to manufacture curtains and curtain rollers for automobiles. In those days, no automobile worthy of the name could be found without curtains at its windows.

In 1919 Carey & Company was consolidated with McFall Manufacturing Company; four years later the organization was incorporated under the name Carey-McFall Company.

During that period the automobile manufacturers decided that curtains could be eliminated from all cars. Once again, a new product had to be found. Edward Reukauf, Jr., and Walter Stuber, who had become a member of the firm, decided that a great future lay in window coverings called "venetian blinds." The Philadelphia plant was much too small for this new venture, so in 1935 a plant in Montoursville was purchased.

The 65,000 square feet in several buildings had been a furniture factory. Carey-McFall bought it with the aid of The Committee of 100 and government incentives. The one-and-three-quarter-inch wooden slats of "Betsy Ross" blinds were hand-shaped and -carved. The area not only supplied the right kind of wood, but also provided the master craftsmen, such as Adolph and Connie Strittmatter, needed to do the delicate work.

It was a long, hard pull through the Depression years, but by 1941 Betsy Ross venetian blinds had

The Montoursville plant was occupied by the firm from 1935 to 1982.

become the best-known quality venetian blinds in the country. Later, in 1941, when the United States entered World War II, Carey-McFall converted to the production of war goods. The Montoursville plant manufactured camouflage materials and hand and rifle grenades. In 1945 the company was awarded the Army/Navy "E" Award for outstanding production contribution to the war effort.

William B. Reukauf joined Carey-McFall in 1945, after service with the Coast Guard. In 1949 he became vice-president, and in 1956 he was elected president and served until 1975.

During the late 1940s the shift started from wood slats to steel and then to aluminum slat blinds. Carey-McFall also manufactured roller shades, saw blades and key chains.

Quality jalousie windows and doors were manufactured during the early 1950s. Other products of that

This new office building for Marathon Carey-McFall Company was completed in 1983.

time included Alumashade, planter stakes, metal picket fences, trellises, canopies, trailer skirting, piano hinges, and novelty desk items. Carey-McFall became the largest lawn-edging supplier in the United States.

The products manufactured kept changing as the market changed. The 1960s saw fence filler, welded steel tubing, and tomato stakes as part of the mix. An important product introduced about that time was the aluminum Christmas tree. In 1964 the company began the manufacture of PVC brush Christmas trees. Carey-McFall became the second-largest manufacturer of artificial Christmas trees in the United States. The Christmas tree operation was sold in 1982.

In 1970 family ownership of Carey-McFall ended when Marathon Manufacturing Company of Houston, Texas, bought the concern and changed its name to Marathon Carey-McFall Company. Products being manufactured during the decade included strawberry planters and soakers, growing domes, plant

A few of the 1,700 blinds created each day.

and tool hangers, and artificial shrubbery.

BALI Mini Blinds had been introduced in the late 1960s and Marathon Carey-McFall is now the second-largest manufacturer of venetian blinds in the United States. The 1970s saw these versatile window coverings take all kinds of shapes, including arched, cylindrical, circular, A-frame, triangular, corner, inclined, and cut-out. Over 100 colors were developed.

Marathon Manufacturing Company was acquired by Penn Central Corporation in December 1979.

In May 1982 all manufacturing activities were consolidated into a 240,000-square-foot building on Route 405 between Montgomery and Muncy.

Sunlight Thru-Vu Enterprises, an Elmsford, New York, manufacturer of vertical and pleated fabric blinds, was acquired by Marathon Carey-McFall in July 1983, and moved to Montgomery. The vertical blinds are made of fabric, plastic, metal, or macrame in a wide variety of shapes and colors. The addition of vertical and pleated blinds positions the company as a

The Lutheran Brotherhood building in Minneapolis, Minnesota. Hundreds of Marathon Carey-McFall blinds adorn the windows.

major factor in the window-covering industry.

A new office building in Montgomery was completed in 1983, and the Montoursville facilities were sold. Assembly plants in Houston, Texas, and Chicago, Illinois, were added in 1984.

In 1984 Marathon Carey-McFall products were used in decorating over three million windows.

STONE CONTAINER CORPORATION
CORRUGATED CONTAINER DIVISION

In the spring of 1950 a native of Williamsport, with a geology degree from Princeton, returned home to establish a box factory after having worked with several large paper companies. Frank F. Winters founded Penn Central Containers, Inc., and rented a building from Darling Valve at the foot of Walnut Street. He started with four employees, manufacturing corrugated shipping containers and corrugated inner packing.

As the business grew, more space was needed. In 1956 an 18,000-square-foot building was constructed in the Garden View Section of Old Lycoming Township; five additions were subsequently added, expanding the plant to 65,000 square feet.

Initially the facility was a "sheet plant," which purchased sheets of corrugated board and made them into boxes. In 1957 the first corrugating machine was purchased and the plant became a "combiner plant," which uses large rolls of kraft liner board to make its own corrugated board to be formed into a wide variety of box styles.

Frank F. Winters was sole proprietor of Penn Central Containers, Inc., until his death in

An architectural rendering of the Stone Container plant in Williamsport's Industrial Park, which was first occupied in 1975.

1967, by which time the firm's sales were $1.75 million a year. Northern Central Bank operated the company for the estate's trust until May 1969; Stone Container Corporation of Chicago then acquired the facility and renamed it Stone Container Corporation-Corrugated Container Division.

The steady growth of the company again required more space for the 68 employees and a large volume of material. A 10-acre tract in the Industrial Park was purchased, and a 120,000-square-foot building was erected. It was occupied in 1975.

Stone Container Corporation is the number-one producer in the United States of kraft liner board. With five paper mills that manufacture the raw material for its 33 box plants, it is the sixth-largest manufacturer of corrugated containers and corrugated materials in the nation. The purchase of the Williamsport facility was part of the Chicago-headquartered firm's plan to expand its East Coast market; experienced workers in the area and

the excellent market within a 125-mile radius were major factors in the acquisition.

With the deregulation of the trucking industry, the market has opened up to a 200-mile radius. Fifty-two company trailers—plus common carriers when needed—haul products from the Williamsport Industrial Park plant, which records over $20 million annually in sales.

A 1984 expansion project added 15,000 square feet to house the 150 employees and modern equipment.

This montage reflects the various containers produced at Stone Container Corporation.

JAMES C. MANEVAL FUNERAL HOME

Clyde L. Maneval's decision to become a funeral director was the result of a friendship he formed as a young man with the undertaker in rural Liberty, Pennsylvania.

After attending Susquehanna University, Maneval graduated from Muncy Normal School. He taught school for several years in Liberty, then attended the Renouard Training School for Embalmers in New York City—where he was one of its first graduates in the class of May 1918.

During World War I Maneval entered the Army Medical Corps, aiding victims of the flu epidemic at Camp Lee, Virginia.

After the war he opened a combination furniture and funeral business in Everett, Pennsylvania, just east of Bedford. In a typical arrangement for that time, furniture was sold out front—and funeral preparations were made in the back. Undertakers usually had no facilities for viewings, which were held in the home of the deceased or at the church. Services were held either in the home, in church, at the cemetery, or in some combination of these.

In 1923 Maneval and Romaine Bastian established the Bastian and Maneval Funeral Home in Williamsport at 829 West Fourth Street. They dissolved the partnership in 1936, and the Maneval Funeral Home was founded that same year. The founder purchased the former Vandergrift Funeral Home at 711 West Fourth Street. The building, facing Annunciation Catholic Church, was originally a "Millionaires' Row" mansion.

Following in his father's footsteps, James C. Maneval graduated from the Cincinnati School of Mortuary

Clyde L. Maneval founded the Maneval Funeral Home in 1936.

James C. Maneval, son of the founder, carries on the family traditions.

Science prior to entering the service in World War II. After returning from the Air Force in 1945, James joined his father in the business; he became a partner in 1961.

The firm survived the 1936 and 1946 floods. Although the home was flooded, it was possible to work out of the hospitals until the water receded.

On the morning of December 1, 1959, an Allegheny Airlines plane crashed into Bald Eagle Mountain, directly south of the airport. There was only one survivor of the 26 on board, and Maneval Funeral Home joined other such establishments in working around the clock until all the bodies were identified and shipped to their proper destinations.

Clyde L. Maneval died on March 6, 1968. Later that same year James purchased a funeral home at 500 West Fourth Street, the present location.

The beautiful James C. Maneval Funeral Home is located at 500 West Fourth Street.

LUNDY

THE LUNDY FAMILY

At the age of 14, Maurice Lundy left his home in Ireland and was a stowaway in a peat barge. When the vessel arrived in Boston, its captain sold him for passage to a lumberman in Maine. About the time he worked off his indentureship, Major Perkins was recruiting boom rats, so Maurice walked to Williamsport in 1850. He worked on the Susquehanna Boom for almost 50 years, eventually becoming chief algerine and an independent raft contractor.

Maurice built the second house on Third Street west of Hepburn Street. He was a U.S. marshal for the district and served for six years on on the city council.

His son, Frank B. Lundy, was born in 1870 and worked for the Williamsport Planing Mill until 1922, when he and Richard H. Lundy started the Lundy Lumber Company. They were joined by John W. Lundy in 1927. Frank B. Lundy was president of the Williamsport Merchant's Association and served on the Committee of 100, which helped attract industry after the Depression.

Lundy-Jessell Homes continues its tradition of professional planning and quality construction on individual lots and subdivisions such as Greenbriar, shown here.

LUNDY-JESSELL HOMES

For over 60 years the Lundy family has been constructing homes in the Williamsport area. The first were built in the 1920s by Lundy Lumber Company. In 1933 this division was reorganized as Lundy Construction Company, which remained a leader in housing for many years.

In the 1950s a new division of Lundy Lumber was formed, called Lundy Homes. Lundy Homes built over 2,000 homes in the Susquehanna Valley and developed the communities of Lundy Park, West Hills, and East Hills.

After Lundy Lumber and Lundy Homes were acquired by Lloyd Lumber in 1981, a new enterprise, Lundy-Jessell Homes, was formed to continue the tradition of quality housing. Excellent designs in all types of housing, including town houses, passive solar, and traditional, have established Lundy-Jessell as the leader in a wide price range. The firm builds in its professionally planned subdivisions of Countryside, Spring Grove, Greenbriar, and The Heights, as well as on individual lots.

With tradition rooted in the past and with a strong commitment to the future, Lundy-Jessell Homes is a partner in progress for the Susquehanna Valley.

LUNDY CONSTRUCTION

Lundy Construction has been building commercial, institutional, and industrial facilities in the Williamsport area for over 50 years. Many of the major local landmarks have been built by Lundy Construction, including the Lycoming County Courthouse and the Historical Museum; the Little League stadium, headquarters, and museum; Roosevelt Junior High School; and much of both Lycoming College and Williamsport Area Community College. Industrial jobs include buildings for Avco, Bethlehem Steel, and most of the Williamsport Industrial Park.

The Butler Metal Building System, coupled with experienced staff and crews, makes Lundy Construction a leading design-and-build contractor in north-central Pennsylvania, noted for its on-time, within-budget performance.

Proud of the extensive part played in the building of this area, Lundy Construction looks forward to participation in the future growth of Lycoming County.

Richard H. Lundy, Jr. (left), and his father, Richard H. Lundy, Sr., on the site of the fourth addition of the Wundies plant, which now totals 243,000 square feet.

PATRONS

The following individuals, companies, and organizations have made a valuable commitment to the quality of this publication. Windsor Publications and the Williamsport-Lycoming Chamber of Commerce gratefully acknowledge their participation in *Williamsport: Frontier Village to Regional Center.*

Ralph S. Alberts Company, Inc.*
Alcan Cable*
Anchor/Darling Valve Company*
Avco Lycoming Williamsport Division*
Ball Travel Service
Bank of Central Pennsylvania*
Brodart Co.
John L. Bruch Agency, Inc.
Canada Dry Bottling Company, Inc., of Williamsport*
Candor, Youngman, Gibson, & Gault*
Canteen Vending Company, Inc.*
Confair Bottling Co., Inc./Cenpro, Inc.*
Data Papers, Inc.*
Divine Providence Hospital*
H.A. Ecker, M.D., D.D.S. Inc.
Mr. & Mrs. Allen E. Ertel
Eureka Paper Box Company, Inc.*
Family Practice Group

Ferno Ille, a Division of Ferno Washington, Inc.
Founders Federal Savings and Loan Association*
Frito-Lay, Inc.*
Bill Fry Ford-Toyota
Harry & Helene Glazewski
Glyco Inc.*
Marc Williams Goldsmith
Grit Publishing Company*
Grumman Allied Industries, Inc.*
GTE Products Corp.
Mr. & Mrs. Rollin E. Hain
Hartman Agency, Inc.*
John Hoffman Architect
Hope Enterprises, Inc.*
Insoport Industries, Inc.*
Jersey Shore Steel Company*
Jones Specialty Shop
Keeler/Dorr-Oliver*
Keystone Filler & Mfg. Co.*
Keystone Friction Hinge Company*
Kline & Company*
Koppers Company, Inc.*
Lamco Communications Inc.*
Lawrence Volkswagen
Peggy L'Heureux Real Estate
Liberty Mutual Insurance Company
Little League Baseball®*
George E. Logue, Inc.*
Mrs. Charles, A. Lucas
Lundy*

James C. Maneval Funeral Home*
Marathon Carey-McFall Company*
Neyharts's/Mary Lib's*
Northern Central Bank*
Pennsylvania Power & Light Company
PMF Industries, Inc.*
Pullman Power Products Corporation*
C. A. Reed Incorporated*
John Savoy & Son, Inc.*
Shop-Vac Corporation*
Sarah Foresman Spofford
Stone Container Corporation Corrugated Container Division*
Stroehmann Brothers Company*
Susquehanna Supply Company*
West Branch School Association
Williamsport Area Community College
The Williamsport Hospital*
Williamsport Sun-Gazette
Woolrich, Inc.*
Wundies Incorporated*
WWPA/Summit Enterprises*

*Partners in Progress of *Williamsport: Frontier Village to Regional Center.* The histories of these companies and organizations appear in Chapter 8, beginning on page 133.

BIBLIOGRAPHY

Anspach, Marshall R., ed. *Historical Sketches of the Bench and Bar of Lycoming County, Pennsylvania, 1795-1960.*Williamsport: Lycoming Law Association, 1961.

Beach, Nichols. *Atlas of Lycoming County, Pennsylvania.* Philadelphia: A. Pomeroy and Co., 1873.

Bey, Theophilus. *Williamsport Illustrated: A Presentation in Pictures from Original Photographs and in Text of the Places of Greatest Beauty and of the Religious, Educational, Financial, Manufacturing, and Commerce Factors that have made Williamsport one of the Leading Progressive Cities of the Nation.* Williamsport: Bey, 1910.

Blair, W.C., & McMath, J.B. *Condensed History of Williamsport.* Williamsport: Williamsport Gazette, 1873.

Blakesley, Alfred M. "The West Branch Front, A Summary of the War Effort in the West Branch Valley." Unpublished Paper, Williamsport: James V. Brown Library, 1945.

Boyd, Andrew, and Boyd, W. Harry. *Directory of Williamsport.* Pottsville: W.H. Boyd Co., 1867-1950.

Boyd, Julian, and Taylor, Robert J. *Susquehanna Company Papers.* Ithica: Cornell University Press, 1962-1971.

Building a Sense of Community. Williamsport: Williamsport Area School District, 1972.

Burgess, George H., and Kennedy, Miles C. *Centennial History of the Pennsylvania Railroad Company.* Philadelphia: Pennsylvania Railroad Co., 1949.

Burrows, John. *Sketch of the Life of General John Burrows: Furnished by Himself at the Request of His Numerous Relatives.* Williamsport: N. Bubb, 1917.

Clarke, W.P. *The Life and Times of the Honorable William Fisher Packer.* Williamsport: Lycoming Historical Society, 1937.

Collins, Michael. "A History of the Lycoming Hotel." Unpublished Paper, Williamsport: Lycoming College, 1983.

Coryell, Tunison. "Autobiographical Sketch of Tunison Coryell, 1791-1881." Williamsport: James V. Brown Library. (mimeograph)

DePol, John. *Lycoming College: Six Woodengravings Printed Directly from the Blocks in a Limited Edition.* Williamsport: Lycoming College, 1962.

Dugan, Jeffrey W. *The Bands of Williamsport Pennsylvania.* Unpublished Master's Paper, Pennsylvania State University, 1975.

Ebbert, George. "The Decision to Move Williamsport's City Hall." Unpublished Paper, Williamsport: Lycoming College, 1982.

Eckel, Edward Henry. *Chronicles of Christ Church Parish, Williamsport, PA., 1840-1896.* Williamsport: Press of the Gazette and Bulletin, 1910.

Faulkner, Harold U. *American Economic History.* New York: Harper & Brothers, 1938.

Fisher, Sydney George. *The Making of Pennsylvania.* Philadelphia: J.B. Lippencott Co., 1896.

Garben, Werner M. "The Rebuilding of St. Boniface Church." Unpublished Paper, Williamsport: Lycoming College, 1982.

Gazette and Bulletin. 1890-1955.

Goodrich, Carter. *Canals and American Economic Development.* New York: Columbia University Press, 1961.

Goodrich, Carter. *Government Promotion of American Canals and Railroads.* Westport: Greenwood Press, 1974.

Graves and Steinbarger. *Atlas of the City of Williamsport, PA., and Suburbs.* Philadelphia: Graves and Steinbarger, 1898.

Greater Williamsport Arts Council. *A Picture of Lycoming County, Vol. II.* Williamsport: Williamsport Arts Council, 1978.

The Grit. 1882-1984.

Harlow, Alvin F. *Old Towpaths: The Story of the American Canal Era.* New York: D. Appleton and Company, 1926.

Heitman, Francis. *Historical Register of the Officers of the Continental Army.* Rev. ed., Washington, D.C.: Rare Bookshop Publishing, 1914.

History of Lycoming County, Illustrated. Philadelphia: J.B. Lippincott and Co., 1876.

Homes and Heritage of the West Branch Valley. Williamsport: Junior League of Williamsport, Inc., 1968.

Humes, James C. *Sweet Dreams Tales of a River City.* Williamsport: Grit Publishing, 1966.

Hulslander, Steve. *From Lumberjacks to Smoke Stacks.* Williamsport: Williamsport Area School District, 1981.

Hunter, C.M. *Atlas of the City of Williamsport, PA.* Philadelphia: C.M. Hunter, 1888.

Huston, Charles. *Artwork of Williamsport.* Chicago: Parish, 1892.

Inglis, William. "The First National Bank of Williamsport." Unpublished Paper, Williamsport: Lycoming College, 1983.

Johnson, Allen, and Malone, Dumas, eds. *Dictionary of American Biography.* New York: Scribners, 1931.

Kane, Robert. "Annunciation Church: History of the Structural and Decorative Design 1889-1979." Unpublished Paper, Williamsport: Lycoming College, 1979.

Klein, Philip S., and Hoogenboom,Ari. *A History of Pennsylvania.* New York: McGraw-Hill, 1973.

Kulikoff, Allan. "The Progress of Inequality in Revolutionary Boston." *William and Mary Quarterly.* 3rd Ser. 28, (1971), pp. 375-412.

Lemon, James T., and Nash, Gary. "The Distribution of Wealth in Chester County, Pennsylvania, 1693-1802." *Journal of Social History.*

2 (1968) pp. 1-24.

Let's Take a Walk. The Greater Williamsport Community Arts Council and the Junior League of Williamsport, Inc., 1976.

Lycoming County Historical Preservation Plan. Prepared by Lycoming County Planning Commission, 1974.

Lycoming County Historical Society Journal. "Vanderbelt Papers." Williamsport: 1955-1984

Lycoming Gazette. 1807-1836.

McDonald, Gregory. "City Government and the Board of Trade: Progress and Reform in Williamsport, 1900-1917." Unpublished Honors Thesis, Williamsport: Lycoming College, 1980.

McMinn, J.H. *Complete History of First Baptist Church.* Williamsport: Williamsport Evening News, 1904.

Marsh, Warrern L., ed. "History of Covenant Central Presbyterian Church, Williamsport, PA; 1840-1952." Williamsport: James V. Brown Library, 1952. (mimeograph).

Meador, Yolanda, ed. *Loyalsock: The Evolution of A Modern Township.* Bicentennial Committee of Loyalsock Township.

Meginnes, John F. *Genealogy and History of the Hepburn Family of the Susquehanna Valley, With Reference to Other Families of the Same Name.* Williamsport: Gazette and Bulletin Printing, 1894.

Meginnes, John F. *History of Lycoming County Including Its Aboriginal History.* Chicago: Brown, 1892.

Meginnes, J.F., ed. *Resources and Industries of the City of Williamsport and the County of Lycoming.* Williamsport: Williamsport Gazette, 1886.

Minutes of the Provincial Council of Pennsylvania from the Organization to the Termination of the Proprietary Government. Harrisburg: Theophilus Fenn, 1852.

Motter, Alton M., ed. *Religion in Lycoming County.* Williamsport: United Churches of Lycoming County, 1982.

Murray, J.F. "History of the War Work of the Public Schools of Williamsport." Unpublished Paper, Williamsport: James V. Brown Library, 1920.

Nunan, Frank. "Little League Baseball: A Study of Its Growth and Effects in America." Unpublished Paper, Williamsport: Lycoming College, 1979.

Pennsylvania Archives. Philadelphia and Harrisburg: Joseph Severns, 1896-1935.

Pennsylvania Writers Projects of the W.P.A. *A Picture of Lycoming County.* Williamsport: Commissioners of Lycoming County, 1939.

Pessen, Edward. *Jacksonian America: Society, Personality, and Politics.* Rev. ed. Homewood: Dorsey Press, 1978.

Pierce, Edward L. "Lycoming County in the Civil War." Unpublished Master's Thesis, Pennsylvania State University, 1934.

Plankenhorn, William Frederick. "Geographic Study of the Growth of Greater Williamsport." Unpublished Ph.D. dissertation, Pennsylvania State University, 1957.

Protasio, John. "Italian Americans in Williamsport." Unpublished Paper, Williamsport: Lycoming College, 1979.

Repasz Band. *Repasz Band Williamsport, PA., The Oldest Band in America.* Williamsport: Grit Publishing, 1915.

Rhian, Terry. "Williamsport's Economic Development During the Canal Period, 1820-1850." Unpublished Paper, Williamsport: Lycoming College, 1980.

Richards, David. "The 109th Infantry Regiment in the Battle of Huertgen Forest." Unpublished Paper, Williamsport: Lycoming College, 1982.

Rick, William F. *A Brief History of St. Marks Ev. Lutheran Church: The Pioneer Church of Lutheranism in this City 1852-1890.* Williamsport: Gazette and Bulletin Printing, 1896.

Roman, Paul. "Rationing in Williamsport During World War II." Unpublished Paper, Williamsport: Lycoming College, 1980.

Rosenberger, Homer T. *The Philadelphia and Erie Railroad: Its Place in American Economic History.* Potomac: The Fox Hills Press, 1975.

Russell, Helen H. *The Tiadaghton Tale: A History of the Area and Its People.* Compiled by Carol F. Baker. Williamsport: Scaife's Valley Press, 1975.

Russell, Mary L. "History of Music of Williamsport." Unpublished Master's Thesis, Pennsylvania State University, 1957.

Schlesinger, Arthur M., Jr. *The Age of Jackson.* Boston: Little Brown, 1945.

Shannon, Joseph. "Impact of Industrialization on the Wealth Distribution of Williamsport." Unpublished Paper, Williamsport: Lycoming College, 1983.

Sipes, William D. *Pennsylvania Railroad: Its Origin, Construction, Condition, and Connections.* Evansville: Unigraphic, Inc., 1975.

Stotz, Carl E., with Baldwin, M.W. *At Bat with the Little League.* Philadelphia: Macrae Smith, 1952.

Taber, Thomas T., III. *Sunset Along Susquehanna Waters.* Williamsport: Lycoming Printing Company, Inc., 1972.

Taylor, George R. *The Transportation Revolution.* New York: Rinehart, 1951.

Turnbaugh, William A. *Man, Land, and Time.* Evansville: Unigraphic, Inc., 1977. Published for the Lycoming County Historical Society, Williamsport

Turnbaugh, William A. "Six Cheers and a Volley." Unpublished

Manuscript, 1969.

U.S. Bureau of the Census. "Population of the Second Census of the United States 1800." Roll 41, Pennsylvania, Vol. 7, National Archives: Washington, D.C., 1957.

U.S. Bureau of the Census. "Population of the Thirteenth Census of the United States, 1910." Roll 1372-1373 Lycoming County, National Archives: Washington, D.C.

United States Department of Commerce. *Sixteenth Census of the United States; 1940 Population.* Washington, D.C.: Government Printing Office, 1942.

United States Department of Commerce. *Report on Vital and Social Statistics in the United States at the Eleventh Census, 1890.* Washington, D.C.: Government Printing Office, 1896.

U.S. Government Printing Office. *Heads of Families at the First Census of the United States Taken in the Year 1790, Pennsylvania.* Baltimore: Genealogical Publishing Co., 1977.

Updegraff, Christine. "The Transformation of Farming in Lycoming County." History Internship, Lycoming County Planning Commission, 1975.

Wallace, Paul A. *Pennsylvania: Seed of a Nation.* New York: Harper & Row, 1962.

Weaver, Craig. "Internship on Michael Ross." Unpublished Paper, Williamsport: Lycoming College, 1976.

White, Bonnie. "Women in Employment During World War II: The Nation and Williamsport." Unpublished Paper, Williamsport: Lycoming College, 1979.

"Williamsport Tax Records 1808-1844." Lycoming County Historical Society, Williamsport, PA.

Williamsport Junior League. *The West Fourth Street Story.* Williamsport: Grit Publishing, 1975.

Williamsport-Lycoming Chamber of Commerce. "Minutes and Annual Reports of the Williamsport Chamber of Commerce, 1927-1937." Williamsport.

Williamsport-Lycoming Chamber of Commerce. "Minutes and Annual Reports of the Williamsport Board of Trade and Chamber of Commerce, 1919-1927." Williamsport.

Williamsport-Lycoming Chamber of Commerce. "Minutes of the Committee of 100, 1935-1937." Williamsport

Wilson, David S. "The History of the North-Central Chapter of the Society for Pennsylvania Archaeology." Unpublished Paper, Williamsport: Lycoming College, 1980.

Wilson, William B. *History of the Pennsylvania Railroad Company.* Philadelphia: H.T. Coates & Co., 1895.

Woolever, Naomi L. "The Street Railway Era in Williamsport, PA." *The Bulletin of the National Railway Historical Society.* Vol. 40, No. 4, 1975, pp. 35-48.

Yount, Paul L. *An Historical Survey of St. Mark's Lutheran Church of Williamsport, PA.* Williamsport: Grit Publishing, 1927.

Zamarra, Jacqueline. "The Water Company of Williamsport, Pennsylvania: From Private Ownership to Municipal Acquisition." Unpublished Paper, Williamsport: Lycoming College, 1981.

INDEX